Classics in Linguistics

Chief Editors: Martin Haspelmath, Stefan Müller

In this series:

1. Lehmann, Christian. Thoughts on grammaticalization

2. Schütze, Carson T. The empirical base of linguistics: Grammaticality judgments and linguistic methodology

3. Bickerton, Derek. Roots of Language

Thoughts on grammaticalization

3rd edition 2015

Christian Lehmann

Christian Lehmann. 2015. *Thoughts on grammaticalization*. 3rd edition 2015 (Classics in Linguistics 1). Berlin: Language Science Press.

This title can be downloaded at:
http://langsci-press.org/catalog/book/88
© 2015, Christian Lehmann
Published under the Creative Commons Attribution 4.0 Licence (CC BY 4.0):
http://creativecommons.org/licenses/by/4.0/
ISBN: 978-3-946234-05-0 (Digital)
       978-3-946234-06-7 (Hardcover)
       978-3-946234-07-4 (Softcover)

Cover and concept of design: Ulrike Harbort
Typesetting: Felix Kopecky, Sebastian Nordhoff
Proofreading: Martin Haspelmath, Christian Lehmann, Sebastian Nordhoff
Fonts: Linux Libertine, Arimo, DejaVu Sans Mono
Typesetting software: X⇊LATEX

Language Science Press
Habelschwerdter Allee 45
14195 Berlin, Germany
langsci-press.org

Storage and cataloguing done by FU Berlin

Language Science Press has no responsibility for the persistence or accuracy of URLs for external or third-party Internet websites referred to in this publication, and does not guarantee that any content on such websites is, or will remain, accurate or appropriate. Information regarding prices, travel timetables and other factual information given in this work are correct at the time of first publication but Language Science Press does not guarantee the accuracy of such information thereafter.

Contents

Prospect of Volume II   v

Series Editors' preface to the 3rd edition   vii

Preface to the 1982 working paper version   ix

Preface to the 1995/2002 editions   xi

Abbreviations   xiii

1   The history of research in grammaticalization   1

2   Grammaticalization: characterization and delimitation of the concept   11
    2.1   The term "grammaticalization"   11
    2.2   The meaning of "grammaticalization"   13
    2.3   Degrammaticalization   18
    2.4   Renovation and innovation   22
    2.5   Reinforcement   24

3   Grammatical domains   27
    3.1   Verbal complexes   28
       3.1.1   Existence and possession   28
       3.1.2   The copula   28
       3.1.3   Modals and moods   29
       3.1.4   Tense and aspect   31
       3.1.5   Passive and emphasis   34
       3.1.6   Auxiliaries and alternative sources   35
    3.2   Pronominal elements   40
       3.2.1   Definite pronominal elements   40
       3.2.2   Indefinite pronominal elements   52
    3.3   Nominal complexes   58
       3.3.1   Nominal categories   58

Contents

		3.3.2	Nominalization	65
		3.3.3	Attribution	72
	3.4	Clause level relations		79
		3.4.1	Adverbial relations	79
		3.4.2	Main actant relations	115
	3.5	Conclusion		128

4 Parameters of grammaticalization — **129**
- 4.1 Theoretical prerequisites — 129
- 4.2 Paradigmatic parameters — 134
  - 4.2.1 Integrity — 134
  - 4.2.2 Paradigmaticity — 141
  - 4.2.3 Paradigmatic variability — 146
- 4.3 Syntagmatic parameters — 152
  - 4.3.1 Structural scope — 152
  - 4.3.2 Bondedness — 157
  - 4.3.3 Syntagmatic variability — 167
- 4.4 Interaction of parameters — 170
  - 4.4.1 Quantifiability of the parameters — 170
  - 4.4.2 Correlation among the parameters — 173
  - 4.4.3 Lack of correlation — 179
  - 4.4.4 Reduction to zero and fixation of word order — 181

Epilogue to the third edition — **189**

References — **197**

Index — **211**

    Name index — 211

Prospect of Volume II[1]

5. Processes cognate to grammaticalization
    - 5.1. Semantic processes
    - 5.2. Lexicalization
    - 5.3. Phonological processes
    - 5.4. Analogy

6. Traditional problems in new perspective
    - 6.1. Grammatical meaning
    - 6.2. Grammatical levels
    - 6.3. Markedness
    - 6.4. Arbitrariness of the linguistic sign
    - 6.5. Semantic representation

7. Comparison of languages
    - 7.1. Contrastive linguistics
    - 7.2. Language typology
    - 7.3. Language universals

8. Language history and linguistic evolution
    - 8.1. Development of grammatical categories
    - 8.2. Linguistic evolution
    - 8.3. Historical reconstruction

9. Language theory
    - 9.1. Language activity
    - 9.2. The causes of grammaticalization

---

[1] Volume II was planned but was never written; see the preface to the 1995/2002 editions.

Series Editors' preface to the 3rd edition

This is the third edition of Christian Lehmann's *Thoughts on grammaticalization*, a book which has had great impact on the development of grammaticalization studies since the 1980s in spite of its unusual publication history.

The first version was circulated in 1982 as a working paper of the University of Cologne's UNITYP project. At that time, its full title included the indication "Volume I", because the author had planned a second volume. The first published edition appeared in 1995 with Lincom Europa. The second edition appeared again as a working paper, this time of the University of Erfurt (ASSidUE), in 2002.

We are happy that Christian Lehmann accepted our proposal to publish it again as a regular book. We feel that it deserves more prominence, as it provides an excellent overview of grammaticalization processes and its theoretical ideas have not been superseded.

The third edition contains few changes compared to the second edition from 2002; the main addition is an epilogue at the end of the book. Otherwise the author and editors limited themselves to a few stylistic modifications such as corrected typos, more consistent use of abbreviations and a few adaptations to the usual Language Science Press style.

Note that the post-1982 work that corresponds to the various chapters of the planned Volume II is mentioned in the preface of the 1995 edition.

Berlin/Leipzig, October 2015   The Series Editors

Preface to the 1982 working paper version

As we will be going a long way, through involved and ramified discussions, until we arrive at something like a definition of grammaticalization, the reader who wants to know beforehand what this book is all about is asked to accept this as a preliminary characterization: Grammaticalization is a process leading from lexemes to grammatical formatives. A number of semantic, syntactic and phonological processes interact in the grammaticalization of morphemes and of whole constructions. A sign is grammaticalized to the extent that it is devoid of concrete lexical meaning and takes part in obligatory grammatical rules. A simple example is the development of the Latin preposition *ad* 'at, towards' into the Spanish direct object marker *a*.

It must be made clear at the outset that this treatment is preliminary, incomplete and imperfect. It presents little more than what has been found out in the two centuries in which the subject has been studied, and probably it contains even less than that, because I have been unable to take notice of all the relevant literature. I must also warn the reader that I have great conceptual difficulties with the present subject, and I will leave many questions open. The problem is not so much an empirical one: there are sufficient analyzed data, and the empirical phenomena in themselves appear to be reasonably clear. What is highly unclear is how the phenomena are to be interpreted, classified and related to each other. Grammaticalization is such a pervasive process and therefore such a comprehensive notion that it is often difficult to say what does not fall under it. The present essay will therefore be concerned, first and foremost, with the question: what *is* grammaticalization?

The discussion will not be couched in terms of a specific theory of grammar, one reason being that existing grammatical models are inadequate for the representation of the gradual nature which is essential to the phenomena comprised by grammaticalization. As many of the problems involved are traditional ones, they can be discussed in traditional terms.

The theory of language which is to account for the systematicity, goal-directedness and dynamism inherent to grammaticalization must be structural,

Preface to the 1982 working paper version

functional and operational in nature. It is essentially the theory of Wilhelm von Humboldt (1836), which has been elaborated in more recent times by Eugenio Coseriu (1974) and Hansjakob Seiler (1978). This theory has never been made fully explicit; but it will become transparent through all of the present treatment, and an attempt to make it more explicit will be presented in the last chapter.

The work is organized as follows. We start, in Chapter 1, with a brief historical review of the relevant literature. Chapter 2 will supply some first clarifications to the concept of grammaticalization and will delimit it against related concepts. Chapter 3 contains the bulk of the empirical data which illustrate grammaticalization, ordered according to semantically defined domains of grammar. From this evidence, the various basic processes which integrate grammaticalization and which are called its parameters are then extracted and ordered according to how they pertain to the paradigmatic or the syntagmatic aspect, to the content or the expression of the grammaticalized sign. The degree to which these parameters correlate will also be discussed in Chapter 4. The next chapter looks out for analogs to grammaticalization in different parts of the language system and tries to distinguish these from grammaticalization proper. In Chapter 6 we turn to a couple of traditional linguistic problems, asking whether the concept of grammaticalization can contribute anything towards their clarification. The various modes of contrasting different languages, including language typology and universals research, are discussed in the perspective of grammaticalization in Chapter 7. Chapter 8 concentrates on the diachronic aspect of grammaticalization, its role in language change and historical reconstruction. The final chapter tries to formulate the advances that may be made in language theory if grammaticalization is given its proper place in it.

Due to idiosyncrasies in the timing of my research projects, I have had to interrupt the writing of this book after Chapter 4. It was decided that the finished chapters should appear as volume I, while Chapters 5 – 9 should be reserved for a second volume. I have included them in the preceding sketch and also given a prospect on their contents in order that the reader may get an idea of the plan of the complete work. It is my intention to complete volume II for *akup* in 1983.

A cordial word of thanks goes to Bernd Heine and Mechthild Reh, who have been working on grammaticalization and evolutive typology, especially in African languages, simultaneously and partly in cooperation with me. They have been kind and disinterested enough to put their notes and manuscripts at my disposal. References are to this prepublication version; their work is now being published as *akup* 47. Finally, I should like to thank Sonja Schlögel and Ingrid Hoyer, who have taken great care in typing and editing the manuscript.

Cologne, 7.10.1982   Christian Lehmann

Preface to the 1995/2002 editions

A preliminary version of the present work was distributed in 1982 under the following title: *Thoughts on grammaticalization. A programmatic sketch. Vol. I.* Köln: Institut für Sprachwissenschaft der Universität (*Arbeiten des Kölner Universalienprojekts*, 48). It got out of stock immediately, but has been in high demand since. A slightly revised version was released in January 1985, but only in form of a number of xerocopies. The original plan was, of course, to get back to work on grammaticalization as soon as possible, to write up volume II and then publish the whole work. Then the title, too, would have been streamlined a bit. However, I never got around to do that.

The semipublished 1982 paper has played an instrumental role in the development of modern work on grammaticalization. Many people have asked me to at least make it available in published form, even if I should never manage to round it off. This is what I am doing here. Consequently, this publication is slightly anachronistic. I have removed those errors of the preliminary version that I got aware of. I have modified many points of detail. I have updated references to unpublished material. But I have not taken into consideration the vast amount of literature on grammaticalization that has appeared since (including my own more recent contributions) and that would lead me to reformulate substantially some of the ideas expounded here. Readers should be aware that the state of research reflected here is essentially that of 1982.

References to volume II, including even the "Prospect of contents of volume II", have not been deleted. A fair appreciation of what is being published here is only possible if one considers that it was always intended to be only half of what would, at least, be necessary. However, I doubt that volume II will ever be published. Below, I list the articles on grammaticalization that I have published since 1982. Some of them may be considered to fill the lacunae created by the prospect. In particular, the following assignments may be allowed:

Ch. 5.2:   Lehmann (1989a), Lehmann (2002a).

Ch. 6.3:   Lehmann (1989b).

Ch. 7.2:   Lehmann (1985b), Lehmann (1986).

Preface to the 1995/2002 editions

Ch. 8: Lehmann (1985a), Lehmann (1987), Lehmann (1992).

Ch. 9: Lehmann (1993), Lehmann (1995).

I have been unable to get my English grammar and style revised by a native speaker, and I must apologize for the inconveniences resulting therefrom. Finally, cordial thanks go to Cornelia Sünner for the effort she has made in editing the typescript. I also thank the numerous colleagues who have reacted to the preliminary version and whose comments would deserve fuller attention.

Bielefeld, 21.07.1995   Christian Lehmann

For the second edition, some changes and corrections have been made.

Erfurt, 08.07.2002   Christian Lehmann

Abbreviations

Grammatical categories in interlinear morphemic translations

ABL	ablative	EL	elative
ABS	absolutive	ERG	ergative
ACC	accusative	EXIST	existence
ADJVR	adjectivizer	F	feminine
ALL	allative	FIN	finite
AN	animate	FOC	focus
ART	article	FUT	future
ASP	aspect	GEN	genitive
AT	attributor	GER	gerund
AUX	auxiliary	HAB	habitual
CL	noun class	HON	honorific
COLL	collective	HUM	human
COMPL	completive	ILL	illative
CONN	connective	IMP	imperative
CONT	continuative	IND	indefinite
COP	copula	INDEP	independent
D1	determiner of first person deixis	INESS	inessive
		INF	infinitive
D3	determiner of third person deixis	INST	instrumental
		INT	interrogative
DAT	dative	IO	indirect object
DEF	definite	LAT	lative ($\simeq$ directional)
DEM	demonstrative	LOC	locative
DES	desiderative	M	masculine
DET	determiner	MID	middle voice
DIR	directional	N	neuter
DU	dual	NEG	negative
DYN	dynamic	NHUM	non-human

Abbreviations

NOM	nominative	PTL	particle
NONSG	non-singular	RDP	reduplication
NR	nominalizer	REAL	realized
OBJ	object (verb affix position)	REFL	reflexive
OBL	oblique (affix position)	REL	relative
PART	participle	SBJ	subject (verb affix position)
PAST	past tense	SBJV	subjunctive
PERL	perlative	SEP	separative
PL	plural	SG	singular
POL	polite	SIM	simultaneous
POSS	possessor (nominal affix position)	SR	subordinator
PRAET	praeterlative	SUPER	superlative/-essive
PF	perfect	TERM	terminative
PROG	progressive aspect	TOP	topic
PRS	present	TR	transitive
PST	past	VOL	volitional

Abbreviations of language names

IE	Indo-European	OHG	Old High German
OE	Old English	PIE	Proto-Indo-European

Other abbreviations

id.	idem	op. cit.	opere citato

1 The history of research in grammaticalization

As far as I can see, it was Antoine Meillet (1912) who coined the term "grammaticalization" and first applied it to the concept for which it is still used today. We will return to him in a moment. The concept itself, however, and the ideas behind it, are considerably older. The idea that grammatical formatives evolve from lexemes, that affixes come from free forms, was already expounded by the French philosopher Étienne Bonnot de Condillac. In his work *Essai sur l'origine des connaissances humaines* (1746), he explained the personal endings of the verb through agglutination of personal pronouns and maintained that verbal tense came from the coalescence of a temporal adverb with the stem. Again, John Horne Tooke, in his etymological work Ἔπεα πτερόεντα *or the diversions of Purley* (vol. I: 1786, vol. II: 1805), claimed that prepositions derive from nouns or verbs.[1] We shall see in Chapter 1 that all such processes do, in fact, occur, though not necessarily in the specific cases which these authors had in mind.

Condillac and Horne Tooke were certainly only forerunners to the first evolutive typologists, notably August Wilhelm von Schlegel and Wilhelm von Humboldt. In his *Observations sur la langue et la littérature provençales* (1818), Schlegel deals extensively with the renewal of Latin synthetic morphology by Romance analytic morphology. About the formation of the latter, he writes:

> C'est une invention en quelque façon négative, que celle qui a produit les grammaires analytiques, et la méthode uniformément suivie à cet égard peut se réduire à un seul principe. On dépouille certains mots de leur énergie significative, on ne leur laisse qu'une valeur nominale, pour leur donner un cours plus général et les faire entrer dans la partie élémentaire de la langue. Ces mots deviennent une espèce de papier-monnaie destiné à faciliter la circulation. (1818: 28)

This is followed by a series of Latin-Romance examples of different kinds, including the development of articles, auxiliaries and indefinite pronouns, which

---

[1] Information on Condillac and Horne Tooke from Arens (1969: 109f, 132–134), and Stammerjohann (1975: 119, 452f).

have subsequently become the stock examples of grammaticalization theory. Although Schlegel goes so far as to speak of "la formation d'une nouvelle grammaire" (1818: 30), he views the development essentially as due to linguistic decadence. It will be observed, however, that some of the core aspects of grammaticalization, viz. semantic depletion and expansion of distribution, are foreshadowed here.

Wilhelm von Humboldt arrived at more far-reaching conclusions. In his academic lecture on the origins of grammatical forms, he proposed that "grammatische Bezeichnung" (the signifying of grammatical categories, as opposed to objects) evolves through the following four stages (1822: 54f):

I. "grammatische Bezeichnung durch Redensarten, Phrasen, Sätze": grammatical categories are completely hidden in the lexemes and in the semantosyntactic configurations.

II. "grammatische Bezeichnung durch feste Wortstellungen und zwischen Sach- und Formbedeutung schwankende Wörter".

III. "grammatische Bezeichnung durch Analoga von Formen": here the "vacillating words" have been agglutinated as affixes to the main words. The resulting complexes are not "forms", unitary wholes, but only "aggregates", and therefore mere "analogs to forms".

IV. "grammatische Bezeichnung durch wahre Formen, durch Beugung und rein grammatische Wörter".

These four stages are connected with each other "durch verloren gehende Bedeutung der Elemente und Abschleifung der Laute in langem Gebrauch."

One may simply overlook the "evaluation" of the different stages to which this theory is committed. One may also regard it as a terminological issue whether the term "grammatical form" can be correctly applied only at stage IV, and not also at the other stages. But one must recognize that this account of the evolution of grammatical forms is essentially a theory of grammaticalization, if only a sketchy one. Three things are worth noting here. First, the term "grammatical form" must not mislead one into thinking that this theory deals only with the expression of the language sign. The passages quoted leave no doubt that the evolution in question affects both the meaning and the expression of the grammatical sign. Secondly, the four stages are essentially the morphological types of the linguistic typology of the time: stages I and/or II = isolating, III = agglutinative, IV = flexional. Thirdly, linguistic typology, which in the twentieth century was reduced to a synchronic discipline, is here conceived as evolutive typology. Consequently, the theory of grammaticalization is tied, from the very start, to evolutive typology.

This theory was subsequently widely received under the name of "Agglutinationstheorie". This term appears to refer only to the transition towards stage III, but was later used to comprise all of the four stages.[2] The first to apply the theory, Franz Bopp, who shared ideas with Humboldt through correspondence, actually concentrated on stage III. In his *Über das Conjugationssystem der Sanskritsprache in Vergleichung mit jenem der griechischen, lateinischen, persischen und germanischen Sprache* (1816: 147f; apud Arens 1969: 177), and again in vol. I of his *Vergleichende Grammatik des Sanskrit, Zend, Griechischen, Lateinischen, Litauischen, Altslavischen, Gothischen und Deutschen* (Bopp 1833-52), he derived the personal endings of the Indo-European verb from agglutinated personal pronouns.[3] Several of the neogrammarians, among them Brugmann, were favorably inclined to hypotheses of this kind. Again, the typological version of agglutination theory was most vigorously promoted by August Schleicher; he followed Humboldt in making agglutination theory the center of his evolutive typology.

Another prominent representative of agglutination theory is Georg von der Gabelentz. The essential passage from his *Die Sprachwissenschaft*, which remained unaltered in the second edition (1891: 251 = 1901: 256), will be quoted in full here, because it summarizes well what was known or thought about agglutination theory at that time.

> Nun bewegt sich die Geschichte der Sprachen in der Diagonale zweier Kräfte: des Bequemlichkeitstriebes, der zur Abnutzung der Laute führt, und des Deutlichkeitstriebes, der jene Abnutzung nicht zur Zerstörung der Sprache ausarten läßt. Die Affixe verschleifen sich, verschwinden am Ende spurlos; ihre Funktionen aber oder ähnliche drängen wieder nach Ausdruck. Diesen Ausdruck erhalten sie, nach der Methode der isolierenden Sprachen, durch Wortstellung oder verdeutlichende Wörter. Letztere unterliegen wiederum mit der Zeit dem Agglutinationsprozesse, dem Verschliffe und Schwunde, und derweile bereitet sich für das Verderbende neuer Ersatz vor: periphrastische Ausdrücke werden bevorzugt; mögen sie syntaktische Gefüge oder wahre Komposita sein (englisch: *I shall see*, — lateinisch *videbo* = *vide-fuo*); immer gilt das Gleiche: die Entwicklungslinie krümmt sich zurück nach

---

[2] This inadequacy of the term was also felt by Jespersen, who proposed to substitute it by "coalescence theory" (1922: 376).

[3] This application of agglutination theory is not to be confused with Bopp's typology of roots.

> der Seite der Isolation, nicht in die alte Bahn, sondern in eine annähernd parallele. Darum vergleiche ich sie der Spirale.

The extent to which Gabelentz is obliged to Humboldt emerges clearly from this quotation. On the other hand, two things are new here: First, an explanation for grammaticalization is offered, this being seen as the result of two competing forces, the tendency towards ease of articulation and the tendency towards distinctness. We will meet these again and again, in various disguises, in the subsequent literature. Secondly, the evolution is not conceived as linear, as leading from a primitive to an advanced stage, but as basically cyclic, though Gabelentz is cautious enough to use the more precise metaphor of the spiral. With the necessary refinements, this still corresponds to the most recent insights.

In 1912, Antoine Meillet published his article "L'évolution des formes grammaticales". Although the title is reminiscent of Humboldt's lecture, Meillet shows no sign of being acquainted with it or with agglutination theory, though he certainly must have been. In particular, his examples include Schlegel's examples. However, grammaticalization was of interest to him not for its typological implications, but for its capacity to explain certain facts in the history of Indo-European languages. He thus continues the Bopp–neogrammarian tradition. Meillet assumes three main classes of words, "mots principaux", "mots accessoires" and "mots grammaticaux", between which there is a gradual transition.

> L'affaiblissement du sens et l'affaiblissement de la forme des mots accessoires vont de pair; quand l'un et l'autre sont assez avancés, le mot accessoire peut finir par ne plus être qu'un élément privé de sens propre, joint à un mot principal pour en marquer le rôle grammatical. Le changement d'un mot en élément grammatical est accompli. (1912: 139).

This leads Meillet to what appears to be a reformulation of Gabelentz's agglutination theory:

> Les langues suivent ainsi une sorte de développement en spirale; elles ajoutent de mots accessoires pour obtenir une expression intense; ces mots s'affaiblissent, se dégradent et tombent au niveau de simples /141/ outils grammaticaux; on ajoute de nouveaux mots ou des mots différents en vue de l'expression; l'affaiblissement recommence, et ainsi sans fin.

The two driving factors he mentions, "expressivité" and "usage", also have much in common with Gabelentz's tendency towards distinctness and towards ease.

Even when he contends that analytic (= periphrastic) and synthetic constructions do not differ in principle, because they are connected through grammaticalization, citing the example of the Latin-Romance tenses, he only seems to strengthen a point that was already implicit in agglutination theory. However, Meillet does go beyond this. First, he introduces the term "grammaticalization" (1912: 133), though he consistently puts it in quotation marks. He does not define the term, but uses it in the sense of "attribution du caractère grammatical à un mot jadis autonome" (1912: 131). Secondly, Meillet opposes grammaticalization to analogy as the two principal processes of grammatical change (see below §5.4), thus assigning grammaticalization a more narrowly defined place in linguistic theory. And finally (1912: 147f), he offers what appears to be a useful extension of this notion: he considers that the order of constituents may be grammaticalized, too, illustrating from Latin, in which word order signifies expressive nuances, and French, where it expresses syntactic relations.

Three years later, in his article "Le renouvellement des conjonctions", Meillet extends his theory to the historical analysis of conjunctions, especially in Latin-Romance. The recruitment of new words which are then to follow the paths of grammaticalization already well established in the language, is termed "renouvellement" and distinguished from "création", where grammatical and/or formal categories previously absent from the language are introduced. The substitution of Latin *nam* by *quare* > French *car* is an example of "renovation" (renewal).[4]

Continuing in chronological order, we next come to Edward Sapir, who again represents the other, Humboldtian tradition. Sapir's primary interest was neither in grammaticalization as a force in historical change (he does not use the term) nor in agglutination theory or evolutive typology; but in establishing a continuum of the different kinds of linguistic concepts as a basis for his synchronic typology, he actually contributes to both of these theories. In Ch. V of his *Language*, Sapir (1921: 102) defines the following four classes of concepts:

Material content	I.	Basic Concepts
	II.	Derivational Concepts
Relational	III.	Concrete Relational Concepts
	IV.	Pure Relational Concepts.

---

[4] "Renovation" will here be used instead of the traditional "renewal" because it offers a neat counterpart to "innovation".

1 The history of research in grammaticalization

Semantically, there is a gradience through these four classes from the concrete to the abstract; morphologically, there is a parallel gradience from "independent words or radical elements" to expression "by affixing non-radical elements to radical elements ... or by their inner modification, by independent words, or by position". Sapir also mentions the possibility of a word's diachronic passage through this continuum. His most important, and most problematic, innovation is his attempt to give a more precise semantic basis to the different grammaticalization stages. In this, he has had practically no followers. One point which might at first seem to be of minor importance is noteworthy: the expression of grammatical concepts by "position" shows up at the end of Sapir's scale, while it appeared at the beginning of Humboldt's four stages. Take this together with Meillet's contention that word order may be grammaticalized, too, and the problem becomes obvious.

Henri Frei's work may be mentioned in passing. Nothing in his book *La grammaire des fautes* (1929) is intended to be a contribution to grammaticalization theory; but he does adduce a lot of relevant data for "un passage incessant du signe expressif au signe arbitraire", for which he finds two forces responsible, "le besoin d'expressivité" and "la loi de l'usure" (1929: 233). Frei's association of grammaticalization with a change from the expressive to the arbitrary will yet occupy us (1929: 115).

In the period of American and even of European structuralism, topics such as grammaticalization were not fashionable. With the decline of morphological and evolutive typology, this vein of research in grammaticalization virtually broke off. The only work of this time in which agglutination theory figures prominently is the Africanist Carl Meinhof's book *Die Entstehung flektierender Sprachen* (1936), in which he treats the evolution of flexional morphology in Semitic, Hamitic and Indo-European languages. Following Jespersen (1922: 375–388; see ch. V.4), Meinhof in §4 posits two principal ways in which inflection can evolve: (1) through grammaticalization, for instance of nouns or verbs via postpositions to case suffixes; or (2) through the reinterpretation of already existing phonological outgrowths of the word.

Apart from this sporadic recurrence, however, agglutination theory does not, as far as I can see, regain its former popularity until Hodge (1970) and Givón (1971) (the latter apparently being unaware of the venerable tradition which he continues). Two important articles which throw new light on grammaticalization are Roman Jakobson's "Boas's view of grammatical meaning" (1959) and V. M. Žirmunskij's "The word and its boundaries" (1966; Russian original 1961). Jakobson attributes to Boas a distinction between "those concepts which are grammaticalized and consequently obligatory in some languages but lexicalized and merely optional in others" (1959: 492), adducing "the obligatoriness of grammatical categories as the specific feature which distinguishes them from lexical meanings" (1959: 489). This is clearly an advance because it adds an essential syntactic aspect to the until then almost exclusively morphological view of grammaticalization. Here for the first time, too, an opposition between grammaticalization and lexicalization is formulated.

In §3 of his article, Žirmunskij deals with the "unification of the word combination into a single (compound) word." There are two possible directions that this process can take: either towards grammaticalization, which yields "a specific new analytical form of the word", or towards lexicalization, which yields "a phraseological equivalent of the word in the semantic sense." (1966: 83) In the first case, the next stage is a synthetic inflectional word form; in the second case, the next stage is a compound word. Several points should be stressed here. First, there are processes of unification which do not involve the development of one element of the combination into a grammatical formative and which are therefore not regarded as grammaticalization. Second, such processes are called lexicalization. Observe that this use of the term "lexicalization" is quite different from Jakobson's use quoted above; this will constitute one of our problems (§5.2). Thirdly, the term "grammaticalization" is used here not (only) for the transition from the analytic to the synthetic construction, i.e. the agglutination process, but is explicitly applied to the formation of an analytic construction. This is consistent with the meaning of the term which covers an open-ended continuum comprising all of Humboldt's or Sapir's four stages.

Outside structuralism, the Indo-Europeanist tradition of grammaticalization theory remained uninterrupted. Its most important representatives are Jerzy Kuryłowicz and Emile Benveniste. Kuryłowicz applied the concept of grammaticalization systematically in his book *The inflectional categories of Indo-European*, many of which are explained through grammaticalization. In his article "The evolution of grammatical categories" (1965; notice again the tradition of article titles!), Kuryłowicz defines:

> Grammaticalization consists in the increase of the range of a morpheme advancing from a lexical to a grammatical or from a less grammatical to a more grammatical status, e.g. from a derivative formant to an inflectional one. (1965: 52)

By "increasing range" Kuryłowicz means wider distribution, a defining factor of grammaticalization which had hitherto only been hinted at by Schlegel. No-

1 The history of research in grammaticalization

tice that word-formation is reintroduced into the picture, which we might think to have excluded from grammaticalization with Žirmunskij. Kuryłowicz then gives a survey of various Indo-European grammatical categories and their development through grammaticalization. He also opposes grammaticalization to lexicalization in a third sense which will occupy us in §5.2.

Benveniste, who, curiously enough, consistently avoids the term "grammaticalization", has made various contributions to the subject. In his article "Mutations of linguistic categories" (1968), he takes up Meillet's distinction between "création" and "renouvellement", explaining that the former is innovative change, where grammatical categories may disappear or emerge for the first time, while the latter is conservative change, where categories are only formally "renovated". The examples are again the same as in Meillet (1912): the Latin-Romance perfect and future.

Switching back, for the last time, to the conception of evolutive typology, we find this revived in two articles by Carleton T. Hodge and Talmy Givón. In his paper "The linguistic cycle" (1970), Hodge somewhat simplifies the picture by distinguishing only two stages, one with heavy syntax and little morphology (Sm), which roughly comprises Humboldt's stages I and II; and another with little syntax and heavy morphology (sM), which corresponds to Humboldt's stages III and IV. His point is essentially an empirical one: he adduces the history of Egyptian as factual proof for the hypothesis that a single language can pass through a full cycle "sM → Sm → sM". His slogan "that one man's morphology was an earlier man's syntax" (3) is echoed in Givón's formulation "Today's morphology is yesterday's syntax." (1971: 413), which is the central thesis of his article "Historical syntax and synchronic morphology: An archaeologist's field trip". We will deal in §8.3 with the role of grammaticalization in historical reconstruction. Here it suffices to mention that Givón has expanded his theory in various works, proposing, in 1979, the grammaticalization scale which we will discuss in §2.2. The notion of grammaticalization has by now become widely known and is receiving ever greater interest. I will end my review here and discuss more recent work in thematically more specific connections.

Summing up, we can say that the theory of grammaticalization has been developed by two largely independent linguistic traditions, that of Indo-European historical linguistics and that of language typology. The moment has come, I think, where the two threads should be united. One tradition is conspicuously absent from this picture, namely that of structural linguistics, from de Saussure to our day. This is by no means an accident: whereas historical linguistics and typology have been concerned, from their beginning, with processes and continuous phenomena and thus could easily accommodate grammaticalization as a process which creates such phenomena, structural linguistics has tended to favour a static view of language and clear-cut binary distinctions. In Chapter 6 we will try and see whether the perspective of grammaticalization cannot, in fact shed some light on problems traditional in structural linguistics.

2 Grammaticalization: characterization and delimitation of the concept

2.1 The term "grammaticalization"

The derivational pattern which the word *grammaticalization* belongs to suggests that it means a process in which something becomes or is made grammatical (cf. *legalization*). In view of this, the term is unfortunate in several respects. Firstly, the term GRAMMATICAL has various meanings. In the above explication of *grammaticalization*, *grammatical* signifies that which belongs to, is part of, the grammar, as opposed to, e.g., what belongs to the lexicon, to stylistics or discourse. Apart from this, *grammatical* has come to mean something completely unrelated to the notion of grammaticalization: *x is grammatical* is an abbreviation of *x is grammatically correct* and accordingly means that x conforms to (as opposed to: is incompatible with, violates) the rules of grammar. What is particularly distressing about this ambiguity is the fact that while *grammatical* may have either meaning in attributive use, it can only have the second meaning in predicative use; and yet the first meaning is needed in the predicative use which is made of it in the above explication of grammaticalization.

Secondly, in addition to the above explication, *grammaticalization* must mean a process in which something becomes or is made more grammatical (cf. the quotation from Kuryłowicz on p. 7). We defer to §6.2 the problem of what it means to say that something belongs to the grammar to a greater or lesser degree, and observe here that this latter notion should be designated by the noun GRAMMATICALITY. That is, in a theory of grammaticalization, the term "grammaticality" would be needed to mean the degree of grammaticalization which an element has reached. Again, however, this term (or its variant "grammaticalness") is currently based on the other meaning of *grammatical* and therefore means the well-formedness of something according to the rules of grammar.

There would seem to exist a way out. Some authors (e.g. Givón 1975: 49, Bolinger 1978: 489) have used "grammaticization" instead of "grammaticaliza-

2 Grammaticalization: characterization and delimitation of the concept

tion".[1] We might adopt this use and substitute, accordingly, "grammaticity" for "grammaticality" in the intended sense. Unfortunately, this terminological arrangement would soon come to an inconsistent end, because we would not only have to call "grammatic" what we always have called "grammatical"; what is more, this terminological regularization would not be implementable in French, the language in which the term "grammaticalization" was coined in the first place. Finally, it seems paradoxical to give up the well-established "grammaticalization" instead of the rare "grammaticization". We will therefore abide by the terms "grammatical", "grammaticality" and "grammaticalization" and use them exclusively in the sense in which *grammatical* designates that which belongs to the grammar. It seems more convenient to leave the resolution of the terminological conflict to the other side; one might, for example, resort to the expression *grammatically well-formed* if one wants to signify 'grammatically well-formed'.

A more serious question is whether the term "grammaticalization" is not unduly stretched if we apply it to such a large range of phenomena. On the one hand, I intend to follow Žirmunskij in subsuming the formation of analytic constructions under grammaticalization. On the other hand, the process does not stop at the level of inflectional morphology. The English pronoun *him*, after having been grammaticalized to a verb-suffixal object marker *-im* in Tok Pisin, has further evolved into an invariable transitive verb marker. Such linear extensions of grammaticalization processes into derivational morphology are not at all rare. On the one hand, since such extensions continue the same pattern, they should be called by the same name. On the other hand, it does not seem correct to say that the suffix *-im*, in its change from an object marker to a transitive verb marker, becomes more grammatical. A term slightly more comprehensive than "grammaticalization" would seem to be needed; but the alternatives that have appeared in the literature are no more satisfactory. Li & Thompson (1974), Givón (1979: 209) and Brettschneider (1980: 94) have offered the term "condensation" essentially for what is here called grammaticalization.[2] A precursor of this term is Gabelentz's (1891: 433, 436) "Verdichtungsprozess". In a loose sense, *condensation* may be used to designate one aspect of grammaticalization, namely the narrowing down of the level of grammatical structure (see §4.3.1); and this is actually what the above authors have in mind. However, if we take the word literally, it would have to mean that something becomes denser, compacter in the course

---

[1] A further abbreviation is represented in Werner's (1979: 965f) German participle *grammatisiert*, formed on an unattested *grammatisieren* "to grammatize" (i.e. grammaticalize).

[2] Brettschneider, Li and Thompson actually apply this term only to one specific grammaticalization channel, namely the reduction of a (subordinate) clause to a word.

of grammaticalization. On the contrary, the authors quoted in Chapter 1 concur that the meaning of a grammaticalized sign is weakened in the same measure as its expression is weakened; a more grammaticalized sign does not say the same thing as a less grammaticalized one in a smaller space, as seems to be implied by the term "condensation".

The term "reduction" (used, for instance, in Langacker 1977: 103–107) does not have this shortcoming, but displays a different one, which, incidentally, it shares with "condensation". It is not specific enough, because it covers also the reduction of a phrase to a compound word, which is not a grammaticalization process.

Authors depending on A. Martinet have sometimes used the term 'morphématisation' essentially with the meaning 'grammaticalization' (e.g. in Martinet 1968: 1064f). This presupposes Martinet's terminology, in which "morphème" equals other linguists' "grammatical morpheme". Apart from its local character, "morphématisation" has the disadvantage of being too narrow. Although the formation of grammatical morphemes is probably the focus of grammaticalization, it is by no means all of it.

We are thus led back to our term "grammaticalization". I see no way to avoid its extension, in a generic sense, to processes such as the one illustrated above. If one wants to make specific reference to just that type of process, one will, of course, not use the term "grammaticalization"; §5.2 will deal with the question of whether a convenient term can be found.

2.2 The meaning of "grammaticalization"

Having settled on the term, we may now characterize the concept more fully. We will first justify one decision which has been presupposed in the above terminological discussion, namely the interpretation of grammaticalization as a process which may not only change a lexical into a grammatical item, but may also shift an item "from a less grammatical to a more grammatical status", in Kuryłowicz's words. Since adjectives derived in -*al* are commonly non-relative (they have no polar antonyms and do not take part in comparison; cf. *maternal*), one might take the position that the property of being grammatical, of belonging to the grammar, is a binary property and not a matter of degree. As I said, we will postpone discussion of this problem to §5.2. Anyway, if this were accepted, then grammaticalization could not be a gradual, relative process. From this position it would be correct to say that something is either grammaticalized or not grammaticalized. This is the position of Jakobson, Mel'čuk and Lyons. Lyons writes (1977: 234):

2 Grammaticalization: characterization and delimitation of the concept

> Different languages make a different selection, as it were, from the set of possible distinctions that could be made and grammaticalize them (i.e. make them grammatically functional) in terms of such categories as tense, number, gender, case, person, proximity, visibility, shape, animacy, etc.

Throughout his book, Lyons consistently uses the expression "x is grammaticalized in language L" only if x is a semantic category which is represented by a grammatical category in L. At first sight, this appears to provide us with a simple and intuitively satisfactory interpretation of the notion "grammaticalization". But then we must also provide binary criteria which answer the question: which conditions must something fulfill in order to be a grammatical category of a language L? Jakobson (1959: 489; see the quotation above on p. 6f.) and Mel'čuk (1976: 84) answer that the essential criterion is obligatoriness: a meaning is grammatical in L if the speaker cannot choose to leave it unspecified. The criterion of obligatoriness will in fact be used below (§4.2.3); but it does not appear to me to be an absolute one. Something is obligatory relative to the context; i.e. it may be obligatory in one context, optional in another and impossible in a third context. Take, for instance, the category of number. In Latin, every noun form compulsorily belongs either to the singular or to the plural; the speaker cannot choose to leave the number unspecified. Here the criterion correctly decides that number is a grammatical category in Latin. In Turkish, most nouns may be specified for number by adding a plural suffix. Some nouns may not, for instance terms of nationality or profession if they form the predicate. No noun may be specified for number if preceded by a cardinal numeral. In most other contexts, number is optional; i.e. the unmarked form may signify the singular or the plural. Is number obligatory in Turkish or not? Certainly not nearly as obligatory as in Latin. Should we therefore say that number is not a grammatical category in Turkish? Would it not be more illuminating to say that number is more grammaticalized in Latin than in Turkish?

An analogous argument could be made with respect to any other criterion that one might be inclined to propose. Chapter 3 will provide abundant evidence that even the mere transition from a lexeme to a grammatical formative (if we were to restrict grammaticalization to this process) is not a leap, but a gradual shift to a new function. The category of prepositions is a notable example. In many languages, there are some prepositions like English *beyond* which need not be treated individually in the grammar because they obey general rules of syntax like other ordinary lexemes; and there are other prepositions like *of* which require special treatment in the grammar because they are obligatory in a number of constructions. The space in between is filled by the bulk of prepositions,

2.2 The meaning of "grammaticalization"

which are at different stages on their way from lexeme to grammatical formative. I therefore see no way to avoid the conclusion that grammaticalization is a process of gradual change, and that its products may have different degrees of grammaticality.

If grammaticalization is not a binary, but a gradual change of state, then we must face the problem that it may be an open-ended process. Some authors (e.g. Ronneberger-Sibold (1980: 113–115)) have restricted the notion of grammaticalization to the passage from an analytic to a synthetic construction. We have already observed (p. 3) that this passage, the agglutination process, stood godfather to the denomination of agglutination theory. Possibly this transition into the unity of the word is the most salient phase of the grammaticalization process. Nevertheless, the nature of the process is the same before and after this phase. The formation of analytic constructions out of "word combinations" (Žirmunskij), on the one hand, and the melting of an agglutinative to a flexional formation,[3] on the other, are phases of the grammaticalization process. The question naturally arises: where does grammaticalization start, and where does it end? We will provisionally answer this question by the diagram in Figure 2.1, which incorporates the one presented in Givón (1979c: 209).

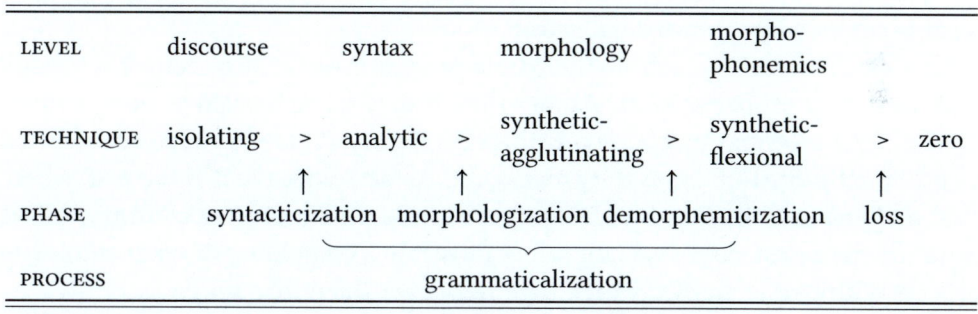

Figure 2.1: The phases of grammaticalization

This picture is incomplete and simplified, because it represents only two of the factors involved in grammaticalization, namely those that will be called condensation and coalescence in §4.3, and because it pretends a perfect correlation be-

---

[3] The terminological confusion associated, especially in German, with the term "Flexion" and its cognates may be resolved in English, for our purposes, by the following convention: "inflection" will be opposed to "word-formation" (esp. "derivation") as the syntax-bound part of morphology; "flexion" will be opposed to "agglutination" (and "isolation") as one of the techniques of morphological typology (namely the fusional or amalgamating one, which Sapir (1921: 129ff) calls "inflective"). Cf. Comrie (1981a: 41f) on the terminological dilemma.

2 Grammaticalization: characterization and delimitation of the concept

tween these two. Nevertheless, it suffices to illustrate, for present purposes, the range of the grammaticalization process and the phases conventionally recognized in it. Thus we assume that grammaticalization starts from a free collocation of potentially uninflected lexical words in discourse. This is converted into a syntactic construction by SYNTACTICIZATION, whereby some of the lexemes assume grammatical functions so that the construction may be called analytic. MORPHOLOGIZATION, which here means the same as agglutination, reduces the analytic construction to a synthetic one, so that grammatical formatives become agglutinating affixes. In the next phase, the unity of the word is tightened, as the morphological technique changes from agglutinative to flexional. This transition from morphology to morphophonemics will here be called DEMORPHEMICIZATION. Givón calls it lexicalization, and this is the fourth sense in which the term appears in the literature. This need not worry us at the moment. We pass over to the final phase, where expression and content of the grammatical category become zero.

I repeat that this account is simplified. It makes it appear as if the grammaticalization process had a clear-cut end, which we will see it has not. On the other hand, the start of the process is not readily identifiable either, and we will defer this problem, too. The sole function of Figure 2.1 is to give a first impression of what is covered by grammaticalization.

A single example to illustrate the whole process is not easy to come by, though such examples probably exist. At any rate, it may be remarked at this juncture that it is not essential to grammaticalization theory that every element affected by grammaticalization enter the process at the start and leave it at the end, where start and end are identified with reference to Figure 2.1. On the contrary, this is certainly the rarest case. I will therefore illustrate a complete grammaticalization process with two examples which together cover the entire range.

From the beginning of the literary tradition up to the postclassical period, the Latin language had an elaborate system of demonstrative pronouns. There was a deictically neutral pronoun *is*, which was also used as an anaphoric personal pronoun. Besides, there were three deictic pronouns, of first (*hic*), second (*iste*) and third (*ille*) person deixis. Apart from their function as NPs, which is our concern here, all four could function as determiners. In Archaic Latin, the members of the deictic triad always had some demonstrative force. Their use was subject to no syntactic rule; they occurred where and how the speaker saw fit. However, *ille* was the unmarked member of the triad and began to assume anaphoric function, thus intruding into the area of *is*, which it finally ousted in Vulgar Latin. At this stage, *ille* was a neutral anaphoric pronoun, witness E1, from the first half of the 6th cent. A.D.

2.2 The meaning of "grammaticalization"

E1   Latin (Pulgram 1978: 288)
duo rustici sic ad hora captum comederunt, et ita illis contigit, et unus illorum sanguinem deiuso produxit nimium. (Anth. *obs.cib.* 25)
'two peasants ate one [turtle dove] just caught, and it so happened to them, and one of them voided too much blood'

Here we have already entered the path of syntacticization, because the function of *ille* is but the grammatical representation of an NP of a previous clause. Still, *ille* is not commonly used as a personal pronoun in subject position. This step has been made, to a varying extent, in the Romance languages. In Standard Italian, for instance, a finite verb does not need an overt subject; *vende* alone may be used to mean 'he sells'. In French, however, the personal pronoun *il* (<*ille*) is obligatory if there is no other subject; the corresponding example would be *il vend*. With this, the phase of syntacticization is completed: we have arrived at an analytical verb form.

The morphologization of this combination would presuppose that *il* remains present even when there is a subject in the same clause. This step has not (yet) been taken; but preparations are being made. In a construction such as *Et lui, vend-il des fleurs?*, the left-dislocated NP is almost the syntactic subject of the clause, and yet the pronoun *il* cannot be absent.[4] It is enclitic to the verb and could, through agglutination, become a suffixal personal ending. (It is improbable that it will do so in French; but this is not essential to the demonstration.) Summarizing then, we have seen that Latin *ille* has started at the beginning of the scale in Figure 2.1 and has advanced, in the shape of French *il*, to the beginning of the morphologization phase.

The second half of this demonstration takes us back to Proto-Indo-European. The so-called secondary personal endings of the active verb were *-m, -s, -t for the three singular persons. Though the details are not recoverable, scholars generally agree that these suffixes derive from the agglutination of personal pronouns. (As will be recalled [p. 3], this was already Bopp's position.) In particular, the third person singular suffix *-t is most probably a reduced form of the neutral demonstrative stem *to- (details in Szemerényi 1970: 302–305 and Seebold 1971). We can therefore be fairly confident that this example takes up at the very point where the former example leaves off.

Still in Proto-Indo-European times, these endings were extended by a suffix *-i, whose nature need not concern us here (cf. p. 39). By the time of Archaic Latin,

---

[4] Cf. also sentences such as *A quelle heure le train arrive-t-il?, La grammaire n'a-t-elle pas le devoir de s'attacher aux fonctions?, Peut-être les hypothèses contraires veulent-elles seulement dire que* ...

this -*i* was again lost. The personal suffixes retained their pronominal function, i.e. their capability of representing the subject, over the most part of the subsequent time. Classical Latin *vendit* means 'he sells' and needs an overt (pronominal) subject even less than Italian *vende* does. However, the pronominal function gradually got lost, and parallel to this the morphological bond between the stem and the personal endings grew tighter. In Latin, the personal endings cannot be neatly separated from the stem, which means that they are not agglutinative but flexional and they are partly different according to conjugation class; so in this sense, and to this extent, they are demorphemicized. This is the transition from morphology to morphophonemics. The phonological substance of the endings is then further reduced; to the Latin *vendo, vendis, vendit* corresponds the Italian *vendo, vendi, vende*. As was mentioned above, the Italian personal endings can still represent, by themselves, the person of the subject. This is no longer so in French. The personal endings have been reduced to zero in the singular (and in the third person plural), which means that apart from exceptions, person is no longer a morphological category of the singular verb. This is the end of the grammaticalization process.

2.3 Degrammaticalization

Various authors (Givón 1975: 96, Langacker 1977: 103f, Vincent 1980a: 56–60) have claimed that grammaticalization is unidirectional; that is, it is an irreversible process, the scale in Figure 2.1 cannot be run through from right to left, there is no DEGRAMMATICALIZATION. Others have adduced examples in favor of degrammaticalization. The few that have come to my knowledge will be briefly discussed.

Kuryłowicz (1965: 52f) maintains that there is a reverse process to grammaticalization which he calls lexicalization. His examples have, according to him, the following structure: derivational category is grammaticalized to inflectional category and is again lexicalized to derivational category. The examples are: Proto-Indo-European *-a* was a derivational nominal affix with collective meaning. In Latin, it was grammaticalized to the plural marker of neuter nouns, e.g. *ovum* 'egg', pl. *ova*. In Italian, the Latin neuter nouns have become masculine and form their plural in -*i*. However, -*a* is again used as a derivational collective suffix, e.g. in *muro* 'wall' — *mura*, *uovo* 'egg' — *uova*.

The Pre-English meaning of the perfect was stative. In Modern English, all the verbs which formerly formed their perfect with *be* use *have* now, and the meaning of the perfect is no longer stative but completive. However, for some verbs the perfect with *be* has been restored in the old stative meaning, e.g. *is come/gone*.

Again, the verbs *can, may, shall, dare* are original perfect forms (known as preterite-presents in Germanic linguistics). While the perfect has changed its meaning in English, today these forms again signify a present state. Furthermore, the hypothesis that they have changed from inflectional forms to derivational stems is evidenced by the fact that they have developed an inflection of their own: *could, might, should, durst*.[5]

None of these examples stands up to closer scrutiny. All of them suffer from the defect that the newly evolved derivational category does not possess a minimum of productivity, whereas those Proto-Indo-European derivational categories which they ultimately go back to (if we may assume, for the sake of argument, that perfect was a derivational category in Proto-Indo-European) must clearly have been highly productive, for otherwise they could not have yielded inflectional categories. Instead, the specific examples which Kuryłowicz adduces are virtually the only ones of their kind; that is, they are lexicalized in quite a different sense (the one we already encountered in Žirmunskij): they are frozen, not amenable to any rule, idiomaticized.

Secondly (and this is a difficulty which most putative examples of degrammaticalization are liable to meet with), these lexicalized forms have not really made their way back from a more grammaticalized, inflectional stage, but instead directly continue the original stage. Italian *uova* is not a modern alternative to *uovi*, nor has the construction *is gone* developed on the basis of an earlier *has gone*, nor do *can* etc. go back to older completive perfect forms. Instead, Italian *uova* continues Latin *ova*, and English *is gone* and *can* etc. continue Proto-Germanic stative perfects or preterite-presents, respectively. Finally, although it must be admitted that the *-a* of Italian *mura* does not go back to Latin, it is not the case that *uova* and *mura* are collectives; they are plural forms. So these examples do not establish a degrammaticalization process.

Kahr (1976: 122) offers a single example of degrammaticalization. Modern Turkish has a postposition *için* 'for', which, like some others, takes nominal complements in their unmarked form, but pronominal complements in the genitive (cf. p. 39 below). In some rare instances, this morpheme is suffixed, e.g. in *on-un-çün* (D3-GEN-for) 'therefore'. Since these suffixed forms are archaic relics, the modern productive postpositional usage must be explained, according to Kahr, as a degrammaticalization of the suffixal construction.

---

[5] As a last example, Kuryłowicz mentions in passing the development of sex to gender to sex from Proto-Indo-European via Proto-Germanic to Modern English. This is a process whose details are complicated; however, it is, in the last analysis, an instance of continuous grammaticalization; see Lehmann (1982b: §7.2).

2 Grammaticalization: characterization and delimitation of the concept

This is just like explaining the prepositional function of Portuguese *com* 'with' through the degrammaticalization of the prefixal construction *comigo, contigo* etc. 'with me, with you' etc. or, for that matter, of the Latin suffixal construction *mecum, tecum* etc. It seems clear that the Turkish case must be just like the Romance one: What was originally an adposition continued to be an adposition in modern times, except in combination with pronouns, where it became affixal already in early times.

A class of possible examples comes from DECLITICIZATION. One factor of the phonological weakening of a grammaticalized element is its deaccentuation and subsequent cliticization. If elements could be found which were exclusively clitic at a former stage, but at a later stage allowed an autonomous use, these would be examples of degrammaticalization. Jeffers & Zwicky (1980: §3) first adduce the Indo-European relative pronouns **yo* and **kwo-*, which may be accentuated in their respective Sanskrit and Latin forms *yas* and *qui*. These are said to derive from clitic connective particles which formed a sequence with clitic anaphoric pronouns. Such a sequence coalesced and was reinterpreted as an inflected relative pronoun.

Two objections must be raised against this argument. First, even granting the etymological correctness of this reconstruction, nobody can guarantee that these connectives were actually clitic at the stage in question. Hittite, for instance, does have such sequences as hypothesized by Jeffers and Zwicky; but the connectives are not clitic. Second, the reconstruction proposed by Jeffers and Zwicky is probably false. The syntax of the clitic connectives in the historical languages (e.g. Hittite *-ya*, Sanskrit *-ca*, Latin *-que*) differs markedly from that assumed by them for Indo-European. The relative pronouns are much more plausibly derived from an anaphoric/demonstrative and an interrogative/indefinite pronoun, respectively (see Lehmann 1984: Ch. VI.1), whose relation to the connectives may well be left open. Given the notorious indeterminacy of reconstruction, everything is, of course, possible. What we need, however, are not hypothetical, but historical examples.

Jeffers' and Zwicky's second case is of a completely different nature. The verb of such ancient Indo-European languages as Vedic could be unaccentuated, especially in main clauses; this appears to be no longer possible at later stages. Though this is probably true, it is not an instance of decliticization, since verbs have never been clitic. Clisis is a lexically inherent property of an element which may manifest itself either independently or in dependence on the semantosyntactic context (Jeffers' and Zwicky's "special" vs. "simple" clitics). In the case at hand, however, we are dealing with a certain pattern of sentence intonation

2.3 Degrammaticalization

which leaves the main verb unaccentuated and which ceases to be usual, or even possible, at a later stage.

The last potential example of degrammaticalization is provided by English. In Proto-Germanic, the genitive suffix *-s* was a flexional ending bound to the word. In Modern English, however, we find such phrases as *the King of England's daughter* and *the man I met yesterday's son*, where the *-s* is agglutinated to a complex NP. This looks like a bona fide case. However, the historical details are complex (see Janda 1980). On the one hand, the originally flexional *-s* became more agglutinative, in Middle English, as a contingent result of the reduction and regularization of the Old English case paradigm. On the other hand, dialects and lower sociolects of Middle English had the alternative construction "NP *his* N" (e.g. *the king (of England) his daughter*) available, which itself became homophonous with the inherited genitive. As a result, the genitive suffix was reanalyzed as a clitic possessive pronoun. Thus, it was not the genitive on its own what expanded to higher syntactic levels. Rather, the (real or putative) clitic possessive pronoun, which had been compatible with these levels from start, got generalized to non-masculine genders.

We may therefore conclude this discussion with the observation that no cogent examples of degrammaticalization have been found. This result is important because it allows us to recognize grammaticalization at the synchronic level. Given two variants which are related by the parameters of grammaticalization to be made explicit in Chapter 4, we can always tell which way the grammaticalization goes, or must have gone.[6] The significance of this for the purposes of internal reconstruction is obvious; see §8.3.

If grammaticalization is really a unidirectional process, one must ask why this should be so. I will not anticipate here the theoretical considerations of the final chapter, but mention only the explanation that Givón (1975: 96) has given. He says that grammaticalization essentially involves a deletion of both semantic and phonological substance. Degrammaticalization would have to be an enrichment in semantic and phonological substance. Now while the result of a deletion process may be predictable, its source is generally not predictable from the result; so the product of an enrichment process, or of degrammaticalization, would also not be predictable. This appears to be a step in the right direction. However, it remains to be seen, first to what extent the results of grammaticalization processes are really predictable, and secondly, if rules for these processes can be found, why natural languages cannot apply them, at least to non-zero elements, in reverse direction.

---

[6] This is true, in the first place, on the synchronic and diachronic axes. The actual historical development may still have deviated from diachronic principles if other factors such as borrowing intervened.

2.4 Renovation and innovation

Grammaticalization changes analytic into synthetic constructions. There are, however, numerous instances in the history where languages have changed from the synthetic to the analytic type. This was in fact the observation on which August W. von Schlegel (1818: 14–30) based his introduction of the terms "analytic" and "synthetic" in the first place. He observed, for instance, that Latin case inflection has been substituted by prepositional constructions in the Romance languages, that certain tenses are no longer formed by verb inflection but by auxiliaries, and so forth. If such changes from the synthetic to the analytic do occur, aren't they instances of degrammaticalization? This has been maintained by Lightfoot (1979: 223–225), but the argument has rightly been rejected by Heine & Reh (1984: 75f). Far from invalidating grammaticalization theory, the evolution synthetic → analytic is predicted by it and has been so predicted since the early days of agglutination theory. If the evolution along grammaticalization scales takes the form of a spiral, this implies that forms which are given up near the end of the scale may be substituted by new forms entering at its beginning. For degrammaticalization to obtain, analytical forms would have to be historical continuants of synthetic forms; but this actually never happens.

This presupposes that we make a clear distinction between the two diachronic relations 'y continues x' and 'y replaces x'. Within a grammaticalization scale, the relation 'y continues x' is equivalent to the relation 'x is grammaticalized to y'. However, the relation 'y replaces x' is neither a relation of grammaticalization nor of degrammaticalization. We shall call it, with Meillet's "renouvellement" in mind, the relation of RENOVATION, also called renewal in the literature. Within a grammaticalization scale, 'y replaces x' is equivalent to 'x is renovated by y'. For brevity's sake, I will employ the following symbolism:

x > y	=	'x is grammaticalized to y';
x /r y	=	'x is renovated by y'.
EXAMPLES		
Latin *ille*	>	French *il*
Latin *clara mente*	>	Italian *chiaramente*
Latin *ille*	/r	French *ce(lui) là*
Latin *clare*	/r	Italian *chiaramente*

2.4 Renovation and innovation

Further examples are the renovation of the future, perfect, passive and adjective comparison, which had been synthetic categories in the ancient Indo-European languages, by the corresponding analytic categories in several of the modern languages, including English and the Romance languages. A particularly rich field of constant renovation are the subordinating conjunctions as already observed by Meillet. All of these examples will be discussed more fully in Chapter 3. A wealth of further material for the development of the synthetic towards the analytic may be found in Tauli (1966: Ch. I).

Now consider the situation where an analytic construction y comes into being, but there is no x such that x /r y. For example, the Latin *ille, illa* has also been grammaticalized into the French definite articles *le, la*. But when we ask what the x is in "Latin x /r French *le, la*", we get no answer. Latin had no grammatical category which corresponded to the French articles, so that nothing has been renovated by these. This is an instance of what Meillet (1915) and Traugott (1980) have called (novel) creation. This is an imprecise term, because all linguistic activity, including renovation, is creative activity. INNOVATION, as used in Benveniste (1968), seems to be a better one, because it expresses the desired meaning and provides a suitable contrast to "renovation".[7] Unfortunately, *to innovate* is intransitive, so that we will resort to *create* in case we need a transitive verb. Further examples of innovation are the introduction of numeral classifiers in Persian, the distinction expressed by *ser* vs. *estar* in Spanish, the progressive form in English and the imperfective vs. perfective aspects in Slavic.

In theory, the distinction between innovation and renovation is entirely clear. Innovation is revolutionary; it creates grammatical categories that had not been in the language before. Renovation is conservative; it only introduces new forms for old categories. The notion of a category which had not been in the language before should cause no problems. Obviously no one would like to commit himself to the claim that no ancestral stage of the Indo-European languages had numeral classifiers, an essence/accidence distinction or a distinction between progressive and neutral or perfective and imperfective aspects. What matters here is the stage immediately preceding the innovation.

In practice, however, there are numerous borderline cases between innovation and renovation. First we must notice that renovation takes its time. There are admittedly cases where the new construction entirely and almost instantly replaces the old one, taking a function and shape maximally similar to the old ones; this has occurred in the renovation of the Latin future in the Romance lan-

---

[7] A wider use of this term has been made in Indo-European linguistics, where it may cover what is here called innovation, renovation and analogical change.

guages. More often, however, the new and the old constructions coexist for some time. An example is provided by the new analytic and the old synthetic perfect ("passé composé" vs. "passé simple") in the Romance languages. As long as such a situation obtains, the two categories tend to be functionally non-identical, so that we have two categories where we formerly only had one. So far this is not really a conservative change. Conservatism asserts itself only when the old construction falls out of use and the new one takes over its function (and possibly its morphosyntactic form). So what is conservative about renovation is not the particular situation brought about by the introduction of the renovative periphrastic construction, but rather the reentering of a grammaticalization channel which, if run through, will lead to a result maximally similar to the situation which had obtained formerly.

Secondly, two grammatical constructions can be functionally similar only to the extent that they are formally similar. If the renovation of a construction enters upon a path that cannot lead to anything formally similar to the former construction, a complete replacement of the old function will never be obtained, and to this extent the change will be partly renovative, partly innovative. Consider the change that is often called the renovation of Latin case inflection by prepositional constructions. Prepositions will never become case suffixes; even their development into case prefixes is relatively rare (cf. §3.4.1.3). Here it suffices to observe that the Latin case suffixes have disappeared, but the Romance prepositions are far from truly fulfilling their function. On the one hand, they do less than that, since strict word order comes in where prepositions (or other means) fail. On the other hand, they do more than that, since prepositions are much more intimately connected with the verb than are case suffixes and may be used to derive compound verbs. Moreover, prepositions can express finer distinctions than cases can because there are more of them. Consequently, the loss of Latin case inflection and the introduction of prepositional constructions is renovative to the extent that the functions of the two constructions overlap, and it is innovative to the extent that they do not.

2.5 Reinforcement

If an element is weakened through grammaticalization, there are, in fact, two possibilities open to linguistic conservatism. The first is to give it up and replace it by a new, but similar one. This is renovation, as we have just seen. The second is to REINFORCE it, thus compensating for and checking the decay. Here are some examples: Latin *aliquis* 'someone' is reinforced by *unus* 'one', yielding **aliqui-*

unu; this is then grammaticalized to Italian *alcuno*, French *aucun* etc. Latin *ille*, which, as we have seen, was grammaticalized to the Romance definite article, was reinforced in its demonstrative function: *eccu illu 'voilà that (one)' resulted in Italian *quello*. Many Latin prepositions have been reinforced on their way into Romance; e.g. Latin *ante* 'in front, before' was strengthened by preposed *ab* 'from' before it developed into French *avant*. We will introduce a symbol for the relation of reinforcement: 'the reinforced form of x is y' will be written 'x ⇒ y'. The three symbols >, /r, and ⇒ will also be used in the converse relations 'y < x', 'y r/ x' and 'y ⇐ x'.

Reinforcement can be reiterated ad libitum. For instance, IE *in 'in' ⇒ *entos > Latin *intus* 'within, inside' ⇒ *de-intus 'of/from within' > French *dans* 'in' ⇒ *dedans* 'inside'. Pre-Latin *is 'that (one)' ⇒ Latin *iste* 'that one on your side' ⇒ Proto-Romance *eccu istu lo 'that one' > It. *questo* 'this' ⇒ *questo... qui* and French *ce...-ci* 'this (one) here'. At the stage where the reinforcement is first made, it sounds to puristic ears like a redundant accumulation,[8] a hypercharacterization (on the latter, see Malkiel (1957) and Tauli (1966: Ch. IV). But the emphasis soon vanishes, and the reinforced expression becomes neutral again.

The examples illustrate the reinforcement of an element by its morphological union with another one. The situation becomes slightly more complicated when an expression is reinforced not by adding an element next to the grammatical marker already present, but at a different place in the construction. Latin *non* 'not' was reinforced by *passum* 'step' in a construction *non V *passu*, to yield French *ne* V *pas*. The particle *ne* can subsequently be dropped, and the negation *pas* ends up at a different position from Latin *non*. Another example, which I have already used in a simplified manner, but which is really quite complex, are the Latin-Romance prepositions. In Proto-Indo-European, we may assume there were agglutinative case suffixes with rather specific functions. When these got more grammaticalized, they were first specified, and thus reinforced, by adverbs; for example, the accusativus directionis was specified by *peri 'around, along' > Latin *per* 'through'. These adverbs were in turn grammaticalized, yielding on the one hand preverbs and on the other adpositions. In Latin we encounter expressions such as *percurrere urbem* or *currere per urbem* 'to run through the city'. We neglect here the possible hypercharacterization *percurrere per urbem* and pay attention to the fact that in no one of these expressions is the suffix substituted by the preposition or preverb. There is no alternative between case suffix and preposition, such as there is between passé simple and passé composé. We see

---

[8] Cf. the telling remark by A. Schlegel, who was the first to observe some of the above cases; according to him (1818: 30), they "ne laissent pas de sentir un peu la barbarie."

2 Grammaticalization: characterization and delimitation of the concept

here that what later on will result in a (partial) renovation, begins as a complex reinforcement (cf. Jakobson 1936: 55). In those many instances where the renovative construction starts as an extension of the renovated one, we may speak of RENOVATION BY REINFORCEMENT; whereas in the other case, where the renovative construction syntagmatically excludes the renovated one, we may speak of PURE RENOVATION.

On the same basis, we are led to distinguish between two types of reinforcement: SIMPLE REINFORCEMENT consists in the morphological union of the bleached element with the specifying one. COMPLEX REINFORCEMENT consists in the introduction of a specifying element in a different position of the construction. We started this chapter with simple reinforcement; this is necessarily conservative. In complex reinforcement, however, if the reinforcing element ousts the reinforced one, we have a source of quite novel constructions.[9] We may even speculate, since no new construction starts ab nihilo, but necessarily uses elements of inherited constructions, that there may be a gradual transition between reinforcement and innovation.[10]

---

[9] Developments of this type are also responsible for a considerable amount of headache caused to the historical linguist by certain grammatical formatives. How would we be able to understand the etymology of, e.g., French *pas, rien, point, personne* or of Italian *cosa* 'what', if we did not know that they arose through reinforcement (cf. §3.2.2.3)?

[10] The distinction between renovation, innovation and reinforcement as made here is also postulated in Kahr (1976: 115), in the terms "renewal", "novel creation" and "hypercharacterization", respectively.

3 Grammatical domains

This chapter deals with what Givón (1979c) and Heine & Reh (1984) have called the various channels of grammaticalization. The term "channel" graphically expresses the fact that the fate of a category in grammaticalization is largely predetermined once we know two things: (1) its meaning, (2) its syntactic function. These conditions are equally necessary. Givón (1979b: 213f) and others have emphasized condition 1, whereas Meillet (1915: 170) had already said: "c'est le rôle dans la phrase qui décide de tout."

The terms "grammaticalization scale" and "grammaticalization channel" will often be used interchangeably. A GRAMMATICALIZATION SCALE is a theoretical construct along which functionally similar signs types are ordered according to their degree of grammaticality as measured by certain parameters to be discussed in Chapter 4. The relation among the elements on such a scale is panchronic. A GRAMMATICALIZATION CHANNEL is a frequently recurring route which signs with a given function may take when they are grammaticalized in language change. The relation among the elements in such a channel is a diachronic one.

The aim of Chapter 3 is twofold. First, a certain amount of examples of grammaticalization will be accumulated in order to give an idea of the nature of this type of process and to provide suitable empirical material to refer to from the more theoretical chapters to follow. Second, although, naturally, not all parts of the grammar can be treated here, the chapter is meant to demonstrate that grammaticalization is omnipresent and not specific to any particular part of the grammar.

The subdivision of the material follows, in part, from the connections established by grammaticalization channels. But as some channels cross, the presentation will necessarily be somewhat repetitive. The amount of material presented is still greatly reduced in comparison with the masses of evidence available for most of the channels. It would be impossible to display it all here; the reader is referred to the cited literature.

3 Grammatical domains

3.1 Verbal complexes

3.1.1 Existence and possession

The various forms of English *be*, as well as of its cognates in other Indo-European languages, go back to three different roots: PIE **bhew-* 'become' yields forms such as English *be*, German *bin*, Spanish *fui*. PIE **Hes-* 'exist, be in a place' yields forms such as English *is*, German *ist*, Spanish *es*. And Proto-Germanic **wes-* 'live' yields forms such as English *was*, German *war*. These are doubtless typical sources of the verb 'to be'. 'He lives' is, for instance, the etymological meaning of the verb *ʔúhki* 'he is' in Tunica (Haas 1941: 41ff). Another source of 'be'-verbs is 'to stand'. This can be seen in Spanish/Portuguese *estar*, French *être*, which derive from Latin *stare*. Among the 15 auxiliaries which Žirmunskij (1966: 85f) cites from Uzbek, there are also *quj-* 'stand, place' and *tur-* 'stand'. 'To remain' is the original meaning of the Portugese verb *ficar*, which is currently taking over some functions of the verb 'to be'. These verbs are usually highly irregular or even suppletive, which points to their grammaticalized status.

English *have*, German *haben* and cognates derive from Proto-Germanic **hafjan* 'seize'. Spanish *tener* 'have' meant 'hold' in Latin. Anticipating future developments of English, we can say that 'receive' is another source: *have* (phonologically /v/ or /z/ or /d/ in the various inflected forms) is currently reinforced by *got* and will soon be entirely renovated by it. These are all, of course, common sources of the possessive verb; see Seiler (1983: 104–106).

Although there are diachronic derivational relations between 'be' and 'have' in many languages, there is, interestingly, no unidirectional grammaticalization relation between them. On the one hand, existence predications are often grammaticalized constructions of the verb 'have'. Thus dialectal German *es hat*, Spanish *ha(y)*, French *il y a*, all 'there is/are'. On the other hand, possessive predications very often contain a verb of existence: Latin *Paulo est liber* 'Paul has a book', Mandarin *wǒ yǒu yí-zhī gǒu* (I Exist one-CL dog) 'I have a dog'; cf. also Russian *est'* and Japanese *arimasu*. This is, by the way, an argument against reducing possession to existence or vice versa.

3.1.2 The copula

A copula is a word which turns a nominal into a predicate. This function will not be considered here because it will be treated in subsequent sections. Here we concentrate on the question: through which grammaticalization channels do elements arise which function as the copula in nominal clauses? There are, in principle, two such channels.

As is familiar from Indo-European languages, a copula may be a grammaticalized 'be'-verb, any one of those treated in the preceding section. In this case, the copula has obviously verbal properties, i.e. it may inflect for person, number, tense etc.; though it may be absent when all the categories are unmarked, as it is, e.g., in Russian.

A less familiar, but equally frequent origin of the copula is a demonstrative or anaphoric pronoun. Consider the case of the Chinese copula, as analyzed by Li & Thompson (1977). In Archaic Chinese, nominal clauses contained no copula. The subject of a nominal predication, especially a relatively heavy one, could be topicalized by left-dislocation. This necessitates a substitute in the subject position of the nominal clause, a demonstrative or personal pronoun which anaphorically takes up the topicalized NP. The resulting nominal clause is, of course, syntactically completely unmarked. The complex sentence structure is as follows: $_S$[NP $_S$[DEM NP]]. The DEM in Archaic Chinese is *shì*. By the 1st century A.D., this construction was sufficiently grammaticalized to be reanalyzed as $_S$[NP DEM NP]. Here *shì* already functions as a copula, one criterion being that it is indifferent as to the person of the subject. About the same time, it ceases to be used as a demonstrative, while in its copula function it becomes increasingly obligatory.

Copulas of this origin may also be found, according to Li and Thompson, in Hebrew, Palestinian Arabic, Wappo and Zway. Such copulas do not, of course, express verbal categories. Since the latter are, in fact, irrelevant to them, they are also not distributed according to marked and unmarked verbal categories, but also appear in what would correspond to a present indicative verbal clause.

The second grammaticalization channel also admits nominal clauses which already contain a copula, which is then reinforced by the pronoun. This is currently happening in French. 'To live is to learn to die' is not *Vivre est apprendre à mourir*, but rather *Vivre c'est apprendre à mourir*, which is pronounced, as Frei (1929: 72) insists, "sans pause".

3.1.3 Modals and moods

Modal verbs or auxiliaries may, of course, derive from full verbs. In what follows, I list some possible sources.

In the Germanic languages, many modal verbs derive from Proto-Indo-European PRETERITE-PRESENTS, i.e. original full verbs whose inherited perfect form was used with stative present function. Among them are OE *can(n)* 'know, be able', *sceal* 'owe', *mæg* 'be able'. These verbs developed a past tense inflection of their own, which made them morphologically highly irregular. Their syntax

3 Grammatical domains

was still that of common verbs in Old English. During the Middle English period, however, they developed those syntactic pecularities which make them constitute the syntactic category of modal verbs; and as such the verbs *can*, *shall*, *may* and others appear in the 16th century. This development is analyzed in detail by Lightfoot (1979: 98ff), though he tries to do without the concept of grammaticalization. A synchronic example for the ambivalence, or transitional status, of a verb between full verb and auxiliary is provided by Romanian *poate* 'can'; see Mallinson & Blake (1981: 198f).

DESIDERATIVE modals such as *will* evolve, of course, from verbs meaning 'want'. As also shown by English, they may subsequently form the basis of subjunctive auxiliaries such as *would*. The German equivalent is *würde*, but this has a different source. The original meaning of *werden* is 'become', and since *würde* is formally subjunctive, its original (still alive) meaning is 'would become'. In this meaning, the verb formed constructions such as OHG *würde lesende* 'would become reading', with a clearly inchoative meaning. The latter, however, disappeared in Middle High German, and in the course of grammaticalization only the subjunctive meaning remained: 'would read'. Once *würde* had become a sign of the subjunctive, the marked participial form of the verb was no longer necessary. In analogy to the other modal verb periphrases, it was simplified to the infinitive form: *würde lesen*. For this account, see Ronneberger-Sibold (1980: 60f). The interesting thing about this development is the solution to the problem of reinforcing the subjunctive mood. This was done by extracting this mood from the main verb and using an auxiliary verb as its bearer whose lexical meaning was necessarily irrelevant since its function was nothing more than to carry the subjunctive. This is why, in this construction, it lost its meaning so soon. Contrast this with the formation of the *werden*-future dealt with in §3.1.4.

The omnipresent existence verb also forms modal constructions, chiefly OBLIGATIVE ones. It combines with nominal verb forms to yield expressions of the type 'my going exists', meaning 'I have to go'. Compare Latin *mihi est eundum* id., but also Yucatec Maya *yàan in bin* (EXIST 1.SG go) id. Once more, the functional similarity of 'have' and 'be' in the existence meaning asserts itself here. Thus we have English *I have to go*, and also Vulgar Latin *cantari habet* 'has to be sung', which, according to Benveniste (1968: §II), ultimately yielded the Romance future (cf. below).

Continuing grammaticalization transforms modal verbs into affixes. Examples for the development of desiderative and obligative modals into future markers have already been mentioned and will yet be seen in the following section. The existence of verbal mood affixes is known; besides the common Indo-European subjunctive suffixes, note in particular the Sanskrit desiderative suffix -*sa*. What is lacking in my data is historical evidence for their development out of modal verbs; but on the basis of the analogy to related categories, such evidence must exist.

3.1.4 Tense and aspect

Tense and aspect are often expressed with the help of periphrastic verb constructions in which an auxiliary is used to support a nominal main verb. The two auxiliaries which predominate in Indo-European languages are presumably widespread everywhere: 'have' and 'be'. Both are used in the analytic perfect of the Germanic and Romance languages. For the origin of this construction, see Meillet (1912: 141–143), Benveniste (1968: §I), Seiler (1973), Rosén (1980), Ramat (1983). In Persian, the auxiliary 'be' has been agglutinated to the main verb and now expresses the personal endings of the PAST TENSE verb. Similarly, Haas (1977) demonstrates that the personal endings in the conjugation of some Muskogean languages go back to an agglutinated auxiliary.

Heine & Reh (1984: 130) show that in Africa, too, past tenses are frequently expressed with the help of 'be'. Following Givón (1973: §5), they posit two other possible origins: verbs of motion, especially 'come'; and verbs meaning 'to be/have finished'. Both can be exemplified from Portuguese: *vem de escrever* (comes from writing) 'has written' (cf. French *vient d'écrire*); *acaba de escrever* (finishes of writing) 'has just written'. Both of these examples illustrate that past tenses often start out as perfects or perfective aspects; the past meaning actually results from a further grammaticalization. The same is to be observed in the development from the Indo-European perfect to the Germanic past and of the Latin perfect to the Romance simple past tense. And the same is again happening with the "passé composé" in French and the *haben*-perfect in Bavarian German.

Passing over to FUTURE TENSES, we again meet 'have' here, viz. in Latin-Romance. The periphrastic construction "infinitive of main verb + form of *habere*" started in Vulgar Latin, according to Benveniste (1968: §ii) in passive clauses, and according to Ineichen (1980) in subordinate clauses. In the course of its expansion, the construction became agglutinative and led to the synthetic Romance future (cf. also Coseriu 1974: 132–151). Overall, 'have' is probably not so common a future tense auxiliary. Much more wide-spread is 'go'. It occurs in periphrastic futures in English and various Romance languages, e.g. Portugese *vou escrever* (go.1.SG write:INF) 'I will write'. An isolated precedence of this may be seen in the Latin passive infinitive of the future, *scriptum iri* 'to be going to be written' (cf. Ultan 1978: 109–114). 'Go' also figures in the Uzbek and Tunica auxiliary lists

3 Grammatical domains

given in Žirmunskij (1966: 85f) and Haas (1941: 41–51), respectively. For African languages, see Givón (1973: §5) and Heine & Reh (1984: 131f).

Since 'be' is the counterpart of 'have' in so many respects, obligative 'be' grammaticalizes to future just as obligative 'have' does. An example is provided by Yucatec Maya. The construction *yàan in bin* mentioned in §3.1.3 is also used colloquially to mean 'I will go'.

Equally often, the future may arise through the grammaticalization of a desiderative modal. English *will* is a known example. In 13th cent. Greek, an impersonal *thélei* 'it wishes' governs a subordinate clause introduced by *ná* 'that'. This is shortened to *thé ná*, then contracted to *thená* and, by the 16th century, yields *thá* FUT. In Swahili, *-taka* 'want' > *-ta-* FUT, as illustrated in E2 (cf. Heine & Reh 1984: 131).

E2 Swahili (Givón 1973: 916)

   a. *n-a-taka   ku-la*
      SBJ.1.SG-PRS-want INF-eat
      'I want to eat'

   b. *ni-ta-ku-la*
      SBJ.1.SG-FUT-INF-eat
      'I will eat'

At a more advanced stage of grammaticalization, we find the Ancient Greek future in *-se/so-*, which derives from a PIE desiderative; see Rix (1976: 224f), and cf. the Sanskrit *-sa-*desiderative mentioned in the preceding section.

Finally, future auxiliaries may evolve from verbs with an inchoative meaning. Givón (1973: 917) adduces the example of SiLuyana (Bantu) *-tamba* 'begin' > *-mba-*FUT, as in *ni-mba-kela* (SBJ.1.SG-FUT-work) 'I will work'. On the other hand, we have the German future with *werden*. This started at the same time and in the same construction as the *würde*-subjunctive mentioned above. Here, again, the original participle of the OHG construction *wird lesende* ('becomes reading') is simplified to an infinitive. However, the inchoative meaning here is not discarded, but grammaticalized to a future meaning.

The main source of PROGRESSIVE ASPECT conjugations is a periphrastic construction formed with the verb 'be' plus a nominalized verb form in some locative dependence. A typical instance of this is the English *she is on working* > *she is a-working* > *she is working*. Compare also the Portuguese variants *está a trabalhar* (stand:3.SG at work:INF; European) and *está trabalhando* (stand:3.SG work:ing, Brazilian). Colloquial German has *ist am arbeiten*, corresponding to the European Portuguese version. One may also be more precise on the nature of the 'be'-verb involved: Since the construction originally expresses a state (position or condition, "Befindlichkeit") of the subject — as is sufficiently proved by the prepositions used —, the verb employed as an auxiliary, if there is a choice, will be the verb 'be at a place'. It could therefore be predicted that Spanish and Portuguese use *estar* rather than *ser* in their progressive constructions. The same can be seen in African languages. Thus, the Ewe progressive construction *éle vavá ḿ* (he:is RDP:come PROG) 'he is coming' originally expresses a location: *m* derives from *me 'inside', so that the original meaning is 'he is in coming' (Heine 1980: 105f). In Abkhaz (Hewitt 1979: 128, 181f), the postposition *-ç'ə̀* 'in' is converted into the intransitive verb 'be in' by adding stative verb inflection. The full verb is put into the masdar, an infinitive-like verbal noun, and is constructed as the oblique complement of the auxiliary, as shown in E3.

E3   Abkhaz (Hewitt 1979: 181)
    a-x°màr-ra   çə̀-wp'
    ART-play-INF in-PRS.INDEP
    'he is playing'

In Uzbek (Žirmunskij 1966: 86), there are four auxiliaries which may be used in the progressive frame "main verb-gerund auxiliary-gerund-inflection", e.g. in *ëz-ib* AUX-*ib-man* 'I am writing', namely *tur-* 'stand', *ŭt* 'sit', *ët* 'lie' and *jur-* 'walk about'. It is palpable how all these verbs characterize the spatial situation of the subject.

Givón (1973: §5) and Heine & Reh (1984: 124–126) also point to a second source of progressive aspect markers, namely verbs of the meaning 'stay', 'remain', 'keep'. This can also be exemplified from Portuguese, which uses *ficar* (beside *estar*) in progressive constructions.

For HABITUAL ASPECT/AKTIONSART, two sources may be mentioned. The first is a periphrasis with the copula, as for progressive aspect. In Imbabura Quechua, the same suffix *-j* which also forms simultaneous relative clauses is used on the full verb. The resulting form is constructed as the predicate complement of the copula. Sentences such as the one in E4 can nevertheless not be analyzed as containing a syntactically regular free relative clause (see Cole 1982: 149).

E4   Quechua (Cole 1982: 149)
    Utavalu-pi trabaja-j   ka-rka-ni.
    Otavalo-LOC work-SIM.NR COP-PAST-1.SG
    'I used to work in Otavalo.'

Subordinate clauses cannot contain validators (a kind of modal particle). However, in habitual sentences such as E4, validators are possible. This shows that there is only one clause in this construction and that non-finite verb plus copula form a periphrastic verb form in it. What started out as a simultaneous nominalizer of clauses ends up as a verb marker of habitual aspect.

The second source of habitual aspect are periphrases which involve the verb 'do'. Sentences such as E5 occur in Irish English.

E5   *He does plough the field for us.* (John Harris p.c.)

In Mayan languages, the predicate focus construction is mainly used in order to express habitual aspect, as in E6 from Yucatec.

E6   Yucatec
     puroh káaltal k-in   bèet-ik
     mere drink   IMPF-ERG.1.SG do-INCOMPL
     'mere drinking was what I did'

Here the full verb becomes non-finite, and the whole predicate is put into focus position. The extrafocal clause reduces to a finite form of *bèet* 'do', to which the nominalized predicate is the direct object.

3.1.5 Passive and emphasis

The analytical PASSIVE with *esse* 'be', which was used, in Latin, only in the perfective categories, replaced the synthetic forms in the Romance languages and yields such passives as Italian *è detto* 'is said'. This is currently being renovated with the auxiliaries *venire* 'come' and *andare* 'go'. Of these, the unmarked form is *viene detto* 'is said'; but the contrast with *va detto* evokes the deictic potential of these auxiliaries: the former then implies 'is said to the speaker', the latter 'is said by the speaker'.

The notion of 'becoming' is at the basis of the auxiliary which serves in German (*werden*) and Persian (*šodan*) passive constructions; it also appears in the English *get*-passive. Because of the basic meaning of the auxiliary, these passives were originally inchoative; *wird grammatikalisiert* would have meant 'becomes grammaticalized', the passive meaning being carried exclusively by the participial form of the main verb. With increasing grammaticalization, however, the auxiliary loses its inchoative meaning and becomes a mere carrier of finite verbal categories. This is another example of renovation through complex reinforcement. For other sources of the passive, see Givón (1979a: 85f).

As for EMPHATIC CONSTRUCTIONS, we will mention here only the auxiliary 'do'. There are different types of emphatic constructions, and in at least three of them the verb 'do' may appear. For the first type, cf. the predicate focus construction mentioned in §3.1.4.

Second, the emphasis may not be on a particular sentence constituent, but rather the assertion itself may be emphasized. This type is exemplified in English. According to Traugott (1980: 55), in Middle English the verb *do* was used as an auxiliary, apart from causative constructions, only if a positive assertion was to be strongly emphasized. By 1700, it came to be used also when the assertion was to be questioned, that is, as an interrogative auxiliary; and by 1900, it appeared also as an auxiliary in negation. The desemanticization accompanying this expansion has led to the situation that *do* is currently being used everywhere with little or no emphasis.

In the third type of emphasis, the main verb is used as a contrastive topic; and due to its being foregrounded, it needs a substitute in the clause. This function is fulfilled by *tun* in Standard German, in sentences such as *Kochen tut sie nicht schlecht* (lit. cooking does she not badly). In Non-Standard German, the auxiliary *tun* has been generalized beyond this context to expressions such as *sie tut nicht schlecht kochen* (cf. p. 123).

3.1.6 Auxiliaries and alternative sources

The discussion in §3.1.2–§3.1.5 has concentrated on auxiliaries and the like. We will first sum it up and then turn briefly to alternative sources of the grammatical categories mentioned.

The common denominator of the above developments can be characterized as follows: main verb becomes auxiliary verb, possibly via modal verb; this then becomes a mood or aspect marker, and the latter finally a tense marker. The most important and most differentiated instance of this development is certainly represented by the verb 'be'. It starts out as a "verbum substantivum", a verb of existence. Subsequently, it comes to be used in location predications, with the meaning 'to be in a place'. Then it appears as the copula in nominal sentences. As such, it may be employed when the predicate is a nominalized verb form, and in this way it ends up as an auxiliary. This development was already posited by Meillet (1912: 131), who exemplifies it as follows:

verbum substantivum:	*je suis celui qui **suis***
'be in a place':	*je **suis** chez moi*
copula:	*je **suis** malade*
auxiliary:	*je **suis** parti*

3 Grammatical domains

As was already mentioned with reference to Persian and Muskogean, further grammaticalization yields inflectional endings.

The grammaticalization of full verbs to auxiliaries shows us two things. First, a piece of methodology: The dispute on whether auxiliaries are main verbs or not (J. Ross: yes; L. Palmer: no; R. Huddleston: yes; etc.) is fruitless. Two grammatical categories connected on a grammaticalization scale are neither the same nor distinct. The difference between them is gradual, and there is no clear-cut dividing line. Secondly, an empirical insight: Grammaticalization can turn syntactic relations around. In a word combination which contains two verb forms, one of which will become the auxiliary in an analytic construction, this latter one starts by being the syntactic (not lexical!) main verb (cf. Givón 1979a: 96f), while the other, governed verb carries the major part of the lexical meaning.[1] However, only a free form can exert government. As, in the course of proceeding grammaticalization, the auxiliary loses its verbal properties, it can no longer be said to govern the lexical verb. When it has become a tense/mood/aspect marker, it depends on the lexical verb, which is now the main verb. Thus, the syntactic relations are almost reversed; though not quite, because within a word there are no syntactic, but morphological relations. We shall find (§4.3.2) that this development of relations is characteristic of grammaticalization processes. For the trouble that intermediate stages of this development may cause to synchronic analysis, see Matthews (1981: 155f).

We now turn to alternative sources of the verbal categories treated above. There appear to be two principal ones: serial verbs and adverbs. Serial verbs will be treated in more detail in §3.4.1.7, as a source of adpositions. They have, in fact, been studied mainly in that connection, and comparably little attention has been devoted to their aspectual or aktionsart function.

I cannot clarify here the complex and much debated issue of the syntactic relations among the verbs in a series. Let us assume the following definition: a SERIAL VERB CONSTRUCTION is the combination of two or more asyndetically juxtaposed verbs with at least one shared argument in order to express a complex, but unitary situation. In the course of grammaticalization of a serial verb construction, one verb in a pair undergoes the usual symptoms of grammaticalization, becoming, in the last event, a grammatical formative, while the other remains virtually

---

[1] The term "main verb" is, unfortunately, ambiguous. In its syntactic sense, it means the governing verb; and in this sense the auxiliary in an analytic verb phrase is the main verb, as is argued above. In its semantic sense, it means, within an analytic verb form, that verb which carries the lexical meaning, and consequently denotes the exact opposite of the first sense. The term denoting the second sense should probably be "full verb".

unaffected.[2] I shall refer to that member of a series which is (destined to be) grammaticalized as the SERIAL VERB in the construction. This terminology is based on the assumption that wherever verb serialization occurs, there is a relatively closed class of verbs with an active serialization potential (the serial verbs), combining with verbs from an open class which are indifferent to serialization. Such serial verbs which develop into adpositions are called "coverbs" in the literature and will be dealt with in §3.4.1.7.

Examples of serial verbs with aspectual function may be adduced from Niger-Congo languages (see also Sasse 1977b: 113–117 on Mba). In Akan (Kwa), there is a verb *bá* 'come' which has developed a grammatical function as the first verb in a series (Welmers 1973: 353f). In this position, it has become a future marker, which is subject to phonologically conditioned allomorphy and has become prefixed, together with its personal prefix, to the following full verb. This is the origin of such forms as *ó-bé-bá* (3.SG-FUT-come) 'he's going to come' or *ò-bé-dìdí* (3.SG-FUT-eat) 'he's going to eat'. In Efik (Benue-Congo), the verb *mà* 'fulfill, accomplish' takes the first position in a series. Here it is grammaticalized to a neutral past marker and undergoes tonal assimilation, as in the following examples (Welmers 1973: 371): *ì-mà í'dí* (we-PAST we-come) 'we came'; *ḿ'má ń-dí* (I-PAST I-come) 'I came'.

More evidence for serial verbs in aspectual function comes from creole languages. Tok Pisin (New Guinea) provides us with the following examples (from Mosel 1980):

E7 Tok Pisin (Mosel 1980: 108)
ol manmeri bilong Papua Niu Gini   i   save kaikai kaukau
PL man   of   Papua New Guinea SBJ.3 HAB eat   sweet.potato
'Papua New Guineans eat sweet potatoes.'

Portuguese provided the verb *saber* 'know, can', which has become *save* 'to do habitually' in Tok Pisin. This enters verbal series as the first member and ends up as an aspectual marker, as in E7.

English *stop* yields *stap* 'live, be located' in Tok Pisin. This enters a verbal series as the last member and develops into a marker of continuous action, as in E8.

---

[2] An alternative development is that a pair of verbs in a series becomes a compound verb; but this is not grammaticalization; see §5.2.

3 Grammatical domains

E8 Tok Pisin (Mosel 1980: 108)
em i   wok i   stap yet
he SBJ.3 work SBJ.3 CONT self
'he is/was still working'

A similar fate has befallen English *finish*; this has become a postverbal completive aspect marker in Tok Pisin:

E9 Tok Pisin (Mosel 1980: 123)
em i   go pinis
he SBJ.3 go COMPL
'he has/had/will have gone'

I shall gloss over several problems in these examples. It is evident, for instance, that in some of them the serial and the full verb each have their own personal prefixes, whereas in others only one of them has. Furthermore, the question naturally arises as to whether we need to treat grammaticalized serial verbs as distinct from auxiliaries or modal verbs. All the examples seem to be interpretable in either of these two terms. This would mean that we have only found a new source of auxiliary verbs, but not a new source of mood/aspect/tense markers, since these would still derive from auxiliaries. Much seems to speak in favor of this position. On the other hand, the morphological difference just mentioned might correlate with a difference among serial, modal, and auxiliary verbs. The latter distinction might also account for the positional differences in the last three examples. Heine & Reh (1984: 128) have an intriguing example from Ewe (Kwa). The language has serial verb constructions in which the serial verb follows the full verb(s). It also has auxiliaries which precede full verbs. There is a verb *nɔ* 'remain, stay' which has been grammaticalized to a habitual aspect marker. In standard Ewe, this is constructed as a serial verb, e.g. *me-yí-na* (I-go-HAB) 'I am in the habit of going'. In the Dahome dialect of Ewe, however, *nɔ* is constructed as an auxiliary, as in *m-nɔ-sa* (I-HAB-sell) 'I am in the habit of selling'.

Faced with problems such as this, I prefer to take no stand on the issue of whether (some of) the grammaticalized serial verbs in the above examples are to be analyzed as auxiliary or modal verbs. It suffices to say that these categories are functionally and structurally quite similar.

We finally turn to a definitely different source of tense markers. Givón (1979b: 218f) raises the question whether tense/mood/aspect distinctions can arise from ADVERBS, and answers it in the negative. Available evidence, however, argues for a more differentiated hypothesis: while modal and aspect markers appear, in fact, to derive exclusively from periphrastic verbal constructions, tenses may come from adverbs (see also Heine & Reh 1984: Ch. 3.1.1.3). There are probably quite a number of languages which use a word meaning 'already' in the function of a past or perfect tense marker; Indonesian *sudah* is one example. Future markers deriving from adverbs can be exemplified from creole languages (Labov 1971). English *by and by* has yielded the free future temporal adverb *baimbai* of the pidgin stage of Tok Pisin (which lacks tense). This was subsequently simplified and grammaticalized to a preverbal future marker, which may cooccur with future adverbs, as in *klostu bai i dai* (soon FUT SBJ.3 die) 'he'll die soon'. In the present creole language, it has become increasingly obligatory and is further phonologically reduced to *be* (cf. also Sankoff & Laberge 1974). Spanish *luego* 'soon' underwent a maximally parallel fate in Papiamento: it was reduced to *lo* and became a preverbal future marker, as in *lo mi kanta* (FUT I sing) 'I will sing'. Adverbs which are grammaticalized to future and past tense markers and adjust their position vis-à-vis the verb accordingly have also been found in the Nilotic languages Luo, Lotuko and Bari (Heine & Reh 1984: 130, 132). Finally, according to an Indo-Europeanist hypothesis of long standing, the final *-i* common to the so-called primary verbal desinences is an original deictic particle. While a reconstruction, obviously, does not count as evidence, the other cases clearly show that the development 'adverb → tense marker' must be posited as a grammaticalization channel.

The developments discussed in the preceding sections may be summarized in Figure 3.1.

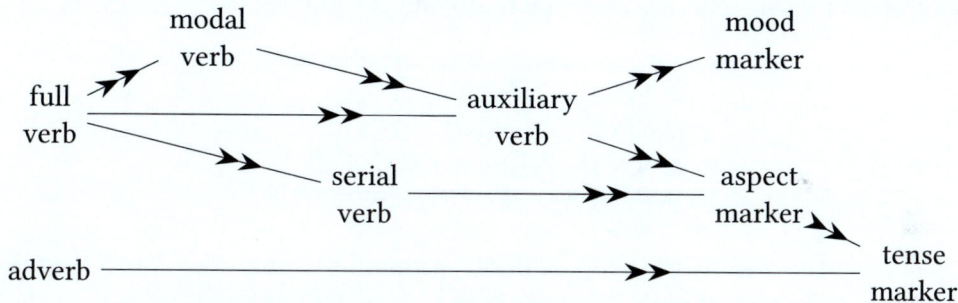

Figure 3.1: Some interrelated grammaticalization channels of verbal categories

3.2 Pronominal elements

I shall not deal here with all the different kinds of pronouns. A major distinction will be made between definite and indefinite pronominal elements. Under the category of definite pronominal elements I will treat demonstratives, definite articles and personal pronouns, as well as their products in grammaticalization. The heading of indefinite pronominal elements will comprise indefinites properly speaking, indefinite articles and interrogative pronouns, and again their grammaticalization products.

3.2.1 Definite pronominal elements

There is one type of pronoun at the root of this family, and this is the free DEMONSTRATIVE PRONOUN. In its full, ideal form, this contains three components, two semantic and one syntactic. First, the demonstrative element in the narrow sense, which embodies definiteness and a pointing gesture. Second, what we may call the deictic element, which directs the attention to something located in regard to the speech situation (speaker vs. hearer, visible vs. invisible, etc.). Third, a categorial element, either NP or DET, which renders the pronoun either syntactically autonomous or dependent. Of these, the deictic component will usually be segmentally expressed at the stage of the free demonstrative pronoun (otherwise it fuses with the demonstrative one). Either the demonstrative or the categorial component will almost always lack expression. The Yucatec Maya discontinuous (or circumfixal) demonstratives express the demonstrative and the deictic components separately. We have the following paradigm:

le NP-*a'*	'this NP'
le NP-*o'*	'that NP'
le NP-*e'*	'aforementioned NP'

The Japanese demonstrative (and other) pronouns express the deictic and the categorial components separately, as shown in the following paradigm:

PRONOUN		PROADJECTIVE	
ko-re	'this one'	*ko-no* N	'this N'
so-re	'that one'	*so-no* N	'that N'
a-re	'yonder one'	*a-no* N	'yonder N'

3.2 Pronominal elements

The first step in the grammaticalization of the demonstrative pronouns is the weakening of the deictic component. Deictic distinctions tend to be neutralized, the paradigm is reduced, and at the same time its unmarked member, namely that of third person deixis, assumes a primarily anaphoric function. An example, Latin *ille*, has already been mentioned in §2.2. A case of extreme reduction is provided by Vulgar Latin **ecce hoc illāc* 'lo this over there'> French *cela* 'that' > *ça* 'it'. We disregard for the moment the fate of the more marked demonstrative pronouns (see §6.3) and concentrate on the further development of the unmarked one. There are two principal grammaticalization channels, corresponding to whether the categorial component is NP or DET; and we will subdivide the discussion accordingly.

3.2.1.1 Definite determiners

At the present stage of the development, we have an adnominal demonstrative pronoun which is deictically neutral and therefore mainly used for anaphoric purposes. Examples, besides Late Latin *ille*, are Gothic *sa, sō, þata*, OE *sē, sēo, þæt* and Homeric *hó, hḗ, to*, all deriving from PIE **so, sā, tod*. Persian *ān* and Japanese *sono* appear to be well on their way towards this stage.

The following development has been described by Greenberg (1978) for African languages (cf. also Givón 1978: §3), but it occurs in languages all over the world. The demonstrative component is gradually reduced to mere definiteness, and the result is a DEFINITE ARTICLE. We thus get French *le, la*, OHG *ther, thiu, thaz*, English *the* and Attic *ho, hē, to*. Further grammaticalization agglutinates the article to the noun. Suffixed articles occur in Romanian, Swedish, Danish, Basque, Ijo (Kwa), Koyo (Kru) and Yuman languages such as Mohave, Diegueño and Yavapai. Prefixed articles occur in Abkhaz (Caucasian) and Arabic vernaculars. The Swedish case illustrates that while the definite article is typically in opposition to a demonstrative, a definite affix starts cooccurring with other definite elements.

At this stage, further semantic weakening leads to a reduction of definiteness to specificity. This is largely true for the Abkhaz article and for the suffixed article of Dagbani (Gur). If this last bit of referential meaning is lost, too, we are left with the categorial component of the erstwhile demonstrative. That is, the element then signals only that the word it is attached to is a noun, and can therefore still be used as a nominalizer (which is an important function of the definite article, anyway). See Greenberg (1978: §3.5) on the nominalizing *-s* of Plateau Penutian.

If the demonstrative pronoun which is at the beginning of this process expresses any noun class or gender distinctions — the primary locus of which is, in fact, the pronoun —, then these will go all the way along, and when the speci-

3 Grammatical domains

ficity of the article is lost, they will be left as NOUN CLASS MARKERS. This appears to be a plausible account of the genesis of nominal gender or class markers as they occur, for instance, in Bantu languages (details in Lehmann 1982b: §7.2).

3.2.1.2 Personal pronouns

We go back again to the stage of Early Latin *is*, Late Latin *ille*, Gothic *sa*, Homeric *hó* and Bambara *ò*. One thing that often happens to such anaphoric pronouns with a slight demonstrative force is that they come to be used as relative pronouns. This happened, for instance, to OHG *ther* and to Homeric *hó*. The development is treated in detail in Lehmann (1984: Ch. V.1.1.2 and 1.2.2). Although this is a deviation from the main channel, it certainly is a grammaticalization, since the pronoun loses its demonstrative force and definiteness (cf. Lehmann 1984: Ch. V.2.3, §2) and becomes syntactically obligatory in a certain construction.

Returning to the main thread, we find the pronouns here losing their demonstrative force, too. The result is a FREE PERSONAL PRONOUN as exemplified by Proto-Romance **illu*, English *he* or German *er*. The latter two derive, in fact, from the PIE demonstrative **ei-s* which also yielded Latin *is*. Having thus arrived at a third person pronoun, let us now turn to first and second person pronouns and discuss briefly their possible origin.

New pronouns, especially for the second person singular, are often obtained by shifting pronouns around in the paradigm, especially by substituting marked forms for unmarked ones. This explains, e.g., the use of German *Sie*, French *vous* and English *you* for the second person singular (see Syromjatnikov 1980: 112 for Japanese). Again, a new first person plural pronoun is being formed in French and Portuguese by what has so far been the non-specific indefinite pronoun 'one', namely *on* and *a gente*, respectively. Here grammaticalization plays no part.

However, new forms may also come from outside the paradigm; nouns may be grammaticalized to pronouns. In Spanish, *vuestra merced* 'your grace' has yielded the honorific second person pronoun *usted*, whose plural *ustedes* has already ousted, in South America, the original plain form *vos(otros)*. The Portuguese product of *vossa mercê*, *você*, is used in most parts of Brasil instead of the original *tu*.[3] Japanese provides the following examples: *watakusi* lit. 'my private affair' > *watasi* 'I' (hon.); *boku* (Chinese loan) 'slave' > 'I'; Old Jap. *kimi* 'lord' > 'you' (hon.) > 'thou'; *anata* lit. 'that part' > 'you' (hon.); *omae* (HON:front) > 'thou' (vulg.) (from Syromjatnikov 1980 and Yoshiko Ono, p.c.). Vietnamese *tôi* 'I' comes from a word meaning 'subject' (Wilfried Kuhn, p.c.). The Indonesian *saya*

---

[3] In Rio de Janeiro, even dogs are addressed by *você*.

'I' derives from a literary word *sahaya* 'servant' (which in turn comes from Sanskrit *sahāya* 'assistant'); and *tuan* 'you' (hon.) is an original Arabic loan meaning 'master' (von der Gabelentz 1891: 152). In East Asia, the use of relational nouns instead of personal pronouns whenever there is a personal relation between the discourse participants is wide-spread and liable to yield rich material for the grammaticalization origin of first and second person pronouns.

We see that personal pronouns derive from two entirely different sources: whereas those of the third person come from demonstratives, those of the first and second persons come from nouns of social relations. There is no a priori reason why the grammaticalization processes which lead to these two kinds of personal pronouns should take a parallel course. It is therefore no wonder that we find many languages where the third person pronouns are not well integrated into the paradigm. Several of the ancient Indo-European languages are examples of this, as their third person pronouns retain a slight demonstrative force which is, of course, absent from the first and second person pronouns. And there are quite a number of languages which are conventionally said to lack third person pronouns altogether, a situation which we might rephrase by saying that what would be the third person pronouns are either too little or too much grammaticalized to be able to fulfill that function. Such languages are Walbiri, Dyirbal, Mangarayi (North Australia; Merlan 1982: 99), Japanese, Lakhota (Sioux) and Basque. This situation repeats itself in the personal affixes of many languages: there are paradigms in which the third person (singular) affix is zero (although this may also be explained by its semantic unmarkedness). On the other hand, the genetic and functional difference of the two kinds of pronouns does not necessarily prevent them from forming an integrated paradigm and behaving maximally similar, as they do, for instance, in English, German, Russian, Arabic, Turkish and Chinese. Such paradigmatic differences will be disregarded in what follows. For more details on the subsequent development, see Lehmann (1982b: §§6.2 and 7.1).

When personal pronouns are deaccentuated, they become clitic, usually either in Wackernagel's position or to the word which governs them. Examples are the oblique pronouns *le*, *la* etc. in Italian, French and Spanish or the forms *ne*, *se*, *s* of Northern Substandard German (e.g. *Ich habe ne/se/s doch gestern gesehen!* 'But I saw him/her/it yesterday!'). Such forms are frequently phonologically reduced in comparison with possibly coexisting stressed forms. While full personal pronouns may have the same distribution as lexically headed NPs, CLITIC PRONOUNS are often confined to certain positions. Many languages, such as Modern Greek and Romance languages, have a set of primary prepositions which require a full NP or personal pronoun as their complement and do not accept a clitic pronoun.

3 Grammatical domains

Clitic pronouns become fillers of syntactic positions which may not be left open. In Italian, for instance, if the direct object is topicalized by left-dislocation, it must be represented in the clause by a clitic pronoun, as in *Giovanni, l'ho visto ieri.* 'John, I saw (him) yesterday.' (cf. Mallinson & Blake 1981: 154). In Spanish, the clitic object pronoun may even cooccur with a nominal object within a clause, as in *Ayer lo vi a Juan.* 'Yesterday I saw John.' At this stage, the pronoun potentially loses its anaphoric function and becomes an AGREEMENT MARKER. At about the same time, it turns from a clitic into an affix (cf. von Humboldt 1836: 496f on this phase of the development). In this way, the carrier of the affix acquires the morphological categories of person, number and gender/noun class.[4] Simplifying somewhat, we call these PERSONAL AFFIXES. They may appear on verbs (for subject, direct and indirect object), nouns (for the possessor) and adpositions (for the complement). There are a number of languages such as Navaho, Abkhaz or Arosi, which have all three of these types. E10 contains examples from Abkhaz (Hewitt 1979: 105, 116, 103).

E10 Abkhaz

    a. (sarà) a-x°əč'-k°à a-š°q°'-k°à Ø- rá- s- to -yt'.
        I ART-child-PL ART-book-PL ABS.3.PL- IO.3.PL.HUM- ERG.1.SG- give.DYN -INDEP
        'I give the books to the children.'

    b. à-č'k°'ən yə-y°nə̀
        ART-boy OBL.3.SG.M-house
        'the boy's house'

    c. a-yə̀yas a-q'+nə̀
        ART-river OBL.3.SG.NHUM-at
        'at the river'

In the cases cited, the personal agreement affixes may still function (anaphorically) as personal pronouns, when no NP is present in the same construction. Further semantic weakening makes them lose this ability, and they become entirely conditioned by agreement. The personal endings of the finite verb in French, Russian and German illustrate this stage of the development. If grammaticalization proceeds further, the personal agreement affixes become invariable markers. The subject affixes of the verb become elements which identify the category "verb" or the constituent "predicate", and its object affixes become transitivity markers. Both these developments have occurred to the erstwhile pronouns *he* and *him*, respectively, in Tok Pisin. The resulting invariable morphemes, the preverbal *i-* and the postverbal *-im*, are exemplified in E11.

---

[4] On p. 31 it was mentioned that a verb may acquire such categories through the agglutination of an auxiliary which possesses them. Ultimately, however, this is probably not an alternative, since the auxiliary, in turn, must have acquired these categories somehow.

E11   Tok Pisin (Sankoff 1977: 67f)
Man i-mek-im   singsing.
man SBJ.3-make-TR spell
'Men utter a spell.'

This is the final stage in the grammaticalization of personal pronouns before their disappearance.

3.2.1.3 Reflexive pronouns

The grammaticalization of reflexive pronouns has been studied recently by Faltz (1977: esp. Ch. IV), Edmondson (1978: 640–647; largely based on Faltz) and Strunk (1980). Several of my examples are drawn from these sources, and the following discussion, too, is indebted to them. Just as it would be difficult to formulate a common grammatical denominator for all the different phenomena arranged on a grammaticalization scale together with personal pronouns and treated in the preceding section, so it is difficult to find a single grammatical denominator for all the phenomena which are commonly called reflexive and which we will again find to be arranged on a grammaticalization scale. Their common denominator lies precisely in the fact that they are connected by a grammaticalization channel, this in turn being determined by a function which might be roughly characterized as marking identity with or back reference to an entity involved in the same proposition (sentence or clause); cf. Plank (1979a).

I will simplify the discussion a bit by assuming the following four categories, enumerated here in the order of increasing grammaticalization:

(i) autophoric nouns, e.g. Sanskrit *ātmán* 'soul';

(ii) reflexive nouns, e.g. English *self*;

(iii) reflexive pronouns, e.g. German *sich* 'oneself';

(iv) verbal reflexives, e.g. Russian *-sja*.

It does not need to be emphasized that the boundaries between these categories are fluid.

There is a whole set of notions centering around the person, as a whole or in part, which are generalized in many languages to comprise the self and which I call AUTOPHORIC. Typical examples are Sanskrit *tan* 'body, person' and *ātmán* 'breath, soul', Buginese *elena* 'body', Okinawan *dūna* 'body', !Xu *l'esi* 'body',

Basque *burua* 'head', Abkhaz *a-xə̀* 'the head'. In their respective languages, all these nouns are translation equivalents of English *self*. As relational nouns, they are often accompanied by a (reflexive) possessive pronoun. Typical examples from Vedic (Delbrück 1888: 207f) are:

E12 Vedic (RV 7,86,2)
   utá sváyā   tanvā́   sám   vade   tát
   and POSS.REFL:INST.SG.F self:INST.SG.F together speak:I that:ACC.SG.N
   'and I converse thus with myself'

E13 Vedic (RV 9,113,1)
   bálam   dádhāna   ātmáni
   strength:ACC.SG.M put:PART.PF.MID self:LOC.SG
   'putting strength in myself'

At the other end of the spectrum, Old Indic makes use of a middle voice, which will be discussed below.

The difference between an autophoric and a REFLEXIVE NOUN in the present conception is mainly one of transparency or etymologizability. That is, autophoric nouns are ordinary nouns with free non-reflexive uses; reflexive nouns are nouns meaning 'self' and nothing else. Examples are German *selbst*, Latin *ipse*, Spanish *mismo*, Italian *stesso*, Finnish *itse*, Hungarian *magan*, Turkish *kendi*, Japanese *zibun* and Yucatec *báah*. Some illustrative sentences are:

E14 German

   a. *Ich komme selbst.*
      'I am coming myself.'

   b. *Wollen Sie die Karten für sich selbst?* (cf. E15)

E15 Finnish
   Halu-at-ko   lipu-t   itse-lle-si?
   want-2.SG-INT ticket-ACC.PL self-ALL-POSS.2.SG
   'Do you want the tickets for yourself?'

Reflexive nouns are a heterogeneous class. In some languages, for instance Finnish, Hungarian, Turkish and Yucatec, they take possessive affixes, just like autophoric nouns (cf. English *myself, yourself*). In others, such as German or the Romance languages, they are not normally combined with possessive pronouns. Again, in some languages such as Japanese and Yucatec, a reflexive noun can by itself function as a reflexive pronoun; in others such as German, Latin and the Romance languages, a reflexive noun can only accompany appositively a reflexive pronoun or another noun in order to emphasize the identity. Reflexive nouns of the latter subtype are formally similar or identical to the (pro-)noun of identity, 'same'; this is so with German *selb-*, Italian *stesso*, Spanish *mismo*. They are somewhat marginal to the grammaticalization channel; but they may enter it if used in reinforcement; see below.

REFLEXIVE PRONOUNS function syntactically like ordinary personal pronouns. Examples are German *sich*, Russian *sebja*, Latin-Romance *se, si, soi*. Because of their primary function to refer back to the subject, reflexive pronouns normally lack a nominative. Instead, an appositive reflexive noun will normally appear, as in E14.a above. Just as ordinary personal pronouns have reflexive counterparts, so ordinary possessive pronouns may have reflexive counterparts. Examples are Latin *suus* (as opposed to *eius*), Portuguese *seu* (as opposed to *dele*) and Russian *svoj* (as opposed to *ego*). As these examples show, the proper possessive pronouns may be inherently reflexive, while the non-reflexive forms are in fact genitives of the personal pronouns.

VERBAL REFLEXIVES are verb affixes expressing that the action somehow affects the subject. Examples are:

E16   Turkish (Wendt 1972: 156)
      Çocuk yıka-n-dı.
      child   wash-REFL-PAST
      'The child washed himself.'

E17   Mangarayi (Merlan 1982: 135)
      jalṇar Ø-bu-yi-ni   ṇa-ḷandi
      hard   3.SG-hit-REFL-PAST N.INST-stick
      'He hit himself hard with a stick.'

E18   Greek (Pl. *Gor.* 7, 452)
      khrēmatistḕs   hoûtos   állōi   anaphanḗsetai
      businessman:NOM.SG.M D1:NOM.SG.M other:DAT.SG.M show:FUT:MID.3.SG
      khrēmatizómenos
      trade:PART.PRS.MID:NOM.SG.M
      'this businessman will appear to acquire for somebody else'

The verb forms in E16–E18 are opposed to unmarked active verb forms: thus compare *yıka-dı* 'he washed' with E16, *bu-ni* 'he hit' with E17 and *anaphanḗse-*

3 Grammatical domains

tai 'he will show' and *khrēmatízōn* 'trading' with E18. Following traditional terminology, I have dubbed the affixes in Turkish and Mangarayi "reflexive", but the Greek affix "middle (voice)". There is, in fact, a structural difference in that the reflexive affixes here come near the verbal stem and are almost derivational, whereas the morphological category of middle in Greek is amalgamated with the personal desinences. On the other hand, the Turkish and Greek categories have in common that both are largely ambiguous between reflexive and passive, while the Mangarayi category is ambiguous between reflexive and reciprocal. In all three languages, the reflexive fills the position of a voice or valence-changing verbal derivation. Reflexive suffixes with similar function occur in Swedish (-*s*) and Quechua (mostly -*ku*, but -*ri* in Imbabura, Cole 1982: 90f).

This type is to be distinguished from a reflexive affix which fills the position of a personal (agreement) affix on the verb, as it occurs, for instance, in Swahili (*ji-*), Abkhaz (*çə-*, Hewitt 1979: 77), Italian and Portuguese (-*se*). Examples are:

E19 Swahili

    a. *a-li-ji-ona*
       SBJ.CL1-PAST-OBJ.REFL-see
       'he saw himself'

    b. *a-li-mw-ona*
       SBJ.CL1-PAST-OBJ.CL1-see
       'he saw him'

E20 Portuguese

    a. *vende-se*
       sells-REFL
       'sells itself' (i.e. is for sale)

    b. *vende-me*
       sells-me
       'sells me'

However, these morphological differences need not coincide with semantic differences. Thus, both in Greek and in Portuguese the reflexive and the passive are not clearly distinguished; and furthermore there are many reflexive verbs whose meaning differs minimally from that of the corresponding active verb. A Greek example can be seen in E18, where *khrēmatizómenos* may be substituted by *khrēmatízōn* without much consequence. An example from Portuguese is *lembrar-se* = *lembrar* 'to recall'.

As the examples may have rendered plausible, these four categories of reflexive elements are in fact on a scale of increasing grammaticality. We have yet to present evidence for diachronic transitions between these stages. In doing this, I will also comment on some of the semantic differences associated with the structural ones.

The transition from an autophoric to a reflexive noun may be illustrated by Arabic *nafs*. In Classical Arabic this is an autophoric noun with the lexical meaning 'soul'. In Cairene Egyptian Colloquial Arabic it has become a reflexive noun with obligatory possessive suffixes, which regularly functions as a reflexive pronoun (Gary & Gamal-Eldin 1982: 80f). Probably Hungarian *magan* is another example, as it appears to be etymologically related to *mag* 'kernel'.

I have no examples for an accomplished transition from a reflexive noun to a reflexive pronoun, that is, no examples of a stage where a reflexive pronoun stemming from a reflexive noun can no longer be apposed to a noun to emphasize the identity of reference. However, the examples mentioned from Finnish, Hungarian and Arabic illustrate such a change underway. So there is reason to doubt Faltz's assertion (1977: 236–238) that the change does not occur.

There is probably an alternative source for reflexive pronouns (according to Faltz (1977: 248–266) it would be the only one), namely same-subject markers. These are pronominal elements representing the subject of a clause and expressing that it is the same as the one of the preceding clause. Grammaticalization would reduce the structural scope of this device to a single clause. In view of the development of the personal pronoun sketched in the preceding section and of general considerations of grammaticalization (see §4.3.1), this would seem to be a plausible development, though it would more probably result in verbal reflexives than in free reflexive pronouns. Due to empirical uncertainty, I will leave the issue at that.

The development of verbal reflexives out of reflexive pronouns is well attested. Deaccentuation is a common fate of reflexive — as of other personal — pronouns. Thus, the Indo-European reflexive **swe* became the enclitic *-za* in Hittite (the *a* is purely orthographic) and the prefixal *he-* in Greek. The Latin reflexive pronoun *se* became clitic in the Romance languages, and the Russian reflexive pronoun *sebja* (REFL:ACC) was reduced to *-sja*. Sometimes, as in Russian or in French *soi*, the original form subsists beside the reduced one. The latter then tends to become affixal, normally to the verb. Hittite *-za* in postinitial position is definitely a minority here. In Italian, Spanish and Portuguese, *se* may be either proclitic or enclitic (and subsequently suffixal) to the verb. Russian *-sja* occurs exclusively as a verb suffix. Jespersen (1922: 377) adduces the following example: Old Norse

3 Grammatical domains

finna sik 'find themselves' (or 'each other') > *finnask* > *finnast* > *finnaz* > Swedish *finnas* 'are found'.

All the above verbal reflexives have a pronominal source. I know nothing about the genesis of the diathetic verbal reflexives exemplified above for Turkish, Mangarayi, Greek and Quechua (see, however, Szemerényi 1970: 305–309 on the Indo-European middle).

As reflexive pronouns shift from representatives of NPs with a special semantosyntactic feature to markers of a verbal category, they are commonly reduced to MIDDLE VOICE markers, "that is, more or less general intransitivizers" (Faltz 1977: 268f). The semantic development to be posited here may be illustrated by the following series of examples from Russian:

> *Myt'sja* 'wash oneself': Here a transitive action affects an object which is identical to the subject.
>
> *Kusat'sja* 'bite (intr.)': Here the object is not identical to the subject. There is, in fact, no object; the action abides in the sphere of the subject. The reflexive marker renders the verb intransitive.
>
> *Brat'sja* 'take (for oneself)', *idtis'* 'go (away)': Here the reflexive marker does not change the transitivity of the underlying active verb, can even be attached to intransitive verbs and expresses only an autistic nuance in the action of the subject.
>
> *Smejat'sja* 'laugh', *bojat'sja* 'be afraid' (< fear oneself), *ostat'sja* 'remain': These are "reflexiva tantum", where the reflexive marker is obligatory and therefore nearly meaningless. At this stage, we also find morphologically conditioned alternation between reflexive and non-reflexive verb forms, e.g. *stat'* (perf.) vs. *stanovit'sja* (impf.) 'place oneself, become'.

Most of these examples could be doubled by synonyms from other Indo-European languages. They occur with the free reflexive pronoun of German, the clitic reflexive pronouns in Romance and the flexional Greek middle voice; recall the comments on the Greek example E18. This shows that the semantic continuum is not neatly matched by a morphological continuum. To expect this would be expecting too much. We must be content to find tendencies. What we can say is that the semantic transition from the notion of an action affecting the subject along the above stages to zero takes place in the morphological zone from a reflexive pronoun via a verbal reflexive to zero. The approximativity of the correlation is also due to the fact that the semantic phenomena themselves are partly dependent on particular verbal meanings. That is, the transition is not one of pure grammaticalization, but involves some lexicalization.

One phenomenon exhibiting a correlation between the semantic and morphological scales may, however, be mentioned. It concerns the difference between the first of the above semantic stages (*myt'sja*) and the subsequent ones. Edmondson (1978: 646f) posits the following situation: a semantically bivalent verb in an ergative language has a reflexive object. Then with several languages which leave a choice in the expression of the reflexivity, and also cross-linguistically, the following can be observed: If the object is represented by a reflexive noun or free reflexive pronoun, the subject is in the ergative, which means that the verb is syntactically transitive. If there is a verbal reflexive, the subject is in the absolutive, which means that the verb has been detransitivized.

The examples which I have adduced show reflexive elements unmarked for person, and thus possibly referring to the third person. Some languages have reflexive pronouns for the other persons as well. In Greek we have *me* 'me' and *se* 'you (ACC)', but *meautón* 'me myself' and *seautón* 'you yourself'. However, the less differentiated system in which the unmarked pronouns of first and second person are also used in the reflexive function, seems to be more widespread. An alternative, but equally economical development, which often accompanies the grammaticalization of a reflexive element to a verbal reflexive, is the generalization of the form which is unmarked for person to the first and second persons. A notable example is Russian; the paradigm runs as follows:

ja mojus'	'I wash myself'
ty mojéssja	'you wash yourself'
on mojetsja	'he washes himself'

with the allomorphs *-s'* ~ *-sja* being phonologically conditioned. The same phenomenon occurs in the Russian reflexive possessive pronoun; *svoj* 'his (own)' may be substituted for *moj* 'my' and *tvoj* 'your' if reflexivity is involved in the possessive relationship. The same is true for Sanskrit *svá*. Tendencies to use the unmarked *se* instead of the first and second person pronouns have also been observed in substandard French by Frei (1929: 147). His examples are in E21.

E21   French

    a. *On nous prie de s'adresser à vous.*

       'One asks us to address ourselves to you.'

b. *Nous se reverrons.*
   'We shall meet again.'
c. *Veuillez, Monsieur, nous faire le plaisir de s'en occuper.*
   'Will you, sir, do us the favor to take care of it.'
d. *Vous se privez.*
   'You deprive yourself.'

The generalization of the unmarked reflexive pronoun is the first in a long series of phenomena which raise the intricate question of the difference between grammaticalization and analogical extension. On the one hand, it would be easy enough to argue that what we have here is analogical extension. On the other hand, the semantic bleaching of the reflexive element causes it to no longer signify features of a referential entity (or an NP), but rather features of the action (or of the verb), and this involves the loss of the category of person. I will content myself with having stated the problem and not try to solve it here. There will be ample discussion of it in §5.4.

A last feature in the development of reflexive elements which commands attention is their frequent reinforcement. I have said above that reflexive nouns are often used in apposition to reflexive pronouns, as in E14.b. This is essentially an emphatic, intensifying use, and it is therefore no wonder that reflexive pronouns are commonly reinforced by reflexive nouns. The Indo-European reflexive **swe-* had yielded atonic *he-* in Proto-Greek. This was reinforced by the reflexive noun *autós* to yield Greek *heautós* 'he himself'. Latin *se* is itself a renovation (probably via complex reinforcement, see §2.5) of the Indo-European middle voice. Like other personal pronouns, it was commonly intensified by the meaningless suffix *-met* or by *ipse* 'self' or by both, e.g. *semet ipsum*. In Vulgar Latin, this was again strengthened by putting *ipse* in the superlative: **semet ipsimum*. This becomes **se medesimo* > Portugese *se mesmo*, Spanish *sí mismo*. A series of reinforcements of the reflexive is also reconstructed for Southern Paiute in Langacker (1977: 107). Speakers feel the necessity of such renovations whenever the reflexive element characterizes merely the action rather than the identity of some actant; then the latter is underscored by apposing a reflexive noun. Cf. especially Faltz (1977: 238–244) and Strunk (1980: 329–334).

3.2.2 Indefinite pronominal elements

Overall, indefinite pronominal elements play a much weaker role in the grammar than definite ones, mainly because they don't relate to the context. Indefinite pronominal elements contain a semantic component which says that the entity meant is not identical with anything established in the current universe of discourse. In addition, there is a categorial component classifying the word as either a determiner or an NP. In contradistinction to definite pronominal elements, the categorial component is often represented by a morpheme of its own; cf. English *some* vs. *someone, which* vs. *who*.

I shall treat here the following types of indefinite pronominal elements: interrogative pronouns, indefinite pronouns, negative pronouns and indefinite articles.

3.2.2.1 Interrogative pronouns

In a normal pronominal question, the interrogative pronoun is in focus position. This can be proved by the cleft-sentences which it requires or favors in many languages, e.g. in French (see Sasse 1977a, and cf. fn. 42, p. 124). In Japanese, the focus marker *ga* is applied to interrogative subjects. This function of the interrogative pronoun has the consequence that it is normally an accentuated free form. There is thus little room for variation, and a more grammaticalized interrogative pronoun would cease to be an interrogative pronoun. This would also seem to account for the amazing diachronic persistency evinced by interrogative pronouns. Thus, the forms reconstructable for Indo-European, **kwi-s* 'who' and **kwi-d* 'what', have survived into most of the modern languages despite eventual sound changes. However, in some cases they have been reinforced. The French cleft-structures *qui est-ce qui/que* and *qu'est-ce qui/que* may be interpreted as reinforced interrogative pronouns. They are in fact well on their way to becoming new interrogative pronouns /kiɛski, kiɛsk/ and /kɛski, kɛsk/, respectively. In Italian, the neuter *che* 'what' has been reinforced by *cosa* 'thing'. The resulting *che cosa* is currently being reduced to *cosa*. This shows a possible source for interrogative pronouns.

When they are not in focus position and deaccentuated, interrogative pronouns may lose their interrogative force and become mere indefinite pronouns. Examples: Greek *tís, tí* 'who, what' as opposed to *tis, ti* 'someone, something'. The Latin interrogatives *quis, quid*, when atonic, may function as indefinites in certain clause types. Similarly, the German interrogatives *wer, was* are employed, in the substandard language, as indefinites. The same applies, finally, to *man, mā* of Classical Arabic.

3 Grammatical domains

3.2.2.2 Indefinite pronouns

Indefinite pronouns arise from a lot of different sources. The first has just been mentioned in the preceding paragraph: interrogatives, when atonic, may be used as indefinites. A second source is provided by the numeral 'one'. Just like other nominal determiners, it may be used either as a determiner or as an NP. We leave its determinative function for p. 56 and observe here its role in the construction of indefinite pronouns. German *einer*, Italian and Spanish *uno* and Abkhaz *a-k'(ə)* are relevant examples. *One* in its turn may come from a noun meaning 'single' (IE **oinos*). Instead of taking the detour via the numeral 'one', such nouns may also directly be used in indefinite pronouns. Examples are Nahuatl *tlaa* 'something' < *itlaa* 'thing' and the nouns in English *somebody* and *something*.

In the Indo-European area it is generally the case that a language has more than one paradigm of indefinite pronouns. Complex, more or less emphatic indefinites may be built up by combining single ones either with each other or with yet other pronominal elements. The English words formed with a determinative indefinite pronoun — *some* or *any* — and a nominal head have already been mentioned. The German forms *jemand* (ever:man:0) 'someone' and *jemals* (ever:time:ADVR) 'ever' have an analogous structure. These may in turn be reinforced by *irgend* 'any' to yield *irgend jemand, irgend etwas*; but *irgend* may also be combined directly with the more basic atonic interrogative-indefinites to yield the whole paradigm of *irgendwer* 'anyone', *irgendwann* 'any time' etc. Similarly, the Latin interrogative-indefinite *quis* and the other pronouns of its paradigm may be reinforced by *ali-* 'other' to yield *aliquis* 'someone' etc. Alternatively, the reinforcement may be done by suffixing *quam* 'how' ⇒ *quisquam* 'anybody'[5] or by reduplication ⇒ *quisquis* 'whoever'; and there are yet other possibilities.

Another widely favored way of forming complex indefinites is by using the numeral 'one' as a nominal head and expanding it by determinative indefinite elements. Typical examples are English *someone* and *anyone*, corresponding to German *irgendeiner*. 'One' may also be combined with indefinites which are already complex. Thus Latin *aliquis* ⇒ Vulgar Latin **aliqui-unu* > Italian *alcuno* 'someone' (cf. French *aucun*). Similarly, Latin *qualis* 'which' + *quis* yielded Vulgar Latin **quali-qui* > Italian *qualche*, French *quelque*. These function as adjectives and are combined with 'one' to yield the substantival indefinites *qualcuno, quelqu'un*. Much could be added here about the formation and fate of meaning 'whoever', 'every(one)' etc. It will appear from this exemplification that indefi-

---

[5] Analogs to this occur in Japanese (suffix *-mo*) and Imbabura Quechua (suffix *-pash*, Cole 1982: 131).

nite pronouns are a particularly rich field of continuous reinforcements by ever new combinations of old material.

As for the non-specific human indefinite pronoun 'one', two sources have been found. The first is, once more, the numeral 'one', as in English. This occurs also in Cairene Colloquial Arabic (Gary & Gamal-Eldin 1982: 79). The other source are nouns with the general meaning 'person'. Compare French *on* < *hom 'man', German *man* id., Italian *la gente* 'the people' and Abkhaz *a-way°ə̀* ART-man/person (Hewitt 1979: 157f).

While definite, namely personal, pronouns generally have a strong tendency to become clitic and affixal to the term governing them, mostly the verb, such advanced grammaticalizations have been little observed in the case of indefinite pronouns. I am aware of two cases of (former) indefinite pronouns filling the position of a personal verb affix. The Nahuatl indefinite pronoun *tlaa* 'something' may be incorporated into the verb in direct object position, as in E22.

E22 Nahuatl (Misteli 1893: 118)
ni-k-neki   in ti-tla-kwa-s.
SBJ.1-OBJ.3-want SR SBJ.2-OBJ.IND-eat-FUT
'I want you to eat (something).'

In Abkhaz, there is an indefinite pronoun *a-k'ə̀* 'something', which is identical to the numeral 'one' and which may be expanded to *a-k'ə̀-r* 'anything' (Hewitt 1979: 158). A reduced form of this may appear in the absolutive prefix position of a few verbs, as in E23.

E23 Abkhaz (Hewitt 1979: 220)
(a+)k'rə-y-fò-yt'
ABS.ART+IND-ERG.3.SG.M-eat.DYN-INDEP
'he's eating'

In both of these examples, the morphological grammaticalization is matched by a semantic one, since there is no emphasis on an indefinite object, but rather the verb is detransitivized by this device.

So far we have dealt with substantival indefinite pronouns only. I will not comment here on the various morphological differences which often separate indefinite determiners from substantival pronouns. However, just as the definite pronominal elements take a different course, accordingly as they are NPs or determiners, developing into articles in the latter case, the same happens with indefinite pronouns, which also develop into articles when adnominal. In the

3 Grammatical domains

most widely known examples, it is the numeral 'one' which becomes an INDEFINITE ARTICLE (for a recent treatment see Givón 1981). The English, German and Romance cases are too well-known to require exemplification here. The same phenomenon occurs in Persian (*yek*), Turkish (*bir*) and many other languages. The phonological weakening which separates English *a(n)* from *one* is noteworthy, as it is an outer sign of the grammaticalization performed. Similarly, the possibility to pluralize Spanish *un (unos)* marks the grammatical distance from the numeral *un(o)*.

I have been implying here that the development in question passes through the stages numeral 'one' > (determinative) indefinite pronoun > indefinite article (cf. Heine & Reh 1984: 273). One may ask what the evidence for the intermediate stage is. Why not simply pass from the numeral to the article, as most linguists have assumed? The reasons are both theoretical and empirical. Theoretically, we may posit, on the basis of the facts ascertained about definite pronominal elements, the following proportion: Just as an adnominal demonstrative does not directly change into a definite article, but passes through the intermediate stage of a deictically unmarked determiner (e.g. Vulgar Latin *ille*, German *dér*), so the numeral 'one' does not directly become an indefinite article, but passes through the intermediate stage of a numerically neutral indefinite determiner. 'Numerically neutral' does not mean that more than one may be meant, but that the opposition to the other cardinal numbers is lost. If this assumption is correct, we should expect there to be indefinite articles coming from indefinite pronouns other than those based on the numeral 'one'. Such cases do exist. The English atonic *some*, often linguistically rendered as *sm*, is a first example. A more convincing one comes from Kobon (Davies 1981). There is an indefinite pronoun *ap* 'some', usable as a substantive or a determiner, which is unrelated to the numeral 'one' and may even cooccur with it (op. cit. 150), but which possibly comes from a former interrogative 'what' (*nöhön* 'what' would then be a renovation, at the side of *an* 'who'; op. cit. 8). This is regularly used as an obligatory postnominal indefinite article, as in *ni ap* 'a boy' (op. cit. 60). It may also be combined with a partitive morpheme *r̵imn-* to yield *r̵imnap* 'some', which is preferably used with mass nouns, as in *hal̵i r̵imnap* 'some greens' (op. cit. 151). So this is a piece of empirical evidence to prove that the grammaticalization stage immediately preceding the indefinite article is an adnominal indefinite pronoun, which may in turn come from the numeral 'one'.

In §3.2.1.2 we observed that the main grammaticalization channel of the definite pronominal elements allowed for a side-channel which led to relative pronouns. The same repeats itself with the indefinite pronominal elements.

Interrogative-indefinites are often used as relative pronouns, especially in preposed relative clauses. Examples are again IE *kwis*, which yielded the Hittite and Latin relative pronouns *kwis* and *qui*, respectively, and Bambara (Mande) *mìn*. The grammaticalization of the indefinite to the relative pronouns involves the loss of the indefiniteness feature; since relative pronouns are mere placeholders, they are neither definite nor indefinite. Further details in Lehmann (1984: Ch. V.2.3, §2).

3.2.2.3 Negative indefinites

Pronouns equivalent to English *nobody, nothing* are mostly either formed by a negator plus an indefinite pronoun, or the negator is directly combined with an element from the same source that also feeds the indefinites. As for the first alternative negation appears to be the principal context in many languages which allows atonic interrogatives to be used as indefinites, the negator and the interrogative-indefinite then frequently coalescing to a negative pronoun. Thus, from the volitive negation *nē* plus *quis* we get Latin *nēquis* 'nobody'; and in an exactly parallel fashion we get Mangarayi *ŋiñjag ŋiñja* (VOL.NEG who) 'nobody' (Merlan 1982: 36, 119).[6] Non-interrogative indefinites are at the basis of German *niemand* (NEG:someone) 'no one', *nie(mals)* (NEG:ever) 'never' etc., and similarly of Latin *numquam* 'never' etc. Cf. also French *aucun* (*...ne*). The numeral 'one' is also used; cf. English *no one*, Italian *nessuno*, Spanish *ninguno* etc.

Lexical nouns seem to be exploited to a greater degree in the formation of negative indefinites than of plain indefinites, which would be explicable as a consequence of the greater emphasis commonly associated with the former. Thus, while English *nobody, nothing* do correspond to plain indefinites formed with the same nouns, Latin *nemo, nihil* and German *nichts* do not have such counterparts. *Ne* + *ho/emo* 'man' yields *nemo* 'nobody', *ne* + *hilum* 'fiber' > *nihilum* > *nihil* 'nothing', OHG *ni* + *wiht-s* (NEG + thing-GEN) > German *nichts* 'nothing'.

While these forms, even if synchronically not fully analyzable, clearly contain a negative (sub)morphemic unit, we also find negative indefinites which are analyzable, but contain no trace of a negator. The better known cases[7] are French *personne, rien* etc., the former of quite recent origin, the latter going back to Vulgar Latin *rem* 'thing'. In the literary style, these are still combined with the negator *ne*; but they retain their negative meaning even in isolation and will certainly outlive *ne*.

---

[6] I cannot dwell here on the role of volition in this context nor on the obvious similarity – not noted by Merlan – between the volitive negation and the word for 'who'.

[7] For less known cases in Germanic languages see Krahe 1967: 73.

If negative pronouns are further grammaticalized, they commonly become negators. Thus, Latin *nihil* 'nothing' > *nil* and Spanish *nada* id. are often used in the sense of 'not (in the least)'. The Latin negator *non* originates in the combination *ne-oenum 'not one'. In a parallel fashion, we have OHG *nih-ein* (NEG.and-one) 'not even one', which gave German *nein* 'no' (cf. Meillet 1912: 140). The German *nicht* 'not' has the same origin as the pronoun *nichts* mentioned above.

A moment ago we saw that the cooccurrence of a negator with an indefinite pronoun may yield a possibly discontinuous negative pronoun, of which only the latter part may survive as a negative pronoun with no morphological sign of negation. The same may happen with negators when they are intensified. A known example is French *ne…pas*, originally 'not a step', then simply 'not'. The original negative particle is becoming optional now, and we witness new reinforcements of the remaining *pas* ⇒ *pas du tout*, or its renovation by *point*. See already Meillet (1912: 140). Further examples in Givón (1979b: 204). Givón (1979: 204 and 1973: 917) also discusses an alternative source of negative markers, namely verbs with the meaning 'fail', 'lack', 'refuse' etc., which I will not take up here.

3.2.2.4 Conclusion

In conclusion of this §3.2, we may summarize the various grammaticalization channels of pronominal elements in Figure 3.2 (p. 59). What has been put in the same column is at the same stage of grammaticalization or has the same degree of grammaticality. Here as in all grammaticalization scales, there are functional similarities between neighbouring positions in a row; but there are also changes which bring it about that the end of a scale may have little in common with the beginning.

There are some open questions here. For instance, in some cases a category developed in the course of grammaticalization is already presupposed at the beginning of the channel. The reader may well wonder about the origin of the elements posited at the beginning of the process. We will defer this troublesome question to §7.

3.3 Nominal complexes

3.3.1 Nominal categories

Much of what would belong in this section has already been dealt with in the section on the pronoun. Let me briefly repeat the relevant results: Definiteness

3.3 Nominal complexes

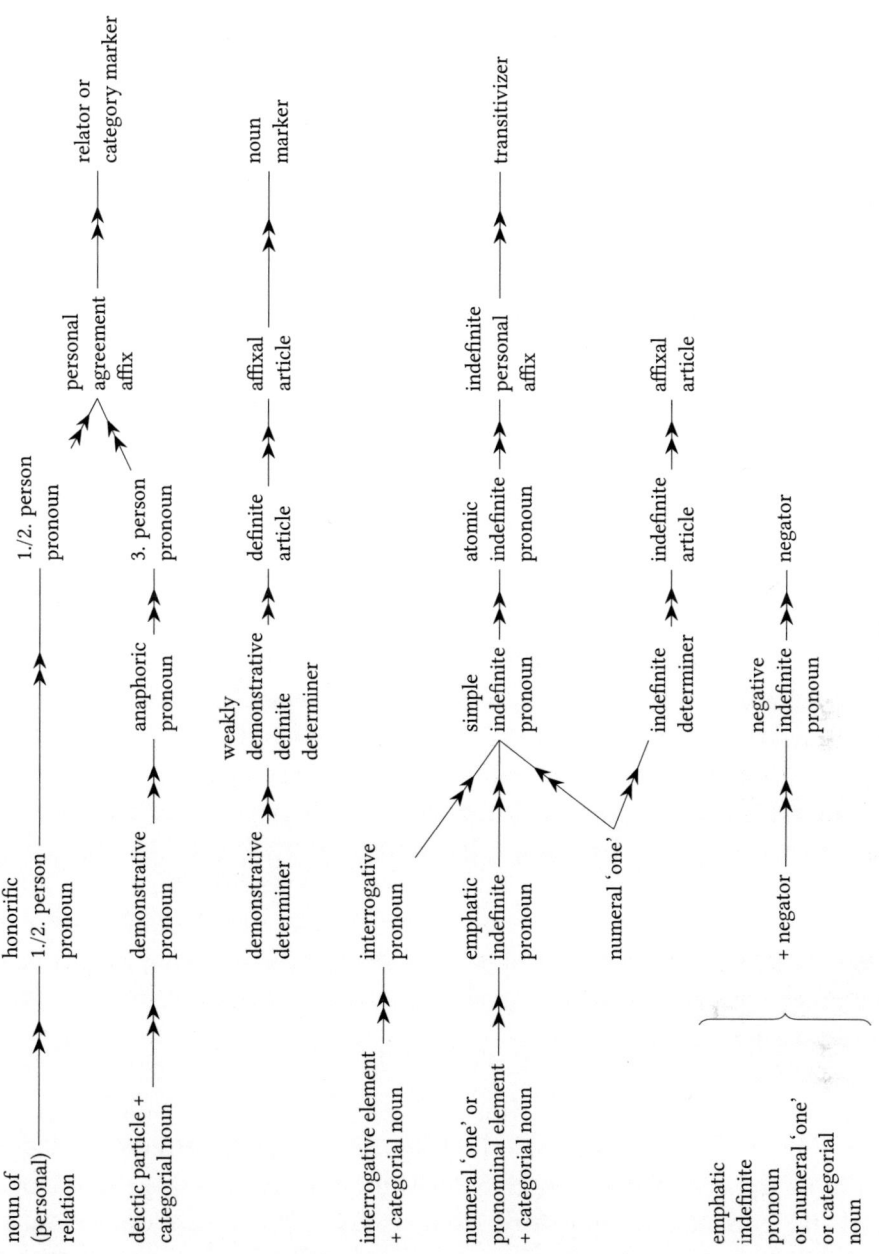

Figure 3.2: Some interrelated grammaticalization channels of pronominal elements

and indefiniteness affixes on nouns derive from pronouns used as determiners. These may ultimately become mere noun markers. Greenberg (1978: §5.3) shows, for instance, that the long vowel in which virtually all nouns in Hausa end may be explained as a former definite article. If such determiners express gender or noun class, then these become, by the agglutination process, categories of the noun.[8] Finally, possessive affixes on nouns originate in possessive pronouns which have undergone the agglutination process described in §3.2.1.2.

The remaining nominal categories to be treated here are number and numeral classifiers. Case will be left for §3.4.

3.3.1.1 Number

Languages without a category of nominal number are not rare. When it seems necessary to focus on a group of individuals, many of these can use morphemes of a COLLECTIVE meaning in combination with the noun. An example is Mandarin *men*, which originally meant 'class', but is now only used as a collective or plural suffix to human nouns, as in *rénmen* (man-COLL) 'people'. Similarly, Hixkaryana has a postnominal particle *komo*, which may be appended only to human nouns and other nouns culturally relevant to humans; e.g. *harye komo* (sweet.potato COLL) 'sweet potatoes'. See also Kölver (1982a: §2.1) on so-called nouns of multitude in Bengali and Heine & Reh (1984: 272) on a collective noun meaning 'kids' in Boni. All these are enclitic or suffixed to nouns and strictly optional; i.e. the unmarked noun may have a singular or plural meaning.

At the next stage of grammaticalization we get agglutinative number affixes, mostly plural suffixes. The change 'collective > plural' is illustrated with historical evidence from Russian, Persian and Arabic in Kuryłowicz (1965: 52). Other examples of agglutinative plural suffixes are Turkish *-ler*, Quechua *-kuna* and Yucatec *-o'b*. These vary in degree of optionality, but none is completely obligatory. In the languages enumerated, the plural suffix is at least absent when the noun is accompanied by a numeral.

In §3.2.1.2 we saw that verbs may acquire the category of number by the agglutination of a personal pronoun. This is also a possible origin of nominal number. We meet here again the two stages just described: first the pronoun accompanies the noun only when there is some special emphasis on plurality; then it becomes affixal and increasingly obligatory. Heine & Reh (1984: 234) adduce Yoruba *awɔn* 'they', which precedes the noun, as an example of the first stage, and Ewe *wó* id.,

---

[8] As explained above, non-grammaticalizational origins of such nominal categories are conceivable.

which is suffixed to the noun, for the second stage. As a result of this, we often find nominal affixes formally similar to third person verb affixes. Compare Yucatec *ch'íich'-o'b* bird-PL with *bin-o'b* go-3.PL. Mangarayi has *wu-r* NONSG-DU and *wu-la* NONSG-PL both as number suffixes to kin terms (other nouns take partly different suffixes) and as pronominal prefixes of third person dual and plural, respectively, to intransitive verbs (Merlan 1982: 88f, 160f).

There is yet a third source of nominal number, and this is numerals and quantifiers. (The three sources are also in Heine & Reh 1984: 273). The numerals 'one' and 'two' may be combined with nouns to yield singular (or singulative) and dual, and a quantifier may provide the plural. In Tok Pisin we get all of these possibilities and in addition a trial. Thus:

E24   Tok Pisin (Mosel 1980: 115, 60)

   a. *dok*
      'a dog, dogs'
   b. *wanpela dok*
      'one/a dog'
   c. *tupela dok*
      'two dogs'
   d. *tripela dok*
      'three dogs'
   e. *ol dok*
      '(the) dogs'

The claim that these elements have at least entered the course of grammaticalization may be proved by the fact that *tupela* and *tripela* may also be suffixed to personal pronouns to signify the respective number categories.

Irrespective of their different origins, the three types of number markers have several grammatical properties in common. One of them is their optionality or incomplete obligatoriness, as already mentioned. Furthermore, they are often restricted to human or animate nouns, or these get different affixes from each other or from inanimate nouns. Cf. Hewitt 1979: 149 on the two number suffixes of Abkhaz. Finally, in this early phase of grammaticalization the paradigm not infrequently comprises more than two numbers. There is a dual in Mangarayi and even a trial in Tok Pisin, and there is a choice among several nouns of multitude in Old Bengali and Hua (Haiman 1980: 221f).

As grammaticalization increases, number affixes become completely obligatory and fusional. This stage is characteristic of several ancient Indo-European languages and also some modern ones such as German. The paradigm tends to be reduced to a binary opposition, which is just what we observe in the development from Proto-Indo-European to the historical languages. Number marking is generalized to all nouns in all contexts, and any formal differences among affixes of the same subcategory either disappear or become purely allomorphic, i.e. they lose their semantic motivation. The penultimate stage of grammaticalization of the number distinction is represented by such alternations as *mouse* vs. *mice*, which are more common in Classical Arabic, and by suppletive forms such as Russian *čelovek* vs. *l'udi* 'man, men' or *god* vs. *leta* 'year, years'. The outlet is always that stage where the grammatical marker becomes zero. In nominal number, this is represented by cases such as German *der Wagen — die Wagen* 'the car — the cars' or English *the fish*.

There is little historical evidence available for this course of events. For the change from the independent to the agglutinative state of the number marker, Bengali (see Kölver 1982a) and Chinese are relevant. The evolution from reconstructed Proto-Indo-European to modern German may be taken to evidence the transition from the agglutinative to the fusional and zero stage.

The various grammatical factors which make up every grammaticalization process will be surveyed in Chapter 4. One of them plays a peculiar role in the development of nominal categories and here appears as the gradual intrusion of the grammatical morpheme into the NP. By this the following is meant: A noun of multitude, personal pronoun or quantifier used as a number marker occurs only once in each NP, normally at its margin. It is a feature of the NP as a whole. With ongoing grammaticalization it may be repeated on the head noun if this does not already carry the marker. This leads to number agreement (and, in the case of the other nominal categories, to gender or case agreement). In this way, number becomes a category of nominal words. A fine example of this phase is Abkhaz; see Hewitt (1979: 222f). At the end of the process, number again disappears from non-nuclear subconstituents, ending up as a category of the noun. This is largely true of English. For details see Lehmann 1982b: §6.3; for the parallel development of case marking see p. 91 below.

We will only touch upon one phenomenon which is very frequent in the development of number marking, but whose counterparts occur throughout the grammar: the paradigm is often simplified by generalizing one allomorph to the detriment of the others. This is particularly common when grammaticalization is already far advanced. Thus, the plural in -*s* has been generalized to practically all nouns in English and in Spanish, though at earlier stages of the languages there had been much irregularity. However, whereas in the above cases a reduction

3.3 Nominal complexes

of the paradigm, i.e. of the semantically distinct subcategories, was observed, here we face a reduction of allomorphy. These two processes are to be clearly distinguished, and we shall see in §4.2.2 that only one of them is a defining characteristic of grammaticalization.

3.3.1.2 Numeral classifiers

Morphemes which express the lexical class into which a noun belongs may be combined with any of its determiners or attributes. According to the category that they attach to, we distinguish between article, possessive and numeral classifiers. Since very little is known about the first two types, I will not treat them here (see Lehmann 1982b: §6.3.3 for some discussion). For detailed information on numeral classifiers, see Kölver 1982b and Serzisko 1980; 1982.

The Indo-European languages originally had no classifiers. In modern Persian (Farsi, Moinfar 1980), nouns may still be accompanied by a bare numeral, as in *do īrānī* 'two Iranians'. The noun is always in the singular. Alternatively, however, we may bestow a classifier on the numeral and form *do nafar īrānī* (two person Iranian). The optionality of the pattern points to its relatively weak grammaticality, as does the size of the paradigm, which consists of 14 classifiers.[9] All of them derive from nouns, whose lexical meanings are still perfectly transparent, and all but two can still be used as nouns. They remain free forms in the numerative construction, and no sandhi phenomena occur. On the other hand, several features indicate that the classifiers are already grammaticalized to a certain degree. First, the paradigm is tightly integrated and hierarchically organized. There are eight forms for different classes of inanimate objects, one for bigger and domestic animals, two for smaller animals and inanimate objects which neutralize the first eight, two for human beings, and one universal classifier which neutralizes all the others. Secondly, although the "Grundbedeutungen" of the classifiers are transparent, some of these do not fit the classifier use. For instance, *dast* means 'hand' but is used in, e.g. *yek dast lebās* (one hand clothing) 'one suit'. The grammatical correlate of this desemanticization is the fact that the construction is not syntactically treated as one of nominal modification, with the classifier as the head noun. If it were, the attributor (izafat) *-e* would have to be appended to the classifier (cf. §3.3.3), which it never is. In short, what we have here is a weakly grammaticalized system of numeral classification.

---

[9] This is not a very reliable criterion, as we shall see in §4.2.2. In the case of numeral classifiers, one must be warned that the figures given in the literature on various languages are often greatly exaggerated, because mensuratives, which designate portions of masses or form collections, are counted as classifiers.

3 Grammatical domains

Contrast this with the Japanese classifier system. First of all, there are two series of numerals, one of native Japanese origin, the other borrowed from Chinese. Some classifiers combine with one number series, some with the other series, with no interchange possible. Apart from those classifiers which represent objects directly counted, such as money and time units, there are only five classifiers in general use: two of Japanese origin for humans and non-humans, and three of Chinese origin for different kinds of objects. Classifiers are completely obligatory; it is impossible to count objects without an intervening classifier. None of the classifiers has an independent use or a meaning of its own. They are suffixed to the numerals, and this is accompanied by assimilations of great irregularity. For instance, *hati* 'eight' + *-hon* 'long, cylindrical object' yields *happon*, whereas with *-satu* 'bound object' it yields *hassatu*. The system is further complicated by the fact that some numerals have allomorphs whose distribution is determined by the following classifier, and vice versa: some classifiers have allomorphs whose distribution is determined by the preceding numeral. This is clearly a strongly grammaticalized classifier system.

Mandarin Chinese has long had a classifier system, which formerly had been, and in the written style still is, fairly differentiated. The classifiers are suffixed to the numeral. In the modern spoken language, the Mandarin dialect, the system is reduced to what had been the most general classifier, *-ge*. Furthermore, the combination *yí-ge* (one-CL) may be reduced to *ge*, whereby *ge* assumes the meaning of unity. Its use has also been generalized to demonstrative pronouns, and here it functions as a marker of singularity. At this stage, it means no more than 'individual, unit' (cf. Serzisko 1980: 24f). This is the end of the grammaticalization of a numeral classifier system.

One feature that characterizes classifier systems to a varying degree is the paradigmatic variability of the classifier (see especially Serzisko 1982). Suppose a noun has a constant, inherent classifier corresponding to its lexical class. Normally this may be substituted by a more general, unmarked classifier, but this is not paradigmatic variability. What is meant by this term in numeral classification is the discretionary combination of a noun with a classifier neither inherent to it nor hierarchically superordinate, by which it is, for the moment, allocated to a different class. The following examples are from Burmese (see Serzisko 1980: 20). The noun *myiʔ* 'river' is inherently classified by itself, yielding the repeater construction *myiʔ tə myiʔ* 'one river', where the order is "noun numeral classifier". However, the classifier may alternatively be *yaʔ* (CL.place), if we refer to the river as, for instance, a place for a picnic; or *tan* (CL.line), meaning, for instance, a river on a map; or *'pa* (CL.sacred object) in dealing with mythological

3.3 Nominal complexes

rivers. This wrong, as it were, classification of a noun is used in various languages for jocular or derogatory effects and points to the relative freedom of the speaker vis-à-vis the system. Paradigmatic variability is more likely among free forms than among bound forms. We may therefore say that it decreases with increasing grammaticalization.

3.3.2 Nominalization

Viewed syntactically, nominalization is the transposition of a clause into a noun; viewed semantically, it is the transposition of a proposition into a concept. As there is a great distance between the two poles of this transition, there are many stages in between, which correspond to different degrees of grammaticalization of the construction. Since I have treated nominalization more comprehensively in Lehmann 1982a, I will here exemplify only some of these stages in order to make the principle apparent.

In Chinese, both classical and modern Mandarin, subject and object complement clauses may be embedded without any sign of subordination, as in E25 from Mandarin.

E25 Mandarin (Bossong 1979: 38)
tā sǐ-le   wǒ zhēn nán-shòu
he die-PF I   very sad
'I am very sad that he has died.'

Similar constructions are frequent in English, where we have *I bet (that) he wins*, with or without the subordinator. There is no structural difference between the embedded and an independent clause, the only hint for the embedding being the syntactic function of the dependent clause as an NP in the superordinate clause. This is why we recognize nominalization here.

The development of subordinators from other conjunctions will be treated on p. 69. Apart from this, there are two main sources of subordinative conjunctions which serve to embed clauses. The first may be exemplified by English *that*, German *daß*, Welsh *a*, Accadic *ša* (< *šu*) and Nahuatl *in*. Here a DEMONSTRATIVE is used to announce the embedded clause. Then a mechanism sets in which prescribes that whatever is preceded (or followed, as the case may be) by a demonstrative as a coconstituent must be a nominal. So the embedded clause is perforce nominalized, and the demonstrative degenerates to a mere subordinator.

The second source of subordinators are VERBA DICENDI. Their grammaticalization to subordinators has been studied in Lord (1976). Ewe has several such verbs, one of them, *bé*, governing indirect speech as in E26.

3 Grammatical domains

E26   Ewe (Lord 1976: 179)
      me-be me-wɔ-e.
      I-say I-do-it
      'I said (that) I did it.'

Subsequently, this verb is used to introduce indirect speech after verbs which cannot govern it, in a type of construction such as 'I argued that it is wrong.' At a further stage of grammaticalization, the indirect speech condition is dropped, and *bé* is used to introduce all types of object clauses, then all types of complement clauses, yielding sentences such as E27.

E27   Ewe (Lord 1976: 180)
      me-dí bé má-ɸle   awua ɖewó.
      I-want SR I:SBJV-buy dress some
      'I want to buy some dresses.'

Bé now has become a complementizer. In such constructions, it no longer behaves like a verb; it takes, for instance, no verbal affixes. Lord adduces similar examples from Efik and Yoruba.

The weak degree of grammaticality of these two types of subordinators is obvious from several facts. They are full words, forming a constituent of their own and not particularly attached to any specific constituent of the subordinate clause. Their etymological meaning is perfectly transparent. In the better known cases (English, German), the subordinator enters into a paradigm with a host of conjunctions which take the same position but differ from it in meaning. Note the optionality of *that* in some contexts.

If the subordinator, instead of preceding the dependent clause, comes at its end, the construction is slightly more grammaticalized. This may be observed in Japanese, as in E28.

E28   Japanese (Kuno 1973)
      Ano hito { ga / no } hon o kai-ta koto ga yoku sirarete iru.
      that person { NOM / GEN } book ACC write-PAST NR NOM well known is
      'That that person has written a book is well known.'

The etymological meaning of the subordinator *koto* 'thing' is still recoverable. It is an independent word and constitutes a paradigm with several other subordinators which can appear in its position (e.g. *no*; cf. p. 73f below). However, the construction is slightly more grammaticalized than the English one, as may be seen by the following criteria. Firstly, the subordinator of complement clauses is non-omissible. Secondly, the construction may be followed by a case particle (*ga* in E28), indicating that syntactically it is treated like any NP. Thirdly, the verbal paradigm of the subordinate clause is reduced, several modal and honorific forms being excluded from it. Lastly, the subject of the subordinate clause may not only be in the nominative, but alternatively in the genitive. On a typological scale, this mostly occurs only if the subordinate verb itself is nominalized (cf. also Bossong 1979: 39), which is clearly not the case in E28. However, diachronic considerations (Bossong 1979: 45–47) make it plausible that the genitive in subordinate clauses such as E28 is a holdover from an earlier embedding construction where the verb did have a nominal form.

At the next stage of grammaticalization, the subordinator becomes affixal, and the subject of the nominalized clause regularly goes into the genitive, as in E29.

E29 Turkish (Wendt 1972: 187)
  Anne-n-in   gel-mey-eceğ-i-ni   söyle-di.
  mother-your-GEN come-NEG-NR.FUT-her-ACC say-PAST
  'He said that your mother will not come.'

There is only one more nominalizer in Turkish which functions like the one in E29, and it indicates non-future. Neither has an independent meaning. Both of them occupy the position of the verbal tense suffix, thus reducing the tense paradigm to a binary opposition. The subject-predicate syntagm of the nominalized clause is maximally likened to a genitive-head noun syntagm, since not only does the subject have a genitive suffix, but also the nominalized verb has an obligatory possessive suffix referring back to the subject. Nevertheless, we do not yet have a deverbal derived noun here; the formation of E29 is entirely a matter of syntax.

However, the next step in the grammaticalization scale does lead us to VERBAL NOUNS which retain few of the properties of the full clause which we started from. English nominalizations in *-ing* are an example. Here it is clear that we are dealing with the nominalization not of a clause, but of a verb. The suffix constitutes a one-member paradigm of nominalizers and cancels all the verbal categories of English. Still, the verbal noun may take arguments and adjuncts almost like the finite verb of a clause. The subject is, of course, in the genitive. In the other modifiers, there is an interesting variation: the object may either remain in the accusative, or it may pass into the genitive, too. In the first alternative, adverbs

3 Grammatical domains

remain such, whereas in the second alternative they become adjective attributes to the verbal noun. A third correlating phenomenon is the possibility of an article in the latter, but not in the former case. Thus:

E30 English

   a. *John's constantly reading magazines*
   b. *John's constant reading of magazines*
   c. **the (constantly) reading magazines*
   d. *the (constant) reading of magazines*

So we have two stages of our grammaticalization scale embodied in the English POSS-*ing* construction. At the latter stage, the nominalized verb has assumed all the relevant features of a noun; *-ing*-nominalizations are even pluralizable.

Extreme grammaticalization leads to the deletion of the grammatical formative. In nominalization, we would be looking for CONVERSION of verbs into nouns without an overt derivative affix. Examples are, of course, known from English: *to run — the run, to love — the love*, etc. However, while virtually all verbs can be nominalized by the *-ing* suffix, most verbs cannot be nominalized by a zero affix. There is a restriction of productivity here which we have so far not found to be typical of grammaticalization. I will return in §5.2 to a conception which can accommodate these heterogeneous facts, and try here another example which apparently does not present this complicating factor. Nominalizations similar to the ones just cited from English are common in Classical Chinese; cf. the following example from Su Shi:

E31 Mandarin (Bossong 1979: 40)

   a. *bīng   bù kě qù.*
      soldier not can leave

      'Military is indispensable.'

   b. *xiān   wáng zhǐ   bīng   zhī bù kě qù.*
      former king   know [soldier GEN not can leave]

      'The former kings were aware of the indispensability of the military.'

There is only an indirect sign of nominality of the verb phrase *bù kě qù* in E31.b, viz. the genitive particle following its semantic subject. We must therefore assume nominalization by a zero affix to have taken place; and this is in fact such a common process in classical Chinese that earlier scholars (e.g. Misteli 1893) had diagnosed a random shift of word classes or, equivalently, the total lack thereof.

3.3 Nominal complexes

However, on the basis of facts about grammaticalization that we have seen up to now, the technique exemplified by E31 fits in the scale as representing an expectable, if extreme, degree of grammaticality of nominalization. There arises, however, the further problem that the difference of nominalizations as exemplified by E31 and such others as exemplified above by E25, which we have posited at opposite ends of the grammaticalization scale, appears to be minimal. This will be dealt with in §4.4.4.

The renovation of a nominalizing construction may be either complete or partial. We may call it complete if no feature of an inherited nominalizing construction is used in the renovation. This has happened during the change from classical to modern Japanese (see Bossong 1979: 45f). Classical Japanese had an infinite verb form which was used in nominalizations. By phonological and morphological change, this became indistinguishable from the "finite" main clause verb form, and nominalization was renewed by means of postposed particles of nominal origin, as exemplified in E28. A complete renovation is also the substitution of the Latin accusativus-cum-infinitivo construction by clauses subordinated with the help of *que/che* in the Romance languages.

In partial renovation, only the subordinator is renewed. This process, which is very common in Indo-European languages, was already studied by Meillet (1915). Typically, a subordinate clause introduced by the unmarked subordinator (English *that*, German *daß*, Romance *que/che*, Persian *ke*, Turkish *-diğ-*, etc.) is embedded as the complement to a noun or a preposition. Then either this head coalesces with the subordinator, or the subordinator becomes dispensable, the former head becoming the new subordinator. Examples are Italian *dal momento che* 'since', French *parce que* 'because', *puisque* 'since', *avant que* 'before', Turkish *-diğ-*POSS *zaman/hal-de* (-NR-POSS time/ state-LOC) 'when/although'. The former subordinator has disappeared in English *before*, German *bevor* and *fall-s* (case-ADVR) 'if'.

The MAKING OF CONJUNCTIONS would easily fill a whole book. The process by which local conjunctions become temporal ones and temporal conjunctions become causal, conditional etc. conjunctions, is also a sort of grammaticalization (see §5.1). Examples are German *da* 'at the place where' > 'at the time when' > 'by the reason that', English *since* 'from the time that' > 'from the reason that', Italian *dal momento che* id., *qualora* (which:hour>) 'if'. In the end, conjunctions which mark a semantic relation of the subordinate to the main clause are grammaticalized to mere subordinators, as when Latin *quod* and *quia* 'because' both fuse into Romance *que/che* 'that'. The same phenomena repeat themselves in the prepositions.

3 Grammatical domains

In contradistinction to this evidence of renovation of conjunctions, evidence for their reinforcement is somewhat scant. Possibly French *parce que*, adduced above as an example of renovation, is rather one of reinforcement. This depends on whether the *que*-clause, at the time it was combined with *par ce*, was a mere complement clause (as assumed above) or a causal clause. The parallel case of German *da* > *zumal da* > *zumal* 'since' is somewhat more convincing.

Clearer evidence comes from subordinators derived from verba dicendi (Lord 1976: 183). In Efik and Yoruba, the subordinator *ke*, which comes from a verb meaning 'say', has been reinforced by a second subordinator *ete*, of the same provenience. Example:

E32   Efik (after Lord 1976: 183)
      Kristian ɔdɔhɔ ete ke imɔ idi idikɔ owo...
      K.   say SR SR he COP man wicked
      'Kristian says that he was a wicked man...'

The more recent subordinator then tends to dispense with the former one, just as in some of the above examples of renovation. Similar observations apply to the Abkhaz particle *h̄°a*, which stems from a verb meaning 'say' and develops into a general subordinator (cf. Hewitt 1979: 5–8, 28–35, 43).

A few words must be said about nominalizations in which an argument place — mostly the subject position — of the infinite verb must be left open, so that it can be semantically filled, with the help of syntactic rules, by an NP of the main clause. The INFINITIVES which appear in this function are very often embedded by a particle or affix which derives from a directional adposition. Examples are English *to*, German *zu*, Romance *a*, Swahili *ku-* (cf. Meinhof 1936) and the case suffixes, mostly the dative (see Szemerényi 1970: 298), on Sanskrit infinitival verbal nouns. This is naturally explicable by the final function which infinitival complements usually have at their origin. Similarly, gerundial suffixes are often based on locative markers; cf. what was said on p. 32 on periphrastic progressive aspects. Once a verb form is embedded with the help of such a directional or local marker, the same process as noted above for the demonstrative subordinators takes place: since that which is the complement to an adposition or even a case affix must be of a nominal nature, these signs will suffice to express the nominalization and degenerate to mere nominalizers. This is easily shown for English *to* = German *zu*, which can even introduce infinitivals in subject function.

Certain types of nominalized clauses derive from the combination of an NP of the main clause with an infinitival complement whose subject place the former fills. Thus, there is unanimity among scholars that the Latin ACCUSATIVUS CUM INFINITIVO originated in sentences such as E33.

E33 Latin
Petrus   videt   Paulum   currere.
Peter:NOM.SG see:3.SG Paul:ACC.SG run:INF
'Peter sees Paul run(ning)'

E34 Latin
Carthaginem   deleri   necesse est.
Carthago:ACC.SG destroy:INF.PASS necessary is
'It is necessary that Carthago be destroyed.'

There *Paulum* is the object of the main clause. Its subjecthood vis-à-vis the infinitive at this initial stage is a consequence of a semantosyntactic rule of complex sentence structure. Subsequently, its subject status becomes grammaticalized, and we also get a.c.i. in non-object positions of the main clause, as in E34.

E34 might also be expressed in English by *It is necessary for Carthago to be destroyed.* Here we have another subtype of the complement clause originating in the combination of an NP of the main clause with an infinitival complement whose subject position it fills (see Jespersen 1940: 300–306 on details). While in American English the grammaticalization of this construction is already far advanced, in French it has come up recently and is still classified as "faute" in Frei 1929: 94. Frei's examples are:

E35 French

    a. *m'envoyez son adresse pour moi lui écrire*
       'send me his address so I may write him'
    b. *Où trouver l'argent pour lui voyager?*
       'Where (may I) find the money for him to travel?'
    c. *Ci-joint un timbre pour vous avoir la bonté de répondre.*
       'Here enclosed a stamp for you to be so kind as to answer.'

These examples show very clearly the conditions under which the construction originates: The subsequent subordinate subject must be a beneficiary in the main clause, which is adjoined with the help of the preposition 'for'. The infinitive complement must express the action which the beneficiary is expected to be able to

3 Grammatical domains

accomplish with the help of the benefaction and which, being a purpose or consequence of the main clause action, is introduced by the final preposition 'to'. In the course of grammaticalization, these semantic conditions are gradually weakened or dropped, and the erstwhile beneficiary NP of the main clause becomes the subject of the infinite clause. This may go so far that the subordinate subject is even put into the nominative. Modern Portuguese has reached this advanced stage of grammaticalization of the 'for-to' complement clause, as exemplified in E36.

E36 Portuguese
Ele trouxe um livro para eu ler.
he brought a book for I read:INF

The construction from which E36 must have arisen, namely *Ele trouxe um livro para mim ler* (*mim* 'me'), is nowadays even condemned by the grammarians, though it is still current in the colloquial language.

While infinitival complements may, thus, contribute to form a full complement clause, the reverse process, the reduction of a clause whose argument positions are all filled to a relational infinitival complement which has necessarily an unoccupied argument position, has not been observed. Recall that this is certainly not what is at stake in the grammaticalization process leading from E25 to E31.b above. It appears that the opening of an argument position is not something which comes about by grammaticalization. Therefore, while we often do have paraphrases among *that*-clauses, *for-to* nominalizations and *-ing*-nominalization, *that*-clauses can practically never be used as a paraphrase of an infinitive complement. Consider the infinitive complement in sentences such as *I let him go* or *forced him to go*. The main verb does not leave the possibility of its direct object being different from the semantic subject of the subordinate verb. Therefore, the subject position of the latter must remain unfilled.

3.3.3 Attribution

We will treat here two kinds of attributes, adjective attributes and possessive attributes, traditionally called genitive attributes. Quite a few languages use an attributor, a relational particle, in the combination of either kind of attribute with a head noun. E37 shows a genitive attributor, E38f show relators which may attribute either an NP (a) or an adjectival (b) to the head noun.

3.3 Nominal complexes

E37 Japanese
watakusi no hon
I AT book
'my book'

E38 Mandarin

a. *wǒ de shū*
I AT book
'my book'

b. *yàojin de huà*
important AT discourse
'important words'

E39 Persian

a. *ketāb -e man*
book -AT I
'my book'

b. *dālān -e derāz*
corridor -AT long
'long corridor'

One development which can lead to such constructions is the grammaticalization of ANAPHORIC or substantivized ATTRIBUTES. When a concept (not a referent) is (pronominally or implicitly) resumed in lexical anaphora and combined with a (new) attribute in order to identify a referent, we have an anaphoric attribute. In English, *one* is used as the anaphoric head in such cases. Japanese has a polyfunctional particle *no*. Its former lexical meaning was 'matter, fact, case' (Jorden 1962: 99). It functions as the grammatical head noun in lexical anaphora, as in E40.

E40 Japanese

a. *Dare no hon desu ka? — Watakusi no desu.*
who AT book COP INT I AT COP
'Whose book is it?' — 'It is mine.'

b. *Dono hon desu ka? — Atarasii no desu.*
which book COP INT new AT COP
'Which book is it?' — 'It is the new one.'

3 Grammatical domains

No may also be a nominalizer; in this function it may be substituted for *koto* in E28 above. We may assume it to have taken the following development: The "Grundbedeutung" of a construction "X *no*" is 'the thing characterized by X'. In this construction, X can be either a — possessive or adjective — attribute, as in the answers of E40, or an embedded clause, as in the altered version of E28. The attributive function of *no*, as in E37, is a secondary development. E37 represents the grammaticalization of the appositive combination of a substantivized attribute with a lexical head; its original meaning is 'my thing, the book'. In this way, an older (optionally asyndetic) possessive attribution was renewed. A parallel renovation of adjective attribution did not take place, because adjectives are marked as attributes by their desinence -*i* (cf. E40b).

Similar constructions involving nouns with the meaning 'thing' or 'possession' are elsewhere frequent in the expression of alienable possession. A further example is the possessive NP in Thai (see Mallinson & Blake 1981: 389). It has the form "possessum *khɔɔŋ* possessor". *Khɔɔŋ*, now a preposition, comes from a noun meaning 'thing, goods, possessions'. Many languages, among them Bororo, Bambara and Dyula, have an attributor of alienable possession that stems from an inalienable noun.

A similar renovation of a juxtaposed attribute by an anaphoric one may be posited for Mandarin Chinese. Besides E38b, we have *jàojin huà*, with the same meaning, but less emphasis on the attribute. On the other hand, we have anaphoric or substantivized attributes with *de*, as in *shì yàojin de* 'is (an) important (one)'. An older form of *de* is *zhi*, as exemplified in E31b above. This is known to have been a demonstrative (cf. the *shì* in §3.1.2 above). It is therefore safe to assume that attribution by means of *de* results from an emphatic renovation of the earlier, still subsisting, juxtapositive attribution.

The history of the Persian attributor (izafat) is better known (cf. Lehmann 1984: Ch. VI.3 and the literature cited there). Old Persian and Avestic had a relative pronoun *hya-* or *ya-*, respectively, which, apart from introducing ordinary relative clauses, was also used in the formation of nominal attributes, as in E41.

E41 Avestic

    a. (Yt.10, 65)
       āat̰ yat̰ miθrəm   yim   vouru-gaoyaoitīm
       then SR Mithra:ACC.SG.M REL:ACC.SG.M ample-pasturage:ACC.SG.M
       frāδąm   azəm
       created:1.SG I

      'when I created Mithra, the one with ample pasture lands'

b. (Vd. 5,1)

tam	kəhrpəm	fraŋuharaiti	yam	iristahe
DET:ACC.SG.F	body:ACC.SG.F	eat:3.SG	REL:ACC.SG.F	deceased:GEN.SG.M

mašyehe
man:GEN.SG.M

'he eats the body of the dead man'

Originally, these were nominal relative clauses, with the relative pronoun as the subject. They forfeit this status, however, as soon as the relative pronoun, instead of being in the nominative, agrees with the head noun in case (as does the nominal predicate), as it does in the examples. At this stage, the relative pronoun becomes a mere attributor, though one distinguished from those discussed so far by its agreement. This, however, is subsequently lost, so that the attributor becomes identical to the subordinator also to be seen in E41a. Example:

E42 Avestic (V. 5,39)

mi	aŋhvō	ya	astvainti
DEM:LOK.SG.M	life:LOK.SG.M	AT	bodily:LOK.SG.M

'in this worldly life'

This emphatic attribution gradually gains ground against the inherited juxtapositive attribution, concomitantly with the loss of the agreement of the attribute. The inherited construction is then almost ousted, while the attributor is further reduced phonologically and becomes a suffix of the head noun. The emphatic force of the construction is also lost, and the result is to be seen in E39.

The Persian case is somewhat different from the Japanese and Chinese ones, as in these certainly no relative pronoun is involved. Their common feature is, however, that the resulting attributor comes from a noun anaphorically related to the subsequent head noun of the attribution and representing this vis-à-vis the attribute. This hypothesis provides a natural explanation for the otherwise startling formal identity of the attributor and the nominalizer in some of the above languages as well as several others, e.g. Lahu. It is, I think, the only way to make sense of the phenomenon that an adjective or a possessor noun should need a nominalizer in order to be attributable to a head noun (the alternative, that a dependent clause should receive an attributor in order to become nominalized, makes no sense, anyway).

An anaphoric pronoun which serves as the head of an anaphoric or substantivized attribute may, of course, show gender or noun class agreement with its repraesentatum. When this construction is apposed to the repraesentatum as the head noun, we have agreement of the attributor with the head noun just as in E41. An example is Gothic *hairdeis sa goda* (shepherd:NOM.SG.M that.NOM.SG.M good:NOM.SG.M) as against *hairdeis gods* (good:NOM.SG.M) (with weak and strong adjective declension, respectively; see Ramat 1980: 110). Both constructions mean 'the good shepherd'; the former is emphatic and more recent, the latter inherited and neutral. While in Gothic the demonstrative has not become an attributor, but an article, its fate was different in the Bantu languages (details in Lehmann 1982b: §7.2). In Swahili we find an attributor which agrees with the head noun in noun class. The possessive attribute construction is [CLX-head [CLX-AT CLy-attribute]]. Examples:

E43 Swahili (Welmers 1973: 275)

  a. *ki-su   ch-a   Hamisi*
     CL7-knife CL7-AT Hamisi
     'Hamisi's knife'

  b. *ny-umba y-a   m-tu   yu-le*
     CL9-house CL9-AT CL1-man CL1-that
     'that person's house'

From the origin of the construction as posited, the attributor is a coconstituent of the attribute. It becomes clitic to the attribute; and further grammaticalization, which may be observed in the related language Tswana, leads to its prefixation, as in E44.

E44 Tswana (Cole 1955: 160)
     mo-sadi   w-a+mo-tšomi
     CL1.SG-woman CL1.SG-AT+CL1.SG-hunter
     'the wife of the hunter'

Here the possessive attribute agrees with its head noun in noun class. Possessive attributes are thus treated structurally exactly as adjective attributes, which agree with their head noun by similar prefixes:

E45 Tswana (Cole 1955: 140)
     mo-sadi   yômo-ntlê
     CL1.SG-woman CL1.SG-beautiful
     'a beautiful woman'

On the basis of the facts discussed so far, I venture the hypothesis that the agreement of the — possessive or adjective — attribute with the head noun, as it is to be observed in many languages, in particular Indo-European ones, has one principal diachronic source: It is an advanced stage of the grammaticalization of a pronoun which formerly represented the head noun anaphorically and served as the head for the attribute. By this device, the attribute is substantivized, and then the syntagm is apposed to the lexical head noun. Further grammaticalization of the whole construction turns apposition into attribution and the agreeing attributor into an affix of the attribute.

The history of the Germanic and Romance languages teaches us that further grammaticalization of the agreeing adjective attribute leads to the loss of its inflection and, consequently, of the agreement. The result is an attribute juxtaposed to its head noun without any segmental means of attribution; this is, instead, signalled by the position of the attribute relative to the head noun. As a consequence of this, the positional freedom of the attribute, which is notably great for the agreeing attribute, is lost at the end of the grammaticalization channel. At this stage at the latest, renovation of attribution sets in in the way described.

In the case of the adjective, the head directly occupies an argument position of the attribute. Possessive attribution, on the other hand, is a special case of a dependency relationship in which an NP B depends on A. A relator R which is to bring about such a relation has to have a governing slot for B and may have a modifying slot for A. The latter can be dispensed with in favor of mere apposition between A and R(B). Given that A is a noun, this allows essentially for two syntactically distinct kinds of relators in this construction. If R has the modifying slot, then it is a case relator, i.e. an adposition or a case. If it lacks it, then R is a relational noun that serves as a dummy head to the possessive attribute. In both cases, there may be a paradigm of relators that express specific semantic relations between the dependent NP and the head noun. Consequently, there are different channels through which the possessive attribute may evolve. The use of relational nouns as possessive relators leads to possessive classifiers. If one such noun grammaticalizes to a (genitive) attributor, we get the situation illustrated on pp. 74–74 from Japanese and Thai. We now turn to the use of case relators to make an NP an attribute to a noun.

The genitive may be viewed as a formal case which neutralizes two opposite dynamic relations of the dependent NP to its head: the dependent B may either be "from" A, bearing an ablative kind of relation to A; or it may be "destined for" A, bearing a benefactive/purposive kind of relation to it. Consequently, we find both ablative and benefactive/purposive relators at the origin of genitive relators. The Romance attributor *de* (Italian *di*), English *of*, German *von* etc. illustrate the first alternative. Latin *dē* '(down) from' started out as a concrete local preposition.

3 Grammatical domains

In the classical language, it could not be used to mark a possessive attribute. It did, however, compete with the mere genitive in the expression of the partitive relation, as shown in E46.a and b.

E46   a. Latin
nullum trium horum generum
'none of these three species'

        b. Latin (Cic. Rep. 3, 47)
nullum de tribus his generibus
id.

        c. Spanish
ninguno de estos tres géneros
none   of these three species:PL
id.

From there, *de* generalized to a general nominal attributor, ousting and renewing the genitive. Thus, in Spanish it is not only obligatory in E46.c, but in various kinds of nominal attributes, including possessive ones. While *de*, as a preposition, is not likely to develop into a case affix, elsewhere suffixal genitives may have evolved from postpositions along these lines.

The grammaticalizational relationship between the benefactive/purposive and the genitive may be illustrated from Imbabura Quechua. E47 shows a benefactive adjunct marked by the suffix *-paj*, E48 shows a possessive dependent with the same suffix.

E47   Quechua (Cole 1982: 113)
wasi-ta   rura-rka-ni   ñuka churi-paj
house-ACC make-PST-1.SG I   son-BEN
'I made a house for my son.'

E48   Quechua (Cole 1982: 115)
Juzi-paj   wasi
Joseph-BEN house
'Joe's house'

The same suffix is used on purposive adjuncts (Cole 1982: 116f), but the dative has a different suffix. In other languages, the formal identity of the benefactive/purposive and the genitive crucially includes the dative. In Mangarayi (Merlan 1982: 66–76; cf. Table 3.4), there is one benefactive/purposive/dative case which is distinct from genitive in pronouns, but not in nouns. The possessed noun has possessive suffixes. The same constellation exists in Hungarian and substandard German. Both the evolution of the genitive from an ablative and from a benefactive involve a shift in the modifying slot of the relator from an adverbal to an adnominal relation.

3.4 Clause level relations

This chapter will deal with relations between the verb and the various complements and adjuncts. The reader will notice that, although the difference between these two types of relations is recognized, they are not always kept apart. Similarly, the distinction between semantic roles (or case functions) and syntactic functions, or between semantic and syntactic relations, is sometimes knowingly obscured; and the distinction between functional sentence perspective and syntax or, more specifically, between "pragmatic" and syntactic relations, will fare no better. All of these are valid and useful distinctions. Unfortunately, they are connected by grammaticalization scales; and differences on grammaticalization scales are always gradual. We will take up the discussion of these dichotomies in §3.4.2.1.

3.4.1 Adverbial relations

3.4.1.1 Adverbial relators

Under the heading of adverbial relations, I will comprise such semantic relations as typically exist between a verb and an adjunct, more typically a local adjunct. We must complicate the issue from the start, by viewing such relations from two different angles: from the point of view of the naked verb, and from the point of view of the naked NP. Consider a seemingly simple case: *Peter is standing on the table*. There is an adverbial relation between the verb and the NP *the table*. We may call it locative and be inclined to say that *on* is its segmental expression. But now consider *Peter is standing on top of the table*. Should we say that the same relation here holds between the verb and the NP *top of the table*? This seems unsatisfactory, since *on top of* clearly belongs together as a more or less fixed complex preposition. Should we then say that we again have an adverbial relation between the verb and the NP *the table*, again a locative one, but this time expressed by *on top of*? This might be true; but it would certainly not be the whole truth. Further structural analysis will show that the complex preposition consists of a simple preposition and its nominal complement, and the latter in turn governs, as a possessive attribute formed with the help of *of*, that NP that we have just assumed to be in a relation with the verb. So is this account wrong, too?

The difficulty lies, of course, in our not being clear about the nature of the relator. *On* in the first example and *on top of* in the second are not merely segmental expressions of a relation contracted between two other terms. Instead, the theory sketched at the end of the preceding section (p. 77) on the nature of dependency relators applies in verbal dependency, too. The — simple or complex — preposition itself contracts relations. On the one hand, it governs its nominal complement; on the other, it modifies (together with its complement) the verb. And if it is internally complex, then its parts may contract similar relations among each other. Thus, instead of a single relation between a verb and an adjunct NP, we get a chain of relations joining the two. The case with *on top of* is not fundamentally different from the situation in *Peter is standing on top of the leaf of the table*, where nobody would want to see a direct relation between the verb and *the table*.

For our purposes, we will have enough with two subrelations within an adverbial relation: the relation between the verb and the adverbial relator, a preposition in our example; and the relation between the adverbial relator and the NP. We will call the former the VA and the latter the AN relation. Apart from this, there are of course, pure verb-NP relations. We will call them VN relations and apply this term also when the internal structure of a (possibly adverbial) relation between a verb and an NP is of no concern.

On the one hand, VA relations are by definition not inherent in naked verbs. If they were, there would be no adjunction, but government, and we would not need an adverbial relator in order to mediate the relation of the verb to the NP. On the other hand, AN relations are not inherent in naked NPs; that is, an NP does not contain an argument slot for an adverbial relator with which it is to be combined. In both cases we need the qualification "naked", because as we shall see in this chapter, what the grammaticalization of adverbial relations is all about is precisely the combination of the relator with either the verb or the NP; and this, of course, fundamentally changes the relational situation.

Since VA and AN relations are dependency relations, but not inherent in verbs or NPs, they must consequently be inherent in adverbial relators. On the one hand, these contain an argument place for a verb which they modify; and on the other hand, they contain one for the NP which they govern. Of these two relations, the VA relation is relatively loose, since it corresponds roughly to the relation between a subject and a non-verbal predicate. The AN relation is much stronger, since it is a government relation which throws the NP into an oblique position. Now, if adverbial relators arise through grammaticalization, we may expect the underlying lexemes to be relational in the required sense. This leaves in principle two classes of lexemes as possible sources: transitive verbs, with slots for a subject and oblique argument; and relational nouns, which may modify a subject as nominal predicates (though the corresponding argument slot may be weak or absent) and which have a second slot for an oblique argument. We shall first discuss relational nouns, then transitive verbs. The phenomena dealt with in the following sections have been studied on a cross-linguistic scale in Kahr (1975; 1976) and Austerlitz (1980: esp. 240).

3.4.1.2 Relational nouns

In this section we will deal with nouns designating spatial regions, such as 'top', 'side', 'back' etc. The fact that such designations of spatial regions often derive from designations of parts of the body (e.g. English *foot*, Latin *frons* 'forehead' > Spanish/Portugese *frente* 'front') will not concern us here. These nouns necessarily have an argument slot for a possessor NP, designating the object with respect to which the location is made. If a language opposes unmarked juxtaposed possessor NPs to marked genitives, the possessors of these relational nouns will remain unmarked, as, e.g., in Sumerian or Malak (Mallinson & Blake 1981: 389). Similarly, if a language has possessive affixes, such relational nouns will certainly admit of them.[10] On the other hand, if the possessor is not expressed, it is always understood from the context, cf. Seiler (1983: §5.2.3.1). Thus, if I say *it is in front*, you will only understand me if you know what it is in front of. Cf. also E62f below.

The incidence of such relational nouns varies a lot among different languages. For instance, Latin has almost none, German has few basic ones (though composition yields many more of them), English has quite a few, and Turkish and Japanese possess a rich paradigm of relational nouns. These may behave like ordinary nouns; in Japanese, they may even be determined by a demonstrative pronoun, as in *ko-no saki* (D1-AT direction.ahead; lit. this forward-direction) '(the direction) ahead from here'.

---

[10] Mallinson & Blake (1981: 50f) report about nominal case suffixes in Wangkumara (Pama Nyungan), which appear to derive from personal pronouns. If this is correct, it may be a variant of the developments described in what follows. Relational nouns with possessive affixes develop into adpositions with personal affixes referring to their complement. This product may be indistinguishable from a personal pronoun with a case affix. Such a complex may then agglutinate to the noun that the personal element referred to.

3 Grammatical domains

Furthermore, relational nouns, like any other nouns, admit of case affixes. In Turkish, for instance, we have, among others, the case suffixes displayed in E49.

E49 Turkish
ev-e /-de /-den
house-DIR /-LOC /-ABL
'to/in/from the house'

The relational nouns, such as *alt* 'lower side', *ön* 'front', *arka* 'back', *yan* 'side' etc., enter into the following construction: they take a preposed complement in the genitive (suffix *-in*), resume this by a possessive suffix (3.PERS. =-*i(n)*), and terminate in a case suffix. This yields the subparadigm of E50.a, exemplified in b.

E50 Turkish (Wendt 1972: 258f)

a. *ev-in* { *alt* / *ön* / *arka* / *yan* } *-in* { *-e* / *-de* / *-den* }

b. *evin altından* 'from under the house'
evin önünde 'in front of the house'
evin yanına 'to the side of the house'

Similar constructions are widespread in the languages of the world; they may be found in many other Turkic, in Finno-Ugric languages such as Finnish and Hungarian, in Basque, Japanese, Quechua etc. They provide for a rich and maximally regular paradigm of locative expressions, almost untranslatable in languages such as Latin, and imitable in German only with the help of clumsy circumlocutions.

The Japanese system is almost perfectly parallel to the Turkish one, except that there are no possessive suffixes. An example will suffice here:

E51 Japanese (Jorden 1962: 97)
A-no kuroi kuruma no usiro de tome-te kudasai.
D3-AT black car GEN back LOC stop-GER grant
'Please stop in back of that black car.'

Japanese, however, has one peculiarity which should be mentioned here. Noun phrases based on local relational nouns may be used to describe the location of an object, as in E52.

E52 Japanese (cf. Jorden 1962: 84f)
Ginkoo wa taisikan no mukoo /mae /yoko /temae /migi desu.
bank TOP embassy GEN yonder.part /front /side /this.side /right.side COP
'The bank is beyond/in front of/beside/this side/to the right of the embassy.'

Two things are remarkable about this construction. Firstly, the relational nouns are not used here as adverbial relators, but as nominal predicates. This proves that the modifying relation in which they take part can be explicated as the relation of the subject to the nominal predicate, as was claimed above. Secondly, they do not require a locative (or other case) suffix in this type of clause. The literal meaning of such sentences is: 'The bank is the yonder part / the front etc. of the embassy.' This makes sense, of course, only if these relational nouns designate not a part of the possessor as a whole, but a region of space identified with respect to the possessor. That is, they do not require a locative suffix because "location" is one of their lexical features. We shall see below that this feature plays a prominent role in the grammaticalization of such constructions.

The above examples mark the starting-point for the development of adpositions through grammaticalization (cf. Mallinson & Blake 1981: 446, fn 5 for more examples). Agglutinative (or even free) case markers, as in Turkish and Japanese, mostly attach to an NP as a whole. Therefore, the final locational case markers in the adverbial phrases of E50 and E51 are not coconstituents of (or appended to) the relational nouns (N_{rel}). Instead, the structure must be represented as in Figure 3.3.a.

a. *Initial structure* [[NP-GEN N_{rel}] -CASE]
b. *Syntactic reanalysis* [NP-GEN [Adposition -CASE]]

Figure 3.3: Structure of complex adpositional phrase

Now, the very first thing that happens in the grammaticalization of such adverbial phrases is the syntactic reanalysis which yields the structure in Figure 3.3.b. We may hypothesize that taking step b also means treating the governing term no longer as a relational noun, but as a (complex) adposition. This implies, among other things, that it can no longer be modified by attributes. This entails, in turn, that its complement may no longer manifest in form of a possessive pronoun.

E53 French

a. * *à votre côté*
   'at your side'

b. *à côté de vous*
    'beside you'

Thus, if French *côté* had remained a noun in E53, E53.a should be possible. However, the correct expression is b. The same goes for German complex prepositions such as *anstatt* 'instead', but not, e.g., for the Arabic preposition illustrated in E55.b below. As a further consequence of the above reanalysis, the removal of the syntactic boundary between the relational noun and the case marker clears the way for their subsequent coalescence.

However, we must recognize that not all languages follow this idealized diachronic development. On the one hand, not all grammaticalization processes need begin at the start. We have already met several examples of constructions which enter grammaticalization channels in the middle. This is particularly common in reinforcement. We shall see more such examples below; they do not really upset any theoretical commitments which we have made so far. What is somewhat more disturbing, however, is that a language may take the second step before the first one, as it were. I shall try to provide a theoretical account of this in §7.2. An example will suffice here. The relational noun may form a constituent with the case marker without stage Figure 3.3.a having ever existed, although the adposition is clearly analyzable as a relational noun. This is so in postpositions such as Latin *causā* (reason:ABL) 'because of' and *gratiā* (favor:ABL) 'for the sake of'. In view of the fact that Latin does not have agglutinative case suffixes, it could hardly be otherwise.

Figure 3.3 must be understood as an abbreviation of several structural alternatives. On the one hand, it is meant to be indifferent as to the position of the relational noun before or after its complement and, accordingly, its development into a preposition or postposition, respectively. I will disregard this difference except where relevant. On the other hand, the postpositive or suffixal case marker in Figure 3.3 may as well be a preposition. This allows us to take examples such as the following into account: *beside, because (of)*, German *mithilfe* 'with the help (of)', *infolge* = Russian *vsledstvie* 'as a consequence (of)', German *anstatt* = *instead (of)* etc. These illustrate the coalescence of the primary, "outer" preposition with the relational noun to a complex preposition.

3.4.1.3 From adposition to case affix

In the situation represented by Figure 3.3.b, various alternative developments may set in; there is no unitary grammaticalization channel. Let me list those developments which I will trace in some detail:

1. Reduction of the complex adposition. The outer case marker is either dropped or fuses with the erstwhile relational noun. The result is in either case a simple adposition.

2. Deletion of the (genitive) case marker on the complement NP.

3. Affixation of the adpostion to its erstwhile complement NP.

As we will see, these three processes are hardly ordered with respect to each other. They may occur in the sequence as enumerated, or number 2 may occur before number 1. Number 3 may occur without number 2 having occured (although 2 may probably then no longer occur).

Let me begin by the reduction of the complex adposition by deletion of the outer case marker. This has occurred in most of the Turkish genuine postpositions, i.e. other than those analyzable as regularly inflected relational nouns, which we have seen in E50. Here I will slur over the fact that most of them govern cases other than the genitive (this will be taken up in §3.4.1.4) and exemplify from that subclass which does govern a complement in the genitive if this is a pronoun. Thus: *sen-in için* (you-GEN for) 'for you', *sen-in ile* 'with you'. *İçin* is still partly analyzable: *iç-i* (interior-POSS.3.SG) functions, at the same time, as a regular relational noun of the postpositional meaning 'in', according to the paradigm E50. The deletion of the location case marker of the postposition presupposes, of course, that the latter is interpreted as expressing a locational case function of its complement NP. Recall what was said above on the Japanese construction of E52.

The analog to the deletion of the outer case marker in the development of complex prepositions is the deletion of the introductory simple preposition. Examples from German include *zum Trotz* 'in spite' > *trotz* 'despite', *anstatt* > *statt* 'instead', *in Kraft* > *kraft* 'by virtue'.

The reduction of the complex adposition to a simple one may also be seen in the Semitic languages. All of the prepositions of Accadic and Classical Arabic govern the genitive, even the unanalyzable primary ones. The reason is that all of them go back to nominal forms in the status constructus, though this is not apparent from synchronic morphology and often not even recoverable by etymology. Examples:

E54 Accadic

    a. *ana bullīm*
       to   extinguish:INF:GEN
       'to extinguish'

b. *ina qāt-i-šu*
      in hand-GEN-POSS.3
      'in his hand'

E55 Arabic

   a. *lil   walad-i*
      for:DEF boy-GEN
      'for the boy'

   b. *la -hū*
      for -POSS.3.SG.M
      'for him'

E55 shows that such prepositions may also take a pronominal complement in the form of a possessive affix, just as do the relational nouns in Turkish (E50). Furthermore, the preposition in E55.a fuses with the definite article, which points to a fairly advanced stage of grammaticalization. Nevertheless, despite their own exiguity, they are not affixes of the noun, and they still govern the genitive.

We now pass on to the second process, the deletion of the case marker on the complement NP. As I said above, since inalienable possession is involved here, there may never have been a genitive case marker on this complement even if the language otherwise does have a marked genitive. If this is the case, the bond between the postposition and its complement is tighter from the start, the genitive deletion phase will be skipped, and the last phase, the agglutination of the postposition, is immediately available. Sumerian case suffixes are said to derive from constructions of this type. For lack of historical evidence, I will not distinguish in the following between genitive endings that have been lost and ones that have never been there.

In Imbabura Quechua, all possessed nouns, with an exception to be discussed presently, govern a marked genitive. Furthermore, we have case suffixes, such as those in E56.a, and we have relational nouns combining with these and governing preposed nominal complements, as in b.

E56 Quechua (Cole 1982: 119–121)

   a. *wasi -pi   /-man /-manda /-paj*
      house -LOC /-DIR /-ABL   /-GEN
      'in/to/from/of the house'

   b. *wasi uku   -pi   /-man /-manda*
      house interior -LOC /-DIR /-ABL
      'within/into/from within the house'

3.4 Clause level relations

As in Turkish, Japanese etc., there are a variety of relational nouns such as *ladu-* 'vicinity' (> 'near'), *washa-* 'back' (> 'behind'), *jawa-* 'top' (> 'on'), which can take the place of *uku-* in E56.b. However, there is an essential difference between the present construction and the Turkish and Japanese ones: Firstly, all these relational nouns obligatorily take their local case suffixes; in this respect they are no longer completely free. This indicates that the reanalysis of Figure 3.3.b has been made; cf. Cole (1982: 120). Secondly, they do not govern the genitive of their complement; instead, this remains unmarked for case. This evidently tightens the bond between the complex postposition and its complement; the former is already well on its way to becoming a complex suffix of the latter. The development of the Hungarian case suffixes, which will be discussed below, actually sets in exactly at the point where the Quechua postpositions stop.

Postpositions to caseless NPs may also be illustrated from Turkish. In fact, the same postpositions which govern the genitive if their complement is a pronoun, require a nominal complement in the absolute form. Thus *bu mesele için* (this affair concerning) 'about this affair', *bayan-lar ile* (woman-PL with) 'with the women'. An intermediate case between these and the fully regular formations of E50 is provided by the following examples from Kahr (1975: 30): *bu çocuk hakk-ın-da* (this child right (n.)-POSS.3.SG-LOC) 'concerning this child'. This differs from the examples just given by being fully analyzable morphologically, and from those in E50 in that the composition of the postposition is invariable.

The present examples of postpositions governing an NP unmarked for case have been taken from languages which do possess a case paradigm, including a genitive. However, this construction is, of course, the only one possible in languages which have no cases. With examples like Turkish *bayan-lar ile*, we are, in fact, at the same level of grammaticalization as with English *with the women* or French *avec les femmes*. Some of these prepositions are more grammaticalized than others. Thus, the prepositions English *of*, French *de*, German *von* all had a fuller ablative meaning, but are now largely devoid of it and mostly used as attributors. The fate of English *to*, Romance *a* is similar: they have been grammaticalized from directional prepositions to case markers of the dative (see p. 99) and, in Spanish, even the accusative. The Latin preposition *per* 'through' yields the Romanian case marker *pe* ACC. The Old Church Slavonic preposition *na* 'on' (superessive and super-lative) develops into a genitive and dative marker in Bulgarian (Qvonje 1979).

The same diachronic relation between the so-called concrete and grammatical case functions returns in the evolution of case suffixes. Cf. Turk, *-e* DIR > DAT, Old Persian *rādiy* 'because of, concerning' > *rā* ACC, Quechua *-ta* and Japanese *-o*

PERL > ACC, IE/Latin -*m* DIR > ACC. The change of an instrumental into an ergative case is common in (the evolution of) ergative languages, e.g. in Dyirbal and Mangarayi. Cf. also §3.4.2.2. Such examples speak against a clear-cut dividing line between concrete and grammatical cases, between semantic and syntactic functions. Recall the difficulties in setting a boundary of directional vs. dative between examples such as *I sent the book to him* and *I gave the book to him*. The problem of the greater or lesser grammaticality of a certain nominal case function has its exact counterpart in the problem of determining whether a certain NP in a clause is or is not controlled by the valency of the verb.[11]

Parallel to the desemanticization of the adposition, we observe its phonological erosion and an increase in its cohesion with the governed NP, which will ultimately lead to the adposition becoming a case affix. This is a straightforward and often observed matter in the case of postpositions. As these occur mostly in languages where the head noun ends the NP, there is no syntactic variation at the constituent structure boundary immediately preceding the postposition. The sequence "NP-CASE" is almost indistinguishable from the sequence "NP POSTP" (with no case suffix intervening). Compare Japanese *Tookyoo ga* (Tokyo NOM) with *Tookyoo made* (Tokyo TERM) 'as far as Tokyo', or Turkish *bayan-lar-ı* (woman-PL-ACC) with *bayan-lar ile*. Therefore, analogical pressure will work here to the same effect as grammaticalization itself, assimilating the postpositions completely to the suffixes. As an alternative to the Turkish postposition *ile*, we have, in fact, the suffix *-le* INST, as in *vapurla* 'with/by the steamer' (Wendt 1972: 63). The same grammaticalizational relationship between comitative and instrumental recurs, by the way, in Latin: *ludo cum Paulo* 'I play with Paul', but *ludo pilā* 'I play with a ball'.

However, suffixation of postpositions is not restricted to NPs ending in the head noun. Basque is an example of a language which has agglutinative case suffixes on NPs, appended to whatever may end the NP: the head noun, an adjective or a determiner. Example: *gizon-a-k* (man-DEF-ERG) vs. *gizon andi-a-k* (man big-DEF-ERG; Brettschneider 1978: 69).

The chance that adpositions will hit upon determiners, instead of on nouns, is much greater for prepositions than for postpositions. Despite the general reluctance to affix elements to varying types of subconstituents, prefixation of prepositions does occur, just as does suffixation of postpositions to non-substantival

---

[11] Meillet (1934: 357–359) holds that the Proto-Indo-European verb had no valency (at least not for non-subjects) and that the dependent NPs were adjuncts whose case was not governed by the verb but chosen according to the sense. Coseriu (1979) makes a similar point about Japanese. Cf. also p. 100 below and Lehmann (1983: §4.2) on the evolution of government.

subconstituents of NPs in Basque. As is to be expected, the most desemanticized prepositions are the first to fuse with the articles. We observe this in French forms such as *du* 'of the', *au* 'to the' etc., which have no counterpart in prepositions such as *dans* or *avant*. Similar phenomena occur in Arabic; cf. E55.a above. In German, most of the primary prepositions may univerbate with the articles; however, some of the univerbations are obligatory. Thus, before the infinitive and the superlative (which, if governed by prepositions, nearly always have the definite article), the fused forms of E57.a (all M/N) must not be represented by the respective sequences in E57.b (Vater 1979: 36).

E57   German

	a. *am*	*beim*	*im*	*vom*	*zum*
	b. *an dem*	*bei dem*	*in dem*	*von dem*	*zu dem*
	at the	at the	in the	of the	to the

It so happens that these are just the most grammaticalized German prepositions. Examples of other languages in Kahr (1976: 135–140).[12] In none of these languages have case prefixes on nouns been developed. We shall meet one such language below.

In German we have the combination of simple, strongly grammaticalized prepositions with case affixes on the governed noun. I shall come back to phenomena of this type on p. 98 and here say only a word on the temporal sequence of the last two processes enumerated above, viz. loss of the (genitive) case affix of the governed noun and affixation of the erstwhile adposition. In the cases discussed above, postpositions have been suffixed to caseless nouns or NPs. This is not necessarily so, as can be seen in Greenlandic Eskimo and Basque. Greenlandic has the case paradigm shown in Table 3.2 (according to Woodbury 1977: 310). Except for the perlative, all of the oblique cases are based on the genitive (of which the ergative itself is a further development; cf. §3.4.2.2); under the phonological effect of the erstwhile postpositions, *p* becomes *m*.

Basque has a prolative suffix with the meaning 'for'. This has either the form *-entzat* or *-tzat*. The prolative suffix proper is only *-tzat*, while *-en* is the regular genitive suffix, which is optional before the erstwhile prolative postposition. Combinations of other case suffixes also occur in Basque and will be discussed in §3.4.1.4.

---

[12] In French, e.g., one cannot say *à l'auteur ou le siège de ce processus* 'to the originator or undergoer of this process', instead of *à l'auteur ou au siège de ce processus*. Cf. p. 159, E106.

3 Grammatical domains

Table 3.2: Greenlandic case paradigm

absolutive	Ø
ergative/genitive	*-p*
instrumental	*-mik*
locative	*-mi*
ablative	*-mit*
allative	*-mut*
perlative	*-kut*

Again, the internal reduction of the complex adposition does not necessarily precede its affixation to the complement. Hungarian, for instance, in its preliterary period (i.e. before 1200 A.D.), had postpositions constructed exactly like the Quechua ones in E56. From the beginning of the literary tradition, these appear as nominal suffixes, but are still readily analyzable. The following examples are from the old literary language.

E58   Hungarian (Tauli 1966: 117)

   a. *vilag-bele*

      'into the world'

   b. *iov-ben*

      'in the good (n.)'

   c. *hely-belöl*

      'out of the place'

The first two examples still lack the vowel harmony to which these suffixes are subject in modern Hungarian. The complex suffixes are based on the relational noun *bél* 'innards' and are to be analyzed as shown in Table 3.3 (cf. also Kahr 1976: 118–121):

The development which these suffixes have taken in modern Hungarian has rendered them simple and largely unanalyzable.

If grammaticalization proceeds, the case affixes will become even shorter and express more basic functions. The Turkish case paradigm is typical for this stage: nominative Ø, accusative *-i*, dative *-e*, genitive *-in*, locative *-de* and ablative *-den* (plus allomorphs). Notice in particular that the suffixes of the most grammaticalized cases are the shortest, while those of the more concrete cases are phonologically more complex. The picture is, of course, not always that neat.

Table 3.3: Development of case suffixes in Hungarian

components				Old Hungarian		Modern Hungarian	
bél	+	-é	LAT	>	-bele	> -be/-ba	ILL
bél	+	-n	LOC	>	-benn	> -ben/-ban	INESS
bél	+	-Vl	ABL	>	-belöl	> -ból/-ből	EL

In the meantime, we should not lose sight of the constituent to which the case affix is attached. At the stage represented by Figure 3.3.a, this was an NP equipped with a case. At a more advanced stage, roughly illustrated by E56, it is a naked NP. At the present stage, the agglutinative affixes are often appended to subconstituents of NPs. Generally, the first subconstituent to get a case affix of its own will be the head noun; but the determiner, too, is a prime candidate. The result of this is case agreement within the NP.[13] This is absent from Turkish, but it does occur in many Australian languages, e.g. Walbiri and Dyirbal. Examples:

E59 Walbiri (Hale 1976: 93)
maliki-li Ø-tji yalku-nu wiri-ŋki.
dog-ERG ASP-OBJ.1.SG bite-PAST big-ERG
'The big dog bit me.'

E60 Dyirbal (Dixon 1972: 100)
bayi yuri baŋgul yaraŋgu bagan.
DET.ABS kangaroo(ABS) DET:ERG man:ERG spear
'The man speared the kangaroo.'

Walbiri represents the incipient phase of the spreading of the case suffixes over the subconstituents of the NP: when the NP is sequentially continuous, it receives, as a whole, only one case suffix; if it is discontinuous, as it is in E59, each subconstituent receives the suffix. In Dyirbal, case marking of determiners (and possessive attributes), besides that of the noun, is obligatory. Recall that on p. 62 above we have observed a parallel intrusion of number marking into the NP.

Further grammaticalization leads to the fusion of the case affixes with morphemes adjacent to it. The examples given above for the univerbation of the preposition with the determiner are at the same time examples of their fusion.

---

[13] Kahr (1976: 117) observes a correlation between the degree of grammaticality of case suffixes and their participation in agreement in Estonian. Cf. also p. 100 below on Georgian.

3 Grammatical domains

Similarly, the declension of the Dyirbal determiner is somewhat irregular and thus no longer completely agglutinative. If the case marker is adjacent to any other inflectional categories, it will fuse with those. Here is an example from Mangarayi (see Table 3.4 for details):

E61   Mangarayi (Merlan 1982: 113)
ŋaḷi-na   ŋaḷa-gaḍugu
F.NOM-D3 F.NOM-woman
'that woman (nom.)'

The prefixes of the demonstratives and the nouns are not morphologically segmentable, but they express distinctly both gender and case. Moreover, this is one example of a language which has case prefixes on subconstituents of NPs, specifically on words, among them nouns; thus they are genuine case prefixes, not prepositions.[14] Distribution of case marking over the subconstituents of the NP and, simultaneously, its complete fusion with the nominal categories of gender and number is known from the ancient Indo-European languages.[15] In some of them, case inflection even affects the inner structure of the nominal stem. In Sanskrit, several subclasses of nouns (substantives, adjectives etc.) inflecting after the consonantal declension undergo a gradation of their stem, with two or even three grades associated with different inflectional subcategories. The determining factor is not the case alone, but also the number. Thus, the stem *bharant* 'bearing' has a weak grade *bharat-*, such that we have, among others, *bharant-ah* in the NOM.PL.M., but *bharat-ah* in the ACC.PL.M.

The penultimate stage of grammaticalization of case marking is reached in the inflection of the personal pronouns of many languages. Here we often have suppletion of the type *I — me*, *we — us*, German *er* 'he' — *ihn* 'him', *du* 'you' — *dich* 'you (acc.)'. This is complete fusion of the case category with the (pro-)nominal stem. Further reduction of case marking leads to its disappearance. Thus, whereas many German nouns still inflect for case, some subclasses do not. The case marking of nouns derived in *-ung*, such as *die Gleichung* 'the equation', appears exclusively on the article and other modifiers, not on the noun itself. Sapir (1921: 164f) claims that the English *-s* genitive has been limited to use with animates in the past and is gradually being replaced by the *of* genitive.

---

[14] There is a widespread belief (e.g. Kahr 1976: 135–140) that such a thing does not exist.
[15] Haudry (1980) adduces empirical evidence for the two developments of case agreement and of agglutinative to fusional case suffixes in Proto-Indo-European, and for their correlation.

3.4.1.4 Adverbs

A verbal action may be modified by local, temporal or modal circumstances. Adverbs contain in their meaning a circumstance of one of these types. They are therefore constitutional modifiers; a VA relation is a head-modifier relation. It is important to keep in mind that the relation between an adverb and its head is lexically contained in the adverb; we say the adverb is relational (for more details about types of relations see Lehmann 1983).

Possibly certain meanings are inherently adverbial; this question may be left alone for the moment. It is a fact that most of the adverbs in every language are synchronically derived from nouns, verbs or adjectives. Etymology usually proves the same to be true for most of the — synchronically — primary adverbs. I will only say a few words here about adverbs derived from adjectives, since these play no role in adverbial relations as introduced in §3.4.1.1. Suffice it here to mention the English adverbs in *-ly* and the Romance ones in *-mente*. Both of these suffixes are grammaticalizations of nouns which formerly served as the heads of the underlying adjectives: Vulgar Latin x-*mente* meant 'in an x-sense', and Proto-Germanic x-*līko* meant 'with an x-appearance'. Both of these nouns were in the ablative. What is interesting about these evolutions for our purposes is that the relationality which the resulting adverbs possess as adverbs is based on the ablative of the underlying nouns.

Local adverbs, just as local adpositions, are lexically predestined to serve as modifiers of something — a verb or, more rarely, a noun, an adjective or another adverb. That means adverbs and adpositions do not differ in their VA relation. Furthermore, both local adverbs and adpositions signify a local aspect (a part, dimension, spatial region) of something or with respect to something. Compare the a- with the b-sentences in E62f.[16]

E62 English

    a. *He is on top of the roof.*
    b. *He is on top.*

---

[16] Similar examples could be adduced from French, where words like *devant, après, en face (de)* are used either as prepositions or as adverbs.

3 Grammatical domains

E63 German

   a. *Er ist über dem Dach.*
      'He is above the roof.'

   b. *Er ist oben.*
      'He is above (or upstairs).'

In the a-examples, the reference point of the local specification is overtly indicated, in the form of an oblique argument of the adposition. The adverbials in the b-sentences mean the same as the adpositions of the a-sentences. E62.b is understood to mean that he is on top of something; and similarly, E63.b necessarily presupposes a reference point "below" with respect to which he is above. The difference is that this reference point is not expressed in the b-sentences. The difference between local adpositions and local adverbs is that the former have a syntactic slot for an oblique complement, while the latter do not. Their reference point must be understood from the situation; often it is the speaker or otherwise inferable from deixis. Cf. Matthews (1981: 150f).

In the present and the preceding sections, I trace the evolution of case affixes out of either adpositions or adverbs. The treatment systematizes the facts in that it assumes that exactly one of the alternatives is at the origin of a given case affix. However, nothing would exclude a syntactically ambiguous item like *above* or *on top* to develop into a case affix. As I have no relevant historical data, I will not speculate on this course of events.

I will not dwell here on the possible origins of local adverbs and mention only a few in passing (there is rich material on adverbs in Germanic languages in Ramat 1980: 173–175). Just like adpositions, they may be based on local nouns. Cf. English *home* = German *heim*, German *zurück* (to:back) 'back(wards)', Gothic *dalapa* (valley:LOC) 'below (adv.)' (for Hittite see below). Or they may come from adjectives specifying a semantically empty local noun, which became elliptical and finally lost. Cf. Latin *supra* 'above', *infra* 'below' < *superā/inferā parte* 'on the upper/lower side'. Often local adverbs are derivatively related to adpositions. Cf. German *unten* 'below (adv.)' vs. *unter* 'below (prep.)' etc. Note again the case endings detectable on some of these adverbs.

Irrespective of such genetic differences, and in spite of their eventual origin in relational local nouns, all of these adverbs have it in common that they can modify a verb without reference to an NP complement, as exemplified in E63.b. There are languages without either adpositions or preverbs, among them Wichita (Caddoan), Dyirbal and Mangarayi, or only three postpositions, such as

Kobon (Davies 1981: 205f). Of these, Wichita does not even have more than two cases (locative and instrumental). Such languages usually abound in very specific adverbs, deictic particles and demonstrative pronouns which dispense with the expression of the reference point by an NP. A typical Mangarayi sentence with locative adjuncts is E64.a. The reference point of the adverb *biwi* is perfectly clear from the context. It may optionally be added, in the dative, as in E64.b.

E64   Mangarayi (Merlan 1982: 80, 81)

   a. *Yuŋgun Ø-yag,   ŋaya biwi   ŋa-ṇiṇa-n-gu.*
      ahead   2.SG-go(IMP) I   behind 1.SG-come-PRS-DES
      'Go ahead, I'll come behind.'

   b. *Biwi   ŋaŋga   ŋa-ṇiṇa-n.*
      behind 2.SG.DAT 1.SG-come-PRS
      'I'll come behind you.'

E65   Mangarayi (Merlan 1982: 82)
   Ja-Ø-yag   jilbuṇ Ø>wam<galama.
   PRS.POS.3-3.SG-go inside <N.ALL>sugarbag
   'It [a bee] goes inside to the sugarbag [honey].'

In E65, either the adverb or the NP adjunct is optional — either can stand alone. They specify each other, the adverb expressing more precisely the local relation, the NP rendering the reference point explicit. E66 is another example of the same type, from Kalkatungu, another Australian language.

E66   Kalkatungu (Mallinson & Blake 1981: 90)
   Juru iŋka-ṇa kunti-pia uṯiŋka.
   man go-PAST house-LOC behind
   'The man went behind the house.'

E66'   *juru iŋka-ṇa uṯiŋka kunti-pia.*
    id.

The adverb *uṯiŋka* is a fossilized nominal form, analyzable as *uṯi* 'back' + -*ŋka* LOC. What is particularly telling in our context is the syntagmatic interchangeability of the adverb and the NP adjunct.

If the adverb is of nominal origin, it is not rare to find both this and the juxtaposed NP equipped with a case marker. Thus, in Māori E67.b is an alternative to a.

3 Grammatical domains

E67 Māori (cf. Kahr 1975: 27)

    a. *ki runga i   NP*
        to top   LOC NP
       'above NP '

    b. *ki runga ki NP*
        to top   to NP
       'on top of NP '

The juxtaposed NP may either have the unmarked locative preposition or receive the same one as the preceding adverb.

We should pause here for a moment to pin down this syntactic structure and compare it with the one we posited in the preceding section as the basis of adpositions which govern the genitive (Figure 3.3). The common denominator of the above constructions may be represented as in Figure 3.4.

$$([\text{NP-Case}_i]) ([\text{ADV}(\text{-Case}_j)])$$

Figure 3.4: Structure of expanded adverbial phrase

The brackets indicate that the two parts of the expanded adverbial phrase do not necessarily form a constituent. In fact, they cannot form one as long as both are potentially independent; this is indicated by the parentheses. The case marker on the adverb is not essential; it may be present if the adverb is of nominal origin. Case$_i$ and case$_j$ will generally be local cases; in particular, case$_i$ is $\neq$ genitive. Case$_i$ and case$_j$ may be identical, as in E67.b, E69.b and E70, or they may not, as in E67.a. In the latter case, they must be somehow compatible; we do not expect to see, e.g., case$_i$ = ablative and case$_j$ = allative. Often, one of them will be an unspecific locative, as in E67.a. Both the adverb and the juxtaposed NP modify the same constituent, generally the verb of the clause; so case$_i$ and case$_j$ are selected in accordance with this function.

The essential difference between Figure 3.3 (either a or b) and E3.4 is this: In Figure 3.3 the NP serving as the reference point of the location has the syntactic status of a complement, governed by the subsequent adposition. In E3.4 the same NP has the status of a modifier of the same constituent of which the subsequent adposition is a modifier; the two are in apposition. Therefore, the case of the NP in Figure 3.3 is governed by the subsequent adposition and is, consequently, the genitive, whereas the case of the NP in E3.4 is not governed at all, but semantically motivated.

According to Indo-Europeanist communis opinio, structures of the general form in Figure 3.4 are at the basis of the development of adpositions in the Indo-European languages. Indeed, some of the archaic Indo-European languages, particular Vedic and Hittite, have hardly any adpositions. Hittite (for which see Starke 1977, part II) has a number of local adverbs of nominal origin, with still recoverable case endings. Some of them pattern in a regular way in that they may take either directional or accusative case endings and function, accordingly, as either a directional or a locative [sic] adverbial. From *ser 'top', for instance, we get both sarā 'to the top' and ser 'on top'. The locative group may function as postpositions and take nominal complements or possessive suffixes. This is essentially like the Turkish situation exemplified by E50 and may be illustrated by E68.

E68   Hittite

   a. (KBO XVII 18 II 8, Starke 1977: 170)
      ta-an   hass-as   pira-n   tia-nzi
      CONN-it hearth-GEN   front-ACC put-3.PL

      'And they put it in front of the hearth.'

   b. (KBO XVII 1 I 32f)
      ERÍN^MEŠ na-n kwi-s   anda   peta-i,   DUMU.È.GAL-s-a
      troops-ACC   REL-NOM.AN   inside:DIR   carry-3.SG   steward-NOM-CONN
      peras-set   ^GIŠ zupari   harz-i.
      front-POSS.3.ACC[17]   torch   hold-3.SG

      'He who brings the troops inside, the steward holds a torch before him.'

If these same relational nouns are put into the directional case, they may only function as adverbs and not take complements. These adverbs may either occur alone, as in E69.a, or they may be followed by an NP in the same case, as in b.

E69   Hittite

   a. (KBO XVII 18 II 5, Starke 1977: 140)
      testa para-a   pā-nzi.
      then front-DIR go-3.PL

      'Then they go outside.'

---

[17] The suffixal possessive pronoun agrees with its head in case. Due to phonological assimilation, the case of the head does not appear.

b. (KBO XXI 90 r. 21, Starke 1977: 154)
   nesta namma para-a   hila   pai-zi.
   then again front-DIR yard:DIR go-3.SG
   'Then he again goes out into the yard.'

A parallel to *para* in E69.a may be seen in *anda* of E68.b. The combination of the adverb with an NP, as in E69.b, is obviously appositive. If the NP were a complement of the adverb, the sense would be different. The spirit of the construction may be rendered by 'to the front, namely to the yard'.

E70 Hittite (KBO VI 2 IV 37', Starke 1977: 152)
     da-san   parn-a   nāwi   pai-zi
     inside:DIR-PTL house-DIR not.yet go-3.SG
     'he has not yet gone into the house'

There are, however, collocations such as that in E70, where the construction is equally appositive, but where the sense would be the same if the NP were a complement of the adverb. In these, the adverb may be reinterpreted as an adposition. This process goes hand in hand with the grammaticalization of the case endings on the NP and on the adverb, which then no longer suffice to express the adverbial relation by themselves. Correspondingly, the collocation of the adverb and the NP becomes increasingly fixed. It is then the adverb which expresses the relation of the NP to the verb. This means that the NP by itself no longer has an immediate relation to the verb; it needs the adverb, which thereby becomes an adposition. This is the stage represented in most of the other ancient Indo-European languages, for instance Latin:

E71 Latin
     a. *Caesar dormit sub arbore.*
        'Caesar is sleeping below a tree.'
     b. *Caesar se iacit sub arborem.*
        'Caesar throws himself under a tree.'

The NP *arbore* in E71.a is in the ablative, which comprises among its functions that of the locative. *Arborem* in b is in the accusative, which still preserves some faint traces of an older directional. Thus, the cases of the NPs are semantically appropriate to their local functions in these sentences. However, in none of them could the preposition be lacking; the cases by themselves do not suffice to express such local meanings.

Further grammaticalization of the adpositional phrase involves a narrowing down of the choice of the case for the NP. Some Latin prepositions are like *sub* in allowing either the ablative or the accusative; but most of them invariably require just one of these cases. Compare E72.a and b.

E72   Latin

   a. *Caesar legatos ad Hannibalem misit.*
      'Caesar sent envoys to Hannibal.'
   b. *Caesar ad Cannas pugnam commisit.*
      'Caesar fought a battle at Cannae.'

Ad can only have a complement in the accusative. While this would be expectable on semantic grounds in sentences such as E72.a, it would be inappropriate in b if the case of an NP dependent on a preposition had an independent semantic function. To the extent that the preposition determines the case of its complement, and to the extent that this case may be without a proper semantic function, the preposition governs its complement and the case of the latter. The consequence is that this line of development results in the same type of construction which results from the grammaticalization of relational nouns with a genitive complement reviewed in the preceding section; the two grammaticalization channels converge.

In the subsequent course of events, a number of things may happen in varying order (cf. the beginning of §3.4.1.3). The case affix of the NP (or noun) will be deleted, and the adposition will become a case affix. Proceeding in the order mentioned, we encounter Italian examples such as E73.

E73   *Cesare mise legati a Annibale.* = E72.a

The morphological difference between E72.a and E73, which consists in the presence vs. absence of case endings, is matched by a syntactic difference: While the prepositional phrase in E72.a is clearly an adjunct, in E73 it is well on its way to becoming a complement of the verb. While *ad Hannibalem* in E72.a might eventually be substituted by the mere dative *Hannibali*, which would represent a complement, no such choice is available in E73, since dative complements in Italian are constructed with the very same preposition. It is important to observe that parallel to the tightening of the AN bond, we have a tightening of the VA bond.

The further fate of prepositions on caseless nouns has already been dealt with on p. 87 and need not be repeated here. Let us finally see what happens when (parallel to Table 3.2 above) the case affix of the noun does not get lost before the adposition becomes affixal. The stacking of a postposition on a case suffix can be illustrated from Basque (cf. Brettschneider 1978: 69). There is an allative suffix *-ra(t)*, as in E74.a.

E74   Basque

    a. *mendi-ra*
       mountain-ALL
       'to the mountain'

    b. *mendi-ra-ntz*
       'towards the mountain'

    c. *mendi-ra-ino*
       'up to the mountain'

This may be expanded either by a suffix *-ntz* to yield a directional, as in b, or by a suffix *-no* to yield a terminative, as in c. Similar phenomena occur, according to Kahr (1976: 123f) and Comrie (1981b: 210f), in Georgian. Here it is particulary noteworthy that while there is nominal agreement in primary cases, the secondary, complex cases are not repeated in the agreement. Recall what was said at the end of §3.4.1.3 on parallelism in the development of agreement and of agglutinative to fusional case affixes.

A recent postposition may fall in with an old case prefix. This situation has been analyzed by Greenberg (1980). It arose in the Ethiopic languages, which, in keeping with their Semitic provenience, had prepositions, but later, under Cushitic influence, developed a number of new syntactic properties, among them postpositions. E75 is an example.

E75   Amharic
    bə-kətəma-w wisṭ
    LOC-town-DEF inside
    'in the town'

Similar phenomena may be found in (non-Persian) Iranian languages. If the adposition becomes affixal, a case circumfix is the result. Such exist in Mangarayi (see Merlan 1982: 57–59). The case paradigm of the masculine noun *malam* 'man' is as in Table 3.4.

The prefixal part codes not only case, but also gender; its form, including the zero, varies among masculine, feminine and neuter nouns. The fusion of case and

Table 3.4: Mangarayi case paradigm

accusative	Ø-malam
nominative	ṇa-malam
genitive/dative/purposive	ṇa-malam-gu
locative	ṇa-malam-gan
allative	Ø-malam-gaḷama
ablative	Ø-malam-gana

gender in the prefixal part, together with the fact that there is no suffixal part in the (most) grammatical cases, warrants the conclusion that the circumfixes are combinations of old prefixes with newly suffixed postpositions. There is, in fact, a prefixless perlative/praeterlative in neuter nouns which still is more enclitic than suffixal (Merlan 1982: 59).

The reverse situation of a more recent preposition hitting upon an old case suffix is, of course, familiar from the western Indo-European languages. However, it is doubtful whether circumfixes will develop here (for instance, in German), since even in those languages where the suffixes have long been lost, the prepositions have not yet become prefixes.

3.4.1.5 Renovations and reinforcements

In the preceding sections we have dealt with two grammaticalization channels which lead to case-marked nouns bearing an immediate relation to a governing term, generally a verb. The input to the channels are constructions in which the relation between a verb and an NP is made maximally explicit, being split up into a VA and an AN relation, with a — possibly complex — relator in between. There is obviously a long way from the input to the output. As there is continuous renovation and reinforcement in this area, most languages have not only one, but several constructions along this grammaticalization scale. Turkish, Basque and German are typical examples. Corresponding to the constant waves of renovation, many languages have several layers of prepositions or of postpositions. A typical situation is the following: The most grammatical case functions, such as the subject, direct (and possibly indirect) object and perhaps also the genitive function, are expressed by case affixes (which may be zero). Above this, there is a layer of primary prepositions, covering such basic adverbial functions as the purposive (final), instrumental, benefactive, comitative, locative, allative/directional, ablative. Then follows a layer of secondary prepositions, representing more complex adverbial relations such as adversative, privative, terminative, sublative, superessive etc. While this set is numerically more comprehensive than the primary one, it still is a closed set. Beyond it, there is an open choice of free constructions involving relational nouns, combinations of prepositions with adverbs and, as we shall see, verbs, for the expression of relations which are seldom or never grammaticalized in languages.[18]

I will return in §3.4.2.2 to the possibility of ordering case functions according to their grammaticality and here draw attention only to some formal points. First, as already indicated, the size of the paradigms tends to grow from the inward to the outward layers, though there may be smaller subparadigms in between. Second, the intimacy of the bond between the relator and the noun decreases from the case affixes to the secondary adpositions and free combinations. Third, the phonological weight of the relators increases in the same way. In particular, the primary adpositions are often all monosyllabic, while the secondary ones may be polysyllabic (cf. also Kahr 1976: 138).

Whenever a case affix (other than genitive) is combined with an adposition, adverb or relational noun, or a preposition is combined with one of these latter devices, or any similar combination is produced, we are presented with a more or less complex reinforcement. Such reinforcement may take place at any of the levels of grammaticality; no construction is so little grammaticalized that it would be exempt from reinforcement. Thus we have seen that concrete, local cases may be reinforced by juxtaposed adverbs. Later on in the development of the same language, the same adverbs, then prepositions, may be used to reinforce dwindling grammatical cases, for instance the dative.

The reinforcement and renovation of prepositions may constantly be observed in the western Indo-European languages. Contemporary German offers a rich selection. Certain combinations of prepositions with relational nouns, such as *infolge* (r/ *durch*) and *mithilfe* (⇐ *mit*), have already been mentioned. These processes are continuing. *Im Zuge* (lit. in the train (of)) 'by, as part of (an action)' is fairly recent; and at the time of this writing, the most fashionable phrases on TV are *im Gefolge* (lit. in the suite) 'as a consequence (of), by', evidently meant to reinforce *infolge*, and *im Wege* (lit. in the way) 'by (way of)', which already exhibits slight traces of grammaticalization, because if ungrammaticalized, it would have to be *auf dem Wege*. Strangely enough, such elaborate locutions are not necessarily more precise than the simple prepositions which they help avoid.

---

[18] This situation was sketched by J. Untermann in an unpublished UNITYP paper of October 2nd, 1980.

of preverbs. The counterparts to the English examples are *auslassen, aufessen, aufstehen, hervor-* or *abstehen*. Here we do have preverbs; but they are separable in certain syntactic environments, mainly in finite main clauses, where we find *läßt etwas aus, ißt etwas auf, steht auf/hervor/ab*, just as in English. Their syntactic behavior is essentially that of adverbials.

We appear to have two parameters here, viz. the syntagmatic variability of the combination of the verb with the preverb and the degree of fusion of their meanings, which are partly independent of each other. Other Indo-European languages whose preverbs would have to be allocated to various places in the two-dimensional space thus set up include Ancient Greek and Russian. Moreover, we would have to distinguish both between different historical stages of these languages and between different layers of preverbs existing together at one stage. In this respect, the situation is analogous to the one sketched on p. 101f for adpositions.

- However, the picture becomes more complicated once we take a further construction into account. In German, there are such verbs as *sich gewöhnen an* 'to get accustomed to', *sich wundern über* 'to wonder at', *halten für* 'regard as' etc., which have counterparts in most of the modern Indo-European languages. Here the verb is said to govern a certain preposition. Prepositions in such a construction have certain properties in common with preverbs. Semantically, the situation is similar to the *eat up/aufessen* type discussed above, in that the adverbial relator ist not — like an adverb — independent of the verbal lexeme, but in some way forms part of it. Some of these "verb + preposition" syntagms can alternatively be rendered by a "preverb-verb" syntagm; thus we have *warten auf* 'wait for' = *erwarten, hoffen auf* 'hope for' = *erhoffen, zweifeln an* 'doubt' = *bezweifeln*, etc. However, the "verb + preposition" complex differs from the constructions reviewed so far in that the adverbial relator governs an NP which constitutes one of the actants of the verb. So adpositions, too, can experience the fate that we have just found to apply to adverbs, namely they lose their independence from the verb and are somehow subsumed under its meaning.

The discussion of the grammaticalization of adpositions in the preceding sections showed us that this commonly proceeds to completion without the intervention of any such factor as semantic irregularity. The development exemplified in the preceding paragraph would seem to be a deviation from the course of grammaticalization, something which may or may not happen, but which clearly is not constitutive of grammaticalization. Looking back at our Indo-European preverbs, we must recognize that semantic irregularity — varying from slight modifications of regular compositionality to complete unpredictability — is characteristic of and essential for them. What is more, preverbation as exemplified

3 Grammatical domains

so far has all the properties of a process of word-formation. It does not apply to all verbs (or to all members of a grammatically defined subclass), but exhibits varying degrees of productivity; and it applies to different verbs with different results. Nothing of the sort has been found in the grammaticalization channels discussed so far. This should warn us against including preverbation, at least of the above type, as one domain of grammaticalization.

It is now legitimate to ask whether semantic irregularity is really a necessary ingredient of preverbation. We are looking for a preverb which does not contribute to the verbal lexeme but which, just like an inflectional affix, alters the grammatical behavior of the verb. In short, we are looking for an adposition which is prefixed to a verb without losing the syntactic properties of an adposition. An example of this has already been presented in E80 above; but as was stated there, this is not a regular grammatical strategy in Latin.

Two types of verbal prefixes come to mind which fulfill the above requirement. The first is maximally similar to the Latin example just mentioned and occurs in Totonac (Penutian, Mexico; see Reid et al. 1968: 24–30). Totonac has SVO as the normal order of the main constituents, no cases and some basic prepositions such as *na(c)* LOC, partly borrowed from Spanish. It has personal prefixes on verbs and relational nouns. The verbal agreement prefixes may cross-reference up to two participants. Nearer to the root, there is a series of slots for preverbs of the kind relevant here. (A bene-/malefactive suffix which figures in Reid et al.'s account will be omitted here.) The use of the preverbs is illustrated by E81.

E81 Totonac

    a. (Reid et al. 1968: 25f)
    Tē-tlahua-lh huanmā cā'-lacchicni'.
    PRAET-do-PAST that   place.of-town
    'He did it passing by that town.'

    b. (Reid et al. 1968: 26f)
    Lī-tucsa qui'hui'.
    INST-hit stick
    'He hits him with a stick.'

It may be seen that the function of these preverbs is strictly comparable to that of adpositions. The Totonac preverbs govern complements, though these may be reduced to verbal agreement prefixes, which in turn are zero for the third person. But if there is a complement NP, there is no additional preposition. For the specific adverbial functions involved — others are COMITATIVE, INESSIVE, and

SEPARATIVE —, there is no alternative to this construction; i.e. there is no way of omitting the prefixes.

A further essential difference from the Latin preverbs consists in the fact that the Totonac preverbs may be combined by rules governing their possible cooccurrence and sequencing. E82 is an example with three preverbs.

E82 Totonac (Reid et al. 1968: 27)
lī-tē-mak-tamāhua tumīn
INST-PRAET-SEP-buy money
'As he passes by it, he buys it from him with money.'

It is evident that this is a means of augmenting the valence of a verb. Now this is something which elsewhere is done by derivation, not by inflection. Although the Totonac preverbs are completely regular and insofar inflectional, it is interesting to note that they occupy affix positions relatively close to the verbal root. The sequence of verbal prefixes is: Tense & Person – Aspect – Preverbs – Transitivity-changing Derivation – Root. With this in view, the grammatical status of the preverbs appears to represent an exceptional, type-constitutive feature of Totonac. It is all the more remarkable as there are no adpositions corresponding to the preverbs.[20]

The second type of grammatical preverb presented here does have adpositions from which it appears to be derived. In Abkhaz,[21] many of the local relators can be shown to derive from relational nouns. Some of them occur only as postpositions, others only as preverbs, and others alternatively as both. It is with the latter subclass that we are concerned here. Furthermore, Abkhaz has a personal prefix slot on relational nouns and postpositions and up to three such slots on verbs. These are agreement prefixes, i.e. they occur independently of whether a complement NP is additionally present or not. The instrumental postposition is *-la*, as in E83.

E83 Abkhaz (Hewitt 1979: 114)
a-žaħ°à   à-la   sə-yə̀-sə-yt'.
ART-hammer OBL.3.SG.NHUM-with ABS.1.SG-IO.3.SG.M-hit-INDEP
'I hit him with the/a hammer.'

E83' *a-žaħ°à   s-a+la-yə̀-sə-yt'.*
ART-hammer ABS.1.SG-OBL.3.SG.NHUM+with-IO.3.SG.M-hit-INDEP

---

[20] Recall, in contrast, the otherwise similar Arosi case mentioned on p. 104.
[21] See Hewitt (1979: 113–149). The facts of closely related Cherkes are similar.

In an alternative, and often preferred, construction, the postposition, together with its personal prefix, is inserted in the series of verbal prefixes, namely between the absolutive and the indirect (or oblique) object slot. The NP complement of the postposition remains in its place. This is exemplified in E83′. It is a grammatically regular construction for quite a number of local and other relators.

If the Abkhaz preverb did not have its personal prefix, it would be more similar to the Totonac one. Being as it is, the combination of preverb with agreement affix is assimilated to a personal agreement prefix. In this respect, it is similar to preverbation in Sumerian (see Falkenstein 1959: 46–49, 59f) and to one agreement prefix class of Swahili (cf. Kahr 1975: 48). There are no preverbs in this language, but instead a number of verbal prefix slots, among them one for the subject and one for the direct object. The subject agreement prefix may also refer to a local adjunct if this is topicalized, as in E84.

E84   Swahili (Polomé 1967: 160)
      ku-le   m-ji-ni   ku-me-ugua wa-tu   wengi
      CL17-D3 CL3-village-LOC CL17-PF-fall.ill CL2-man CL2:many[22]
      'In that town many people are ill.'

The agreement prefix *ku-* on the verb represents the amalgamation of a pronominal element with a locative semantic component, and it refers to an adjunct NP elsewhere in the clause. So far the construction is similar to the Abkhaz one of E83′. On the other hand, the differences are not to be minimized. For one thing, there is, strictly speaking, no local relator in *ku-*, as there is an adverbial relator in the Abkhaz *a+la*. Instead, the locative element constitutes a noun class, whereas in Abkhaz noun classes are represented by the personal prefix, not by the preverb itself. Finally, the reference to local adjuncts by verb prefixes is a narrowly restricted phenomenon in Swahili, whereas it is common in Abkhaz. Nevertheless, the example shows how grammatical preverbation may gradually pass over into verbal agreement.

No grammaticalization channel for preverbation will be set up here. On the one hand, preverbation of the Indo-European type does not appear to be a product of grammaticalization. On the other hand, the evidence for grammatical preverbation is as yet too scant for us to conceive of its evolution; more languages of the Totonac type have to be found. However, what has been seen suffices for us to assert that an adverbial relator, which mediates between a verb and an NP, may

---

[22] *M-ji-ni*, being a locative expression, triggers class 17, i.e. locative, agreement.

take two alternative courses of grammaticalization, according to whether it becomes more noun-bound or more verb-bound. In the former case, it will end up as a case affix, in the latter as a preverb. In this way we might hope to formulate the diachronic basis of the functional equivalence of case affixes and preverbs, as far as it holds.

3.4.1.7 Coverbs

Up to now we have concentrated on adverbial relators derived from relational nouns. However, the only formal condition for something to be able to provide an adverbial relation to an NP is that it contain an oblique argument slot. This condition is fulfilled, among the lexemes, not only by relational nouns but also by transitive verbs. Accordingly, we find adpositions derived from transitive verbs. Sometimes these are finite, as in Italian *un anno fa* (Lit.: a year it makes) 'a year ago'. But more often they are participial, as in Italian *nonostante* = *notwithstanding*, German *während* = *during*, English *concerning* etc. It seems plausible that both relational nouns and transitive verbs are available for languages of any type for the formation of adpositions. While this appears to be true in principle, languages of different types have strong one-sided preferences. Thus Japanese, Turkish, Quechua, Hungarian and typologically similar languages seem to strongly favor relational nouns as the source of their adpositions. When we look for a language which favors transitive verbs, we come across a phenomenon somewhat different from the examples just adduced, namely coverbs. I will assume a COVERB to be a serial verb which assumes the function of an adposition (cf. p. 36), thus restricting somewhat the possible meaning of this term. The development of serial verbs to adpositions has been treated repeatedly in recent times; see, for example, Li & Thompson (1974), Hagège (1975), Givón (1975: esp. p. 93ff), Hyman (1975), Kahr (1975: 33–40), Sasse (1977b: 113–117), Huang (1978), Clark (1979) and Lightfoot (1979: 213–228). Here are some examples:

E85   Hmong (Clark 1979: 6–7)

   a. *Kuv txiv tsis nyob hauv tsev.*
      I   male not be.in inside house
      'My father is not at home.'

   b. *Maivmim npaj   ib roog qav nyob hauv tsev.*
      Maimee prepare one table food in   inside house
      'Maimee is preparing a meal in the house.'

3 Grammatical domains

E86   Efik (Welmers 1973: 369)
      Dá   íkwâ émì sìbé únàm!
      take knife this cut meat
      'Cut the meat with this knife!'

E87   Efik (ibid.)
      Nám útóm émì nɔ̀   mì!
      do   work this give me
      'Do this work for me!'

E88   Mandarin
      Wŏ yòng jiăndao jiăn zhĭ.
      I   use scissors cut paper
      'I cut paper with the scissors.'

E89   Mandarin
      Nĭ jiè gĕi tā sān.
      you lend give he umbrella
      'You lend him an umbrella.'

The examples in E85 show the same element used once as a full verb, then as a serial verb with the force of a preposition. The other examples show verbs only in the latter function. The contrast between the interlinear transmorphemization and the idiomatic translation is meant to suggest that these can still be used, with varying degrees of freedom, as full verbs, but here function like prepositions. The development of coverbs commonly to be observed has been sketched in Clark (1979: 3); her table is reproduced here, with some adaptations, as Figure 3.5. While 1, 2 and 3 are subsequent substages of stage ii, a and b are alternative realizations of the final stage.

Despite the wealth of recent literature — which is more typologically than descriptively oriented —, the details of this development are not yet sufficiently clear. The nature of verb serialization has to be left in the dark here, just as it had to be above on p. 36. However, it seems safe to assume that the juxtapositional serial construction with which we enter stage ii is reanalyzed, during this stage, as a dependency construction in which the subsequent adposition is dependent on its erstwhile fellow verb. Simultaneously, the coverb loses any inflectional characteristics it may have had; i.e., it loses the properties of a verb. As has been stressed by Givón (1975: 82–86), the semantic depletion, the morphological reduction and the loss of syntagmatic variability are all ingredients of the grammaticalization of a verb to an adposition; but they do not need to occur exactly simultaneously. Therefore, there is no sharp boundary between (co-)verb and adposition. Again, since these processes may affect different verbs at different times, not all the serial verbs of a language are necessarily at one and the same stage of Figure 3.5. All of this is exactly parallel to the picture drawn above on 101f for adpositions of nominal origin.

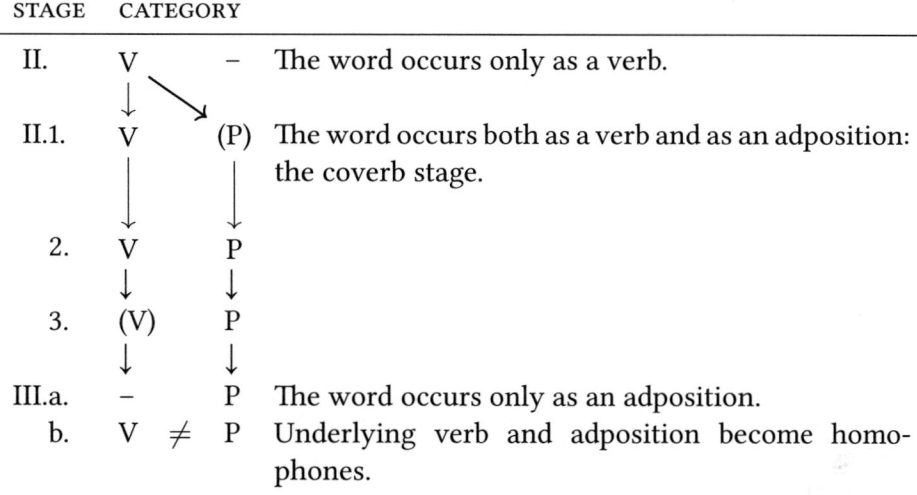

Figure 3.5: Grammaticalization of coverbs

A coverb may be regarded as an adverbial relator providing a relation between a main verb and an NP. In the preceding section we saw that such an adverbial relator may either become noun-bound or verb-bound. The development of serial verbs into adpositions is clearly a case of tightening the bond between the relator and the NP. We may ask whether the alternative, the coalescence of the coverb with the main verb — parallel to the evolution of preverbs —, also occurs. There is, in fact, abundant evidence that it does. E90 and E91 are examples.

E90   Efik (Welmers 1973: 369)
      dá   íkwâ dí!
      take knife come
      'Bring a knife!'

E91 Ewe (W. Kuhn p.c.)
é nò tsī kú.
he drink water die

'He drowned.'

We observe two things here. First, the serial and the main verb form a complex lexical item. Second, this may be discontinuous, as in E90. These facts are exactly parallel to those about preverbation of the Indo-European type as discussed in §3.4.1.6. That is, the composition of two verbs would not be regarded as a case of grammaticalization. I do not want to imply, however, that the grammaticalization and the lexicalization of a serial verb construction are always neatly distinct. In order to dispell this hope, it suffices to compare E90 with E86. The difficulty of keeping verbal compounds and grammaticalized constructions of full (infinite) verb + auxiliary distinct in Dravidian languages may be seen in Bloch (1954: 90–96, 109–112) and Kachru (1980).

The various evolutions of adverbial relators may then be summarized as follows. The lexical source of an adverbial relator is basically either a relational noun or a transitive verb. No matter which source it is, the relator may either become more noun-bound and develop into an adposition, or it may become more verb-bound and form a compound verb. That is, the paths starting from the two distinct sources first branch off and then converge cross-wise, as in Figure 3.6.

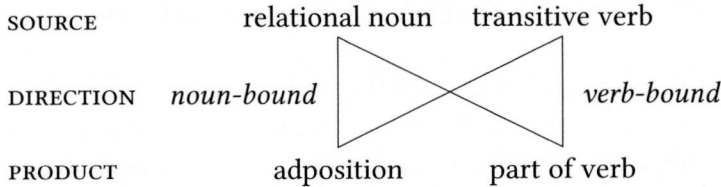

Figure 3.6: Evolution of adverbial relators

While the path leading to an adposition is a grammaticalization channel, the one leading to verbal composition is not. Only in some cases of preverbation which one would not call verbal composition (e.g. Totonac and Abkhaz) can we speak of grammaticalization.

Once the paths have merged, the genetic differences become irrelevant. In particular, an adposition stemming from a coverb may develop into a case affix just as one stemming from a relational noun. Gilyak, e.g., has a couple of cases of this origin, among them the instrumental. This need not be pursued further here. We should, however, look back at the difference in the sources and ask whether it is typologically relevant (for some hints, see Hagège 1975: 257–260). Obviously, the languages which favor relational nouns as the source of their adverbial relators are not the same as those which favor coverbs. We do not know which typological differences are at the basis of these alternative choices, but we may suspect that they have to do with the ways in which the speakers prefer to raise sentential complexity, namely by putting in either more nouns or more verbs.

3.4.2 Main actant relations

3.4.2.1 Terminology

The following distinctions will be made in this section (cf. Hagège 1978: 34ff):

1. At the level of communicative sentence perspective, we have, on the one hand, the polar opposites of THEME and RHEME (that about which something is said, and what is said about it), and on the other hand the two isolated notions of TOPIC (the exposition or reference-frame of a sentence, usually marked by left-dislocation) and of FOCUS (an element emphasized by contrastive stress or even by a cleft-construction).

2. At the level of sentence semantics, we have SEMANTIC (or case) ROLES, such as the agent, the patient, the experiencer etc.

3. At the level of syntax, we have SYNTACTIC FUNCTIONS such as the subject and direct object, or the absolutive and the ergative functions, the indirect object and perhaps some more.

4. At the level of morphology, we have CASES such as the nominative and accusative, or the absolutive and ergative, the dative, locative etc.

Distinctions such as these must be made, but it is not always clear how they are to be made. Complications arise at least from the following interrelations: The matching of a content with an expression, applied to the field of grammar, produces an association of semantic roles with morphological cases. This is generally rather indirect and complicated in the strongly grammaticalized cases; not every agent is in the nominative, nor does every nominative represent an agent, and so on. It becomes increasingly direct and biunique in the more concrete cases; consider, for instance, the association of an instrumental role with an instrumental case, or of a goal with an allative case. Wherever a semantic role is not inherent in the lexical meaning of a verb, but has a separate representation, it becomes less necessary to keep semantic role and morphological case apart; they may be treated as content and expression of a sign.

Furthermore, the concept of syntactic function becomes obscure when we ask for (adverbal) syntactic functions beyond that of the indirect object, i.e. beyond those which have been dubbed "term functions" in relational grammar and which we may call pure syntactic functions. Is there a syntactic function of a locative, or instrumental, complement, or even adjunct? It appears that syntactic functions gradually turn into semantic functions. I have just said that case roles and morphological cases may be treated as paired at this level. Would it make sense to double these case signs, which really express different sorts of grammatical functions, by a distinct concept of syntactic function? Could all the numerous functions which figure here really be kept distinct on purely syntactic grounds? I will assume (with Matthews 1981: 17–21) that they cannot, and will therefore collapse them into the two groups of complements and adjuncts, which are syntactically distinct. The pure syntactic functions are all functions of complements. Those more semantic functions establish the various kinds of adjuncts, but at least some of them (e.g. the locative) may also figure among the complements.

The two kinds of interrelationships discussed in the foregoing two paragraphs obviously depend on each other. It appears that the concept of distinct syntactic functions is useful exactly in that domain where there is no biunique mapping of semantic roles onto morphological cases. The syntactic functions mediate, as it were, between the two. Furthermore, the measure of arbitrariness in the association of semantic roles with morphological cases which is represented in the pure syntactic functions must somehow be connected with the fact that all of them are functions of complements, that is, of terms governed by the verb.

A further problem which has provided the issue for the recent debate on ergativity is hidden by the polysemous use of the terms "absolutive" and "ergative" above. While it is clear that these terms are correctly used at the morphological level, it is controversial whether syntactic functions different from those of the subject and the direct object must be assumed for ergative systems; maybe the syntactic functions "absolutive" and "ergative" result only from an illegitimate transposition of morphological concepts into syntax. To the extent that I will not resolve this dilemma here, the few remarks below which touch on it will remain obscure. On the basis of the criterion of verbal agreement, however, I will favor the view that the fundamental syntactic functions in ergative systems differ from those in accusative systems.

§3.4.2 concentrates on the marking of main actant relations by cases. Their marking by personal agreement affixes has been treated in §3.2.1.2. Independently of such morphological marking, the question, of course, arises whether the syntactic functions themselves can originate by grammaticalization of case roles. This question will be touched upon at the end of §3.4.2.3, but will not be resolved here.

3.4.2.2 Grammatical cases

We have seen in §3.4.1 that adpositions may develop into case markers. However, we averted our attention from this development as soon as the stage of case marking was reached; i.e. we have not pursued any further developments within the case marking system. The consequence of this is that we have seen how concrete cases may emerge by grammaticalization; but we have seen little about grammatical cases. Apart from some remarks on p. 87, the essential exception to this is the genitive, which had to be treated in §3.3.3, since here we are talking about main actant relations. On the following, cf. Givón (1979b: 218).

We will start here with the DATIVE. There are basically two sources for it, the directional and the benefactive. The first one is best known from English *to*, formerly only a directional preposition. The same development led from Latin *ad* 'to' to Romance *a*, which functions, among other things, as a dative marker (cf. E73). It also befell Quechua *-man*,[23] Turkish *-e*, Burmese *-kou* and Japanese *-ni*. The development of the benefactive into the dative may be exemplified from Brazilian Portuguese, where the preposition *para* 'for' is increasingly used instead of *a* in the dative function, e.g. in *dar para* 'give to', *perguntar para* 'ask (someone)'.

A dative marker may further develop into an ACCUSATIVE marker. In keeping with its origin, this will first be used to mark direct objects with a relative independence, mainly human and/or definite/specific objects. Examples are Spanish *a* and Burmese *-kou*.[24] Another case in point is English *him*, which originally was a dative, but replaced the OE accusative *hine*. A related origin is the range or referential case meaning 'with respect to', as in the case of Persian *-rā* and Bororo *-ji*.

The accusative, in its turn, is the case of the actant most intimately connected with the meaning of a transitive verb and most directly governed through its rection. It could only be generalized to all immediate actants, thus becoming an absolutive. However, such a development is not attested (cf. Dixon 1979: 101, fn. 49), mainly because most absolutive cases in the world are morphologically unmarked.

---

[23] It is only allative in Ancash, but allative/dative in Imbabura; see Cole (1982: 104).
[24] See Kölver (1985) for Burmese; furthermore, Dixon (1979: 99) for Ngarluma and, more in general, Mallinson & Blake (1981: 48f, 166).

3 Grammatical domains

The ERGATIVE is the case of the agent of a transitive verb. Its diachronic formation may be part of the genesis of an ergative system in a language, but it may also be a renovation within an already existing ergative system. Anyway, the following developments seem to occur (cf. Anderson 1977 and Givón 1980): In a passive construction, the agent may be adjoined in the instrumental case. When this construction becomes more current and the agent becomes increasingly obligatory, it is reinterpreted as a transitive ergative construction, the instrumental serving also as the case of the transitive subject. Accordingly, instrumental and ergative are expressed alike in many ergative languages, among them Classical Tibetan, Dyirbal and Avar. If the original passive construction is in the perfect or some resultative aspect, the achievement denoted by it may be conceived of as a possession of the agent, and this may accordingly be expressed in the dative or locative (see Seiler 1973). With the frequent rise of ergativity in perfect clauses, we also get ergative cases which are morphologically identical to the dative, as in several Indo-Iranian languages, or to the locative, as in Chukchi and some Caucasian languages.

Whenever a (passive) predicate is nominalized — this may occur not only in subordinate, but also in main clauses, namely whenever there is an (analytic) nominal verb form —, its agent may be in the genitive. When such a construction is reinterpreted as transitive, the genitive develops into an ergative. Again, genitive/ergative polysemy is a frequent phenomenon in ergative languages, e.g. in Lak (Caucasian), Eskimo and Sherpa (Tibeto-Burmese).

When the case of the transitive subject is generalized to any subject, the ergative develops into a NOMINATIVE. In Sherpa, for instance, this takes place via the intrusion of the ergative into clauses with an incorporated object, which are less typically transitive. On similar developments in Georgian and Mingrelian, cf. Anderson (1977). In this manner, marked nominatives may arise; and where they occur, they may be taken as a hint to an earlier ergative system. Accordingly, the Indo-European nominative in -s has been interpreted as a relic of an ergative system to be reconstructed for some Pre-Proto-Indo-European. This hypothesis would, at the same time, account for the formal similarity between the nominative and the genitive, at least in some declension classes; cf. Latin *turris* 'tower', nominative or genitive singular.

The stringency of this reconstruction remains to be examined. There are at least two languages with marked nominatives which do not invite the reconstruction of an earlier ergative system. In Burmese, the nominative (both in transitive and in intransitive clauses) is optionally marked by *-ka*, the ablative suffix. And in Japanese, one way of marking the nominative is by appending *ga*, which goes back to a genitive morpheme. In both of these cases, contrastive emphasis is involved.

The grammaticalization phenomena sketched so far may be summarized in Figure 3.7. This scale incorporates some ordering which has not been demonstrated empirically, but which I assume may be demonstrated to be very much the way indicated. It has various interpretations, the grammaticalizational one being the interpretation most relevant here. Alternatively, it shows possible polysemies of case affixes:[25] two functions connected by grammaticalization may be represented by a polysemous case affix. Cf. §4.2.1 on how grammaticalization connects the "Grundbedeutung" with the "Gesamtbedeutung" of an item.

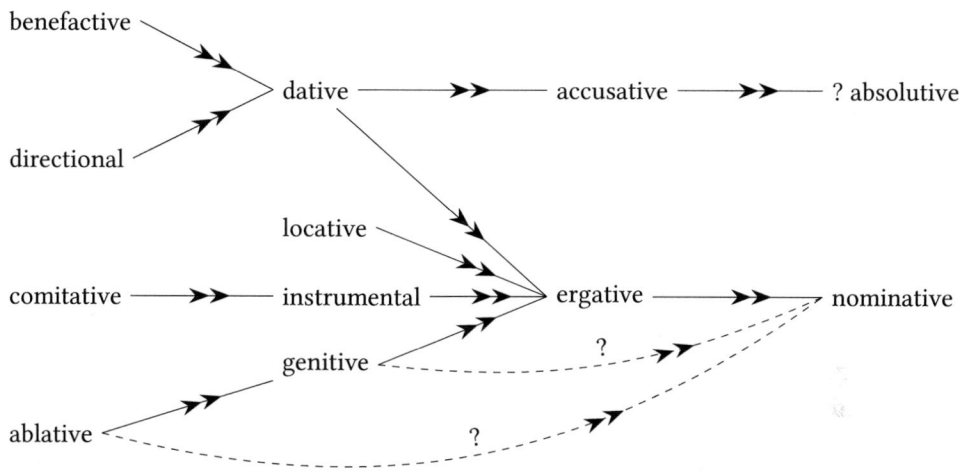

Figure 3.7: Some interrelated grammaticalization channels of cases

More generally, Figure 3.7 may be interpreted as a universal hierarchical layering to be found — presumably with modifications — in the case system of any individual language.[26] The rightmost column constitutes the top of the hierarchy. Moving towards the left and thus descending the hierarchy, we do not arrive at any bottom. The adverbial relations discussed in §3.4.1 may be arranged in similar rows and columns as above and may continue the scale to the left until grammar ceases and the lexicon begins.[27] This layering, introduced already on

---

[25] NB: Such polysemies must be kept distinct from case syncretisms, which affect cases of equal grammaticality (arranged in columns in Figure 3.7), e.g. the instrumental and the ablative.

[26] In the last two columns, the two rows represent, of course, alternative possibilities of systematic cooccurrence; we either have accusative and nominative, or ergative and absolutive.

[27] This fact constitutes another principal challenge to the theory of case grammar; cf. Dillon (1977: 76f).

3 Grammatical domains

p. 101, may be captured by a number of specific hypotheses which use the criteria generally differentiating among degrees of grammaticality (see Chapter 4) and which together may be regarded as rendering the traditional notion of concrete vs. grammatical case more precise. One of these hypotheses, which takes up the considerations of p. 101, will be formulated here (see Lehmann 1983: §4): There is a scale of structural means for the expression of case functions which starts with relational nouns and coverbs and passes through adverbs, adpositions and case markers to morphological zero expression. In every language, this scale is coupled with the scale in Figure 3.7, such that the least grammaticalized case functions are expressed by relational nouns or coverbs and the more grammaticalized ones successively by the other means. Both case functions and means may be skipped, but the order must be observed. Thus, the hypothesis means that each kind of structural means must be employed for a continuous segment of Figure 3.7. One more specific hypothesis entailed by this general one is: if a language has no segmental expression for some of the case functions, these form a continuous segment of Figure 3.7, starting from the right (top). With some minor exceptions, this is empirically true in an overwhelming number of languages.

3.4.2.3 From functional sentence perspective to syntax

The title of this section is reminiscent of Givón's "From discourse to syntax" (1979). In it, I shall report on the arguments presented in the literature (Li & Thompson 1976, Sankoff 1977, Hagège 1978, Givón 1979a, Vincent 1980b) for the grammaticalization of communicative functions to syntactic functions.

The most common way to express a TOPIC is by left-dislocating an NP and adjoining it as a coconstituent to a clause in which it is anaphorically resumed. This construction is becoming increasingly frequent in substandard French; see Ashby (1981). An example is E92.

E92   French
Jean, je l'ai vu hier.
'John, I saw him yesterday.'

There is no syntactic relation between the left-dislocated NP and the following clause or anything in it. One may therefore say that we are here at a level where syntax does not yet govern, where the discourse is structured only by the rules of functional sentence perspective.

Some languages have more or less circumlocutory means for marking the topic by more than mere sequential ordering. In German, we say *was* NP *betrifft/angeht* 'as regards NP ', and in Portuguese and French, somewhat less clumsily, *quanto a = quant à* 'as for'. The first step in the grammaticalization of such a construction is realized in Japanese. There is a postnominal particle *wa*, which indicates that the preceding NP is the topic or the theme of the sentence. It may follow a bare NP, as in E93.a, or one equipped with a case marker, as in b.

E93   Japanese

    a. (Jorden 1962: 43)
    Matti wa arimasen.
    match TOP EXIST:POL:NEG

    'As for matches, there aren't any.' (topic), or:

    'There áren't any matches.' (theme)

    b. (Jorden 1962: 101)
    Kyooto e   wa ikimasen   desita.
    Kyoto   DIR TOP go:POL:NEG AUX:PAST

    'To Kyoto, I did not go.'

The theme is communicatively less salient than the topic; it is not set off by stress or a following pause, and syntactically, it is a constituent of its clause. Correspondingly, *wa* is more grammatical than the topic locutions mentioned above. It is, in fact, in one distribution class, and thus mutually exclusive, with the subject marker *ga* and the object marker *o* (on which see below). Thus, while other NPs may keep their case markers, subject and object are neutralized before *wa*.

Suppose now the following two things happen: First, for every verb, one of its semantically defined actants is destined to be the theme of a grammatically unmarked sentence. This would naturally not be done with arbitrary variation from verb to verb, but with a certain degree of semantic consistency. In particular, the agent will be a preferred theme. Second, the theme is generalized so that every sentence has one. How exactly these two steps are accomplished is largely a mystery; the empirical, in particular historical evidence for them is just not overwhelming. Anyway, both of them imply that the theme is deprived of its communicative function, because it can no longer vary independently of the syntax. It has been syntacticized, i.e. become a syntactic function. Every clause is conceived of as containing a predication about an NP which has this function, namely that of the SUBJECT. We thus get a grammaticalization channel "topic > theme > subject" (cf. Li & Thompson 1976: 484, Givón 1979a: 83–85, Comrie 1981a: 114 and Mallinson & Blake 1981: 99–101).

3 Grammatical domains

A by-product of this development is the subject-verb agreement (cf. p. 44f.). As the left-dislocated NP is gradually integrated into the clause, the anaphoric pronoun referring to it is ousted from the subject position and becomes clitic to the verb. Since its referent is ultimately in the same clause, its function ceases to be anaphora and becomes agreement. Another form of the same development leads to the formation of a copula out of an anaphoric demonstrative, as we saw in §3.1.2.

A somewhat less common way of marking the topic is by right-dislocation. The resulting mode of expression, which is commonly called afterthought-construction, occurs with some frequency in French (cf. Mallinson & Blake 1981: 402, 427). An alternative to E92 is E94.

E94   *Je l'ai vu hier, Jean*

In French, neither left- nor right-dislocation will create new syntactic functions, because the subject and the object are already there. They do, however, lead to the grammaticalization of the anaphoric or cataphoric personal pronouns in the direction of agreement affixes, as the examples suggest. In other languages (see Hyman 1975: 119–121 and Vincent 1980b: 170), the afterthought construction may be the only way of getting a nominal constituent after the verb of the clause. Therefore, if it is grammaticalized, the order of the main constituents may change. In particular, verb-initial basic word order may be assumed to arise in this way. If the subject and object are not universal, but are in complementary distribution with other organizations of the fundamental syntactic relations such as the ergative and absolutive, then these syntactic functions may not only be renovated by changes such as those exemplified or hypothesized above, but may also be created in the first place. The study of the change of accusative to ergative systems or vice versa should be able to provide the necessary empirical elucidations here.

The topicalization of the verb is a further instance of a construction which requires some circumlocution in languages such as German. The construction may be exemplified by E95.

E95   German
      Kochen tut sie nicht schlecht.
      'As for cooking, she is not bad.'

In this analytic construction, the verb is split up into its lexical substance, represented by an infinitive, and its inflectional categories, represented by a finite form of the verb *tun* 'do'. The former is preposed, the latter takes the place of the main verb in the sentence. This is the regular verb topicalization construction

3.4 Clause level relations

in Standard German, to which there is no simpler alternative. The periphrastic expression is entirely motivated by the discourse function to be accomplished. However, in Substandard German this motivation may be absent, and we may have *Sie tut nicht schlecht kochen* instead of the simple *Sie kocht nicht schlecht* (cf. Ronneberger-Sibold 1980: 156 and p. 35 above).

A last example of a construction which starts out at the discourse level with a given functional sentence perspective and then is syntacticized is the Indo-European relative construction which uses the $*k^wi$-/k^wo- pronoun (cf. Lehmann 1984: Ch. VI.1). At the origin of the construction, there is a sequence of two independent sentences which are connected by functional sentence perspective: the first is the topic, the second the comment. One nominal in the first clause is marked by the $*k^wi$-/k^wo- pronoun, which is originally an indefinite pronoun. The complex term which is thus implicitly formed by the first clause is resumed in the next clause by an anaphoric pronoun. A passage such as 'From the tree there will be shoots growing out from the ground; those you should press down into the ground' would be expressed in this way. Its Latin manifestation would look like E96.a.

E96   Latin

   a. (Cat. *agr.* 51)
      Ab arbore abs terra pulli qui nascentur, eos in terram deprimito.
      'The shoots that will grow from the tree from the ground, those you should press down into the ground.'
   b. *In terram deprimito pullos qui ... nascentur.*
      'You should press down into the ground the shoots that will grow ...'

However, at the Latin stage the sequence is already slightly syntacticized into a complex sentence. E96.a shows the so-called correlative diptych. The relative clause is adjoined to the main clause, which means it is not its constituent and it has to either precede or follow it. At the origin, the relative clause always precedes the main clause. Later, the variant b and embedding of the relative clause become possible. Here the erstwhile indefinite pronoun has become a relative pronoun, the anaphoric pronoun vanishes, and the functional sentence perspective is no longer bound up with the construction. The relative construction is fully syntacticized.

Turning now to FOCUS constructions, the most explicit way of marking the focus is the cleft-sentence. Its syntactic construction in the most diverse languages corresponds closely to the English pattern 'it is NP that S'. To the extent that this is an autonomous pattern[28], the communicative function of focus is already minimally grammaticalized. Further grammaticalization will again reduce the syntactic complexity of the construction, simplifying the morphological means to an unanalyzable focus marker, e.g. Quechua *-mi* (Cole 1982: 35f) and Somali *baa* (Sasse 1977a: 348f), and integrating the focus NP into the clause as a constituent with a regular syntactic function.

Focus constructions are grammaticalized as the normal expression of a word question in many languages. The question word is a grammaticalized focus.[29] Accordingly, word questions may be constructed as cleft-sentences, for instance in French and Portuguese.

E97   French
      Qu'est-ce qu'il fait?
      'What is he doing?'

E98   Portuguese
      Quando é que ele vem?
      when   is that he comes
      'When will he come?'

Similarly, focus or rhematic particles will accompany question words:

E99   Quechua (Cole 1982: 18)
      may-pi-mi   pundaniki inga-ka kawsa-rka?
      where-LOC-FOC first   Inka-TOP live-PAST.3
      'Where did the first Inka live?'

E100 Somali (Sasse 1977a: 348)

      a. *las 'aanood b-uu   tegey.*
         Las Anod   FOC-he went
         'He went to Las Anod.'

      b. *ħagg-uu   tegey?*
         where:FOC-he went
         'Where did he go?'[30]

---

[28] The various attempts plainly to derive the cleft-sentence from a relative sentence must be considered failures; see Lehmann 1984: Ch. V.5.3.

[29] This is the message of Sasse (1977a), where the focus is mistakenly called topic. My discussion has also benefited from correspondence with H.-J. Sasse.

Further grammaticalization of this word question construction deletes the focus marker, leaving only the initial position of the question word, which is the unmarked order in numerous languages, including English and German. This is another example of the syntacticization of what was initially motivated by functional sentence perspective.

Another way of grammaticalizing focus markers is to associate them with definite syntactic functions. In Japanese, this concerns the subject and the direct object, while in Burmese it concerns these two and, in addition, the indirect object. If there is no emphasis on these constituents, they are left without case mark. If, however, they are in focus or otherwise stressed, postnominal case particles are attached to them, as shown in the following examples:

E101 Burmese

    a. (Kölver 1985: 4)
    qamei pawa hya-ba-de.
    mother handkerchief search-POL-FIN

    'Mother is looking for a handkerchief.'

    b. *qamei-ga. pawa hya-ba-de.*
    mother-SBJ.FOC handkerchief search-POL-FIN

    'It's mother who is looking for a handkerchief.'

    c. (Kölver 1985: 9)
    qamei pawa-gou hya-ba-de.
    mother handkerchief-OBJ:FOC search-POL-FIN

    'It's a handkerchief that mother is looking for.'

E102 Japanese

    a. = E93.a
    Matti (wa) arimasen.
    match TOP EXIST:POL:NEG

    'There áren't any matches.'

    b. (Jorden 1962: 43)
    Matti ga arimasen.
    match SBJ.FOC EXIST:POL:NEG

    'There aren't any mátches.' or: 'It's matches what is lacking.'

---

[30] *buu = baa+uu, ḥagguu = ḥagge+baa+uu.*

3 Grammatical domains

E103   Japanese (Jorden 1962: 44)

   a. *Tabako (wa) kaimasita.*
      cigarette TOP buy:POL:PAST

   'Cigarettes I bought.'

   b. *Tabako o kaimasita.*
      cigarette OBJ.FOC buy:POL:PAST

   'I bought cigarettes.' or: 'It's cigarettes what I bought.'

As mentioned above, Burmese *-ka.* has the "Grundbedeutung" of an ablative marker, and *-kou* that of a directional. Japanese *ga* goes back to a genitive marker, and *o* to a perlative postposition. Thus, from the point of view of their meaning, these morphemes are relatively little grammaticalized for the syntactic functions which they mark in these examples. It seems therefore natural that they should be optional and only used for emphasis. It may be anticipated with some confidence that further grammaticalization will reduce these particles to plain case markers. The process has already begun in Japanese; the b-sentences may also be used without emphasis.

Despite the scarcity of relevant historical evidence, the development from discourse to syntax has attracted the attention of, and has seemed plausible to, several recent writers, including myself. I should like to quote some passages in order to give an impression of the importance that is being attributed to this matter. Hagège (1978: 22) feels that

> on peut considérer les contraintes syntaxiques comme le résultat du figement, avec démotivation plus ou moins importante, d'opérations qui, de sémantiquement et logiquement interprétables qu'elles ont été, ont pris le caractère mécanique de l'obligation qui définit ce qu'on appelle "la grammaire".

Similarly, Sankoff (1977: 62) states

> that we can describe as syntacticization processes the transition between what initially appear to be ad hoc speaker strategies and what later can be fairly confidently described as syntactic rules.

This may be summarized by Givón's (1979: 107) generalization that "human languages keep renovating their syntax via the grammaticalization of discourse."

In what has been said above, it is implied that topic and focus, as they appear in left-dislocation and clefting, are completely free and wild, as it were, since they transcend the bounds of the simple sentence; whilst theme and rheme may be considered as tamed forms of the topic and the focus, respectively, since they may structure the simple sentence.[31] In a parallel fashion, the intonation contour is narrowed down on the way from topic/focus to theme/rheme: the pause after the topic, and the contrastive stress on the focus, are reduced. This is, of course, not compatible with everything that has been said about these concepts in the rather heterogeneous literature. However, as far as intonation is concerned, D. Bolinger (1978) has expressed a similar view. Among the communicative ("attitudinal") functions of the accent, he has the climatic, which tends to be associated with rightshift, and the emotional, which tends to be associated with backshift. Assuming that by "topic and comment" he means what is here called theme and rheme, we may understand his suggestion (1978: 489): "The intonational treatment of topic and comment ... is probably a diluted and grammaticalized form of both the emotional and the climatic." Such considerations are essential to the approach taken in this work, because they suggest that functional sentence perspective is not a homogeneous domain that could neatly be demarcated from semantics and syntax, but that, on the contrary, some parts of it are closer to free text formation and others are closer to syntax. I propose, then, somewhat reservedly, the grammaticalization scale of Figure 3.8 (cf. Figure 2.1).

The association of all the first elements and all the second elements of the pairs in the second row of Figure 3.8 with each other seems possible, but not compulsory; speaking against this, we have seen subject markers expressing focus. The dots indicate that this is only the initial part of a grammaticalization scale and that it can probably be prolonged. A somewhat speculative guess would be "head/attribute" as the next stage, still within syntax (cf. Lehmann 1984: Ch. IV.2), although this construction also has different grammaticalizational origins, as we saw in §3.3.3.

functional sentence perspective		syntax	morphology
topic/focus	theme/rheme	subject/predicate	...

Figure 3.8: From discourse functions to syntactic functions

All of this was already anticipated by the father of grammaticalization, A. Meillet (1912: 147f). He compares free word order in Latin, which signals "expressive nuances", with rigid word order in French, which expresses syntactic relations. For

---

[31] The theme-rheme structure of the simple sentence is grammaticalized in Imbabura Quechua (Cole 1982: 95–98), which marks the theme by a suffix -ka and the rheme by a suffix -mi.

instance, subject and object of the predicate or the attribute of a head in Latin are identified independently of their sequential position and are distributed in the sentence according to its functional sentence perspective, whereas the same syntactic functions in French are identified exactly by the position of the constituents. This shows — says Meillet — that word order may be grammaticalized. Two comments may be appended to this. First, as we shall see in §4.4, reduction of word order freedom should be considered as one factor in a grammaticalization process which comprises more than that, namely the regulation of functional sentence perspective in terms of syntax, which then continues into morphology and further as indicated in Figure 2.1. Second, Meillet's few remarks would seem to open up a particularly rich field of reliable historical evidence for the sort of development more postulated than demonstrated in this section.

3.5 Conclusion

In this survey of grammaticalization phenomena, the degree of detail has been rather uneven, some sections being comparatively thorough, others rather superficial. What is more, several parts of the grammar have not been mentioned at all. We have seen only some subordinating and no coordinating conjunctions, no sentence-type or other particles, no comparative and only a few possessive constructions, and so on. The material presented, however, should suffice to make my initial claim plausible, namely that grammaticalization is not a process restricted to some particular part of the grammatical system, but that it asserts itself everywhere between discourse structure and morphonology.

While we may safely assume this to be true, it is a different question whether it is possible for every grammatical category to be formed exclusively by grammaticalization. We have seen some examples of the grammaticalization of a periphrastic expression to a simple grammatical formative, where the periphrastic construction was formed not only by lexemes on their way towards grammaticalization, but also with the help of a grammatical formative of just the same category which would emerge as the result of the grammaticalization process. That is, while the grammatical formative of the output did continue a lexeme of the input, the input construction apparently presupposed the grammatical category which the output belonged to. Since reasonable discussion of this problem requires some theoretical background to be laid in the following chapters, we will defer it to §8.3.

4 Parameters of grammaticalization

4.1 Theoretical prerequisites

In the preceding chapter we saw plenty of n-tuples of syntagms whose members were said to be related to each other by grammaticalization and were therefore ordered on a grammaticalization scale. The criteria by which this was done were mentioned sporadically but not made explicit. Since different criteria were, in fact, involved, the reader may well have wondered whether a heterogeneous collection of processes were not subsumed under one heading on no theoretical grounds. In some cases I have even put syntagms on a grammaticalization scale which were not historically related. So while it is certainly time to make the criteria explicit, I should perhaps say first what is not a criterion. Namely, historical relatedness of two syntagms is not a criterion for their ordering on a grammaticalization scale. I will take up this issue in §8.3 and mention here only that grammaticalization asserts itself not only on the diachronic axis and that not all grammatical change is grammaticalization. As to the former point, different structural means synchronically present in a language may be arranged on a grammaticalization scale, e.g. the postpositions and the case suffixes of Turkish. So while the symbolism "x > y" has been used in the meaning 'x is grammaticalized to y', designating, that is, a historical process, this is only a special case of the general relation 'y is grammaticalized more strongly than x' or simply 'y is more grammatical than x'. As to the latter point, it has been made clear from the beginning that analogy goes hand in hand with grammaticalization and drives grammatical change just as much as grammaticalization does. So if y historically continues x, x may have been analogically changed into y. In short, historical relatedness is neither a necessary nor a sufficient condition for two syntagms to be arranged on one grammaticalization scale.

Rather than listing the criteria that have been mentioned unsystematically in Chapter 3 and trying to group them systematically, I shall take here the opposite route and present them deductively. Still, the whole theory behind grammaticalization will not be expounded here, but only as much of it as is necessary to understand why these are genuine criteria of grammaticalization.

4 Parameters of grammaticalization

Language is an activity which consists in the creation of interpersonally available meanings, i.e. signs. This activity can be more free or more regulated; accordingly, the ways in which the signs are formed will either depend more on the actual decision of the language user or more on the social conventions laid down in the grammar. This is the most general way in which we can explain what we mean by saying that a sign may be either less or more grammaticalized, respectively.

The concept of freedom concerns the relation between the language user and the signs he uses. If we abstract from the user, we get a structural analog to this concept, viz. the AUTONOMY of the sign:[1] the more freedom with which a sign is used, the more autonomous it is. Therefore the autonomy of a sign is converse to its grammaticality, and grammaticalization detracts from its autonomy. Consequently, if we want to measure the degree to which a sign is grammaticalized, we will determine its degree of autonomy. This has three principal aspects. First, in order to be autonomous, a sign must have a certain WEIGHT, a property which renders it distinct from the members of its class and endows it with prominence in the syntagm. Second, autonomy decreases to the extent that a sign systematically contracts certain relations with other signs; the factor inherent in such relations which detracts from autonomy will be called COHESION. Third, a sign is the more autonomous the more VARIABILITY it enjoys; this means a momentary mobility or shiftability with respect to other signs.

So far we have three aspects of grammaticalization, namely the decrease in weight and variability and the increase in cohesion. These are still rather abstract and difficult to operationalize as analytic criteria. There are basically two ways provided by linguistic theory in which we might make them more specific and thus more concrete. We might either relate them to the content and expression of the sign, or else to the selection and the combination of the constituents of the sign. From the operational conception assumed here it follows that the first way of subdividing the criteria will be unhelpful. The content and the expression of a sign are insolubly associated with each other. There is a far-reaching isomorphism between them which concerns not only properties of their constitution but also the quantitative aspect of their composition. There tends to be a correspondence between the size, or complexity, of the significans and that of the significatum.[2] This isomorphism is maintained in all the linguistic opera-

---

[1] This notion may go back to Meillet's seminal article, too. Cf. the quotation from Meillet (1912: 131) on p. 4 above.
[2] See Lehmann (1974). The notion of the semantic complexity of a sign is made explicit in Lehmann (1978). The postulate of an isomorphism between significans and significatum of

tions and processes which may affect the sign; whatever may affect the content will have its consequences for the expression, and vice versa. As for linguistic operations, the homomorphism between their application to the content and their application to the expression of a sign (sometimes called "semantics" and "syntax", respectively) is a fundamental postulate of several models of grammatical description, among them Montague Grammar. Grammaticalization belongs rather among the linguistic processes. Here, too, the various factors – to be used as criteria of grammaticalization – apply to the sign as a whole, they do not differentiate between content and expression. This will be seen most clearly in the parameters of variability. If their effects on content and expression can be distinguished – which is sometimes the case with the parameters of weight and cohesion –, they affect both in a parallel fashion. This was already shown by Meillet (1912: 135–139). I will therefore not subdivide the criteria according to this dichotomy, but mention the effects of grammaticalization on the expression and the content of the sign whenever they are discernible as distinct.

On the other hand, the three main aspects of grammaticalization separate into two clearly distinct sets of criteria when they are related to the fundamental aspects of every linguistic operation, viz. the selection and the combination of linguistic signs, which I will henceforth call the PARADIGMATIC and SYNTAGMATIC ASPECTS. The weight of a sign, viewed paradigmatically, is its INTEGRITY, its substantial size, both on the semantic and phonological sides. Viewed syntagmatically, it is its STRUCTURAL SCOPE, that is, the extent of the construction which it enters or helps to form. The cohesion of a sign with other signs in a paradigm will be called its PARADIGMATICITY, that is, the degree to which it enters a paradigm, is integrated into it and dependent on it. The cohesion of a sign with other signs in a syntagm will be called its BONDEDNESS; this is the degree to which it depends on, or attaches to, such other signs.[3] The PARADIGMATIC VARIABILITY of a sign is the possibility of using other signs in its stead or of omitting it altogether. The SYNTAGMATIC VARIABILITY of a sign is the possibility of shifting it around in its construction.

---

the language sign is an implicit cornerstone of the various conceptions of structural linguistics, especially structural semantics, and a recurrent theme in the writings of D. Bolinger. It is, however, rejected by some linguists. Thus, Ronneberger-Sibold (1980: 239) is certainly not alone in claiming that the size of the significans (the "length") of a sign is not related to the size of its significatum but is determined by the frequency of its use. These authors must be asked, first what determines the frequency of the use of a sign, and second, how those cases of isomorphism which have been empirically demonstrated are to be explained.

[3] Bazell (1949: 8) calls cohesion what is here called bondedness.

4 Parameters of grammaticalization

Table 4.1: The parameters of grammaticalization

PARAMETER	AXIS	
	PARADIGMATIC	SYNTAGMATIC
WEIGHT	integrity	structural scope
COHESION	paradigmaticity	bondedness
VARIABILITY	paradigmatic variability	syntagmatic variability

These six criteria (varying subsets of which crop up sporadically in the literature[4]) are displayed, for ease of reference, in Table 4.1. It should be kept in mind that some of these parameters correlate positively, others negatively. As grammaticalization increases, the parameters of cohesion increase as well, while the parameters of weight and variability decrease. This is of no theoretical significance, but merely a consequence of the choice of terms.

Furthermore, it will be seen that while grammaticalization is a process, the six parameters are not processes but properties of signs, though variable properties. Strictly speaking, what these parameters jointly identify is not the grammaticalization but the autonomy or, conversely, the grammaticality of a sign, that is, the degree to which it is grammaticalized (see p. 11f). However, mere variation of one of these properties, namely an increase or decrease in the extent to which a sign has that property, turns it into a process which affects that sign. Thus we may say that grammaticalization as a process consists in a correlative increase or decrease – as the case may be – of all the six parameters taken together. See also Table 4.3, p. 174.

I have been and will be calling these six aspects of grammaticalization variously its parameters, factors or criteria. The term "factor" emphasizes that grammaticalization is a complex phenomenon which is constituted by these aspects and has no existence independently of them; grammaticalization is made up of these six parts. The terms "parameter" and "criterion" focus on the methodological aspects of the problem. The above six properties of linguistic signs are criteria insofar as they can be used to order two functionally similar syntagms on a grammaticalization scale. They are parameters insofar as grammaticalization may be measured along each of them, and it may then be verified to which degree they correlate.

---

[4] Weinreich (1963: 169) uses them to make a principled distinction between lexical and grammatical meaning. van Roey (1974: Ch. I) uses them to distinguish classes of prenominal modifiers.

Insofar as the six grammaticalization parameters have a common deductive basis, they are theoretically dependent on each other. However, the theoretical basis has not been made fully explicit, nor can it be, at least in this study. There are therefore no theoretical grounds on which to expect a 100% correlation between them. The only thing that we can safely assume is that they will correlate to a significant degree. On the other hand, each of the parameters can be examined independently of the others: they are methodically independent of each other. From this viewpoint, the question of whether and to which degree they correlate can legitimately be considered an empirical question. And if they correlate, their correlation may be considered explained by the theory. Naturally, independent application of the parameters to the analysis of natural language syntagms presupposes that they are made explicit to the degree of becoming quantifiable. I will return to this problem in §4.4.

The comparison of two signs with respect to their degree of grammaticality presupposes that they are functionally similar. This is not a formal condition. Theoretically, if all the parameters were made fully explicit and quantifiable, we might compare any two signs at all with respect to their grammaticality, for instance the perfect tense in Latin and the genitive case in Turkish. Obviously, such a comparison would not make sense. Consider the analogous situation in markedness theory: we may well ask whether /s/ or /f/ is more marked in English, but it seems unreasonable to compare /s/ and the progressive aspect as to markedness. The requirement of FUNCTIONAL SIMILARITY thus boils down to the general presupposition of any comparison that two things compared with each other should have something in common. As a methodological prerequisite, the notion of functional similarity will be taken for granted here. The only thing we have to do is to specify what kind of functional similarity we mean. Obviously, the Latin perfect und pluperfect tenses, the Hungarian allative and ablative cases or the English definite and indefinite articles may be said to be functionally similar. But these cannot be ordered against each other on a grammaticalization scale, so that this notion of functional similarity must be excluded. We do not mean that there is a common basis on top of which there may be varying and contrasting differentiae specificae. Instead, what we find in a grammaticalization channel is a function common to all the elements in it, the differences among them being primarily of a quantative nature. This is to say, two adjacent elements on a grammaticalization scale fulfill the same function, but to different degrees. For example, a demonstrative and a definite article both have the function to determine, but the demonstrative determines more specifically than the article. However, the quantitative differences between adjacent items sum up when the distances on a scale become greater, and there must certainly come a point where quantity changes to quality. For example, although a demonstrative pronoun may, in the long run, be grammaticalized into an affixal noun marker (sign of nominality), we would probably not want to say that the difference between these two signs is merely of a quantitative nature. Nevertheless, they still have a common functional basis, which is, so to speak, laid bare in the most grammaticalized member of a scale (e.g. the noun marker), but superposed by more specific functional aspects in the less grammaticalized members (e.g. the demonstrative). In this sense, the functional similarity among the elements of a grammaticalization scale is represented by its last member, something close to their common "Gesamtbedeutung", the smallest common denominator to which the input of the scale reduces in the end.

In what follows, we will discuss each of the six parameters in turn, highlighting its specific aspects and marking it off against other linguistic processes which are similar in appearance and may interact with grammaticalization, but must be kept distinct from it.

4.2 Paradigmatic parameters

4.2.1 Integrity

The paradigmatic weight or integrity of a sign is its possession of a certain substance which allows it to maintain its identity, its distinctness from other signs, and grants it a certain prominence in contrast to other signs in the syntagm. It is this factor of grammaticalization in which semantic and phonological aspects can be most clearly distinguished. Decrease in the semantic integrity of a sign is desemanticization; decrease in the phonological integrity is phonological attrition. The parallelism between these two processes has been emphasized repeatedly in the literature; see Meillet (1912: 135–139) and Lehmann (1974: 114–119). I will subdivide the discussion accordingly.

PHONOLOGICAL ATTRITION (called erosion in Heine & Reh 1984: 21ff and decay elsewhere) is the gradual loss of phonological substance. We may assume here that the significans of a sign is represented as a two-dimensional matrix of marked phonological features. A column in the matrix is a segment, and it must contain at least one such feature. Now attrition may be described as the successive subtraction of phonological features. Depending on where features are subtracted, this may also lead to the loss of segments; then the result is, of course, that the sign becomes shorter. With the loss of the last feature, the whole significans disappears. Since phonological attrition and desemanticization go hand in hand, this accident normally means that the significatum is also lost, so that the sign ceases to exist. However, this is not always so, as we shall see later on. Anyway, this is perhaps the factor which can most straightforwardly be operationalized, since little more than counting of phonological features is involved.

Examples of phonological attrition picked at random from Chapter 3 are the reduction of Latin *ille* to French *le* (frequently /l/), Proto-Indo-European **esti* > Engl. *is* (frequently /z/), PIE **oinos* > Engl. *a* (i.e. /ə/). Heine & Reh (1984: 25) have an impressive example from Duala (Bantu): Proto-Bantu **gide*, probably some verb meaning 'finish', > *-gide* COMPL> *-ide* > *í* > ´ (i.e. high tone). The example shows that phonological attrition may indeed leave exactly one phonological feature of an erstwhile multisegmental significans.

It is obvious that phonological attrition is omnipresent in linguistic change. It plays its role not only in grammaticalization, but affects, in the long run, practically every sign. Examples outside grammaticalization are the reduction of Latin *aqua* 'water' to French *eau* (i.e. /o/) or of PIE **k^wetwores* to Engl. *four* (i.e. /fɔː/). Consequently, it would be wrong to infer from phonological attrition to gramamticalization. We will meet the same situation with some of the other parameters. None of them is by itself sufficient to define grammaticalization; it is only by the interplay of all of them that grammaticalization comes about.

We may preliminarily raise here the question of the causal relationships between phonological attrition and anything else. On the one hand, some linguists believe that virtually all of linguistic change is a consequence of the reductive phonological evolution. The latter leads to the loss of inflection and therefore to grammatical renovation or even innovation, and it leads to the loss of lexical items and therefore to constant neology. Phonological attrition itself, in this conception, is essentially a consequence of the articulatory inertia of the speaker who follows the principle of least effort. Other linguists think rather that phonological attrition is merely a symptom of functional changes going on in the system, that inflectional morphology gets lost not on phonological, but on semantosyntactic grounds. I should prefer to treat this – certainly complex – problem not in such an isolated fashion, but to gather insights on the behavior of each of the parameters and then try to obtain an integrated picture of eventual causal or hierarchical relationships among them. In the other parameters to be discussed, I will therefore not devote special attention to questions of this sort.

We now turn to the semantic integrity or SEMANTICITY of a word. For the sake of simplicity, I will assume that the semantic representation of a sign consists of a set of propositions taken from some semantic metalanguage commonly called semantic components or features, and that those propositions which are conjoined (rather than disjoined) contribute to the semantic complexity or semanticity of the sign (details in Lehmann 1978). DESEMANTICIZATION, or semantic depletion (Weinreich 1963: 180f) or bleaching, is then the decrease in semanticity by the loss of such propositions. As said above, the last proposition is commonly lost at the moment where the last rest of the significans also disappears; but as we shall see, either one can continue, at a submorphemic level, without the other. The operationalization of this criterion is in principle completely parallel to that of phonological attrition, except that semantic representations of the required sort are not always easy to come by.

Here are some examples of desemanticization: Latin *dē* 'down from (the top)' (cf. pp. 77–78) had a delative meaning. That is, in x *dē* y, x is on top of y at some prior time, but then moves down and away from y. In the Romance development, what got lost first was the first, specifically delative component, and what remained was the ablative meaning 'from'. (This is, by the way, an example of a possible leftward prolongation of the scale in Figure 3.7, p. 119). On its way towards French *de* (note the phonological attrition from /dē/ to /d/), the motion component was lost, too, so that the ablative was reduced to the genitive 'of', the sheer notion of a relation between two entities. OE *sceal* 'owe' specifies that what the subject has to do is to pay an amount of money or otherwise to return something to somebody. First this specification is lost, and only the meaning that the subject has to do something is left. Then the deontic component is lost, too, and what remains is an indication that the subject will do something. Finally, Latin *hāc hōrā* 'at this hour' was grammaticalized to Portugese *agora*, Spanish *ahora* 'now'. Here the generic temporal component and the deictic element pointing to the time of the speaker go through to the end, but the specification of the time unit present in the source is lost underway.

Just as phonological attrition, desemanticization occurs outside grammaticalization as well. I will defer discussion of this phenomenon to § 5.1 and dwell here on the manifold aspects of desemanticization within grammaticalization. The principal interest of scholars since W. von Humboldt (1822: 52) has centered around "die Stufenfolge, in welcher die ursprüngliche Bedeutung sich verloren hat". There are descriptive terms available for the kind of semantic variation to be found in a grammaticalized item: at the source of a grammaticalization process, we have the "Grundbedeutung" (core meaning) of the item; at the end, we have its "Gesamtbedeutung" (general meaning; cf. Jakobson 1936). This relationship manifests itself both diachronically, as the semantic gradation that Humboldt had in mind, and synchronically, as a specific kind of polysemy. It is illustrated

4.2 Paradigmatic parameters

with particular clarity by Figure 3.5 on the grammaticalization of coverbs and Figure 3.7 on the grammaticalization of cases. The literature contains a wealth of proposals to account for this kind of ordered semantic variation. Two of them will be selected for review here (see, in additon, Traugott 1980).

The most conservative conception was first formulated by E. Sapir (1921: Ch. V) and has already been shown (p. 5) to continue certain ideas of Humboldt's. Sapir sets up four classes of concepts (displayed on p. 5 above) which run the gamut from the most concrete to the most abstract or, according to his conception, from "material content" to "pure relation". He gives no criteria by which a meaning can be assigned a place between these two poles. His proposal has, nevertheless, appeared attractive to more recent authors and is taken up by Žirmunskij (1966: 83) with the words:

> The grammaticalization of the word combination is connected with a greater or lesser weakening of the lexical meaning of one of its components, its consistent transformation from a lexically meaningful (presentational) word into a semi-relational or relational word ... The grammaticalization presents the result of the abstraction (sometimes more, sometimes less full) of the concrete lexical meaning which the function word initially had.

Here we meet the same pairs 'concrete/abstract' and 'presentational/relational'. It appears that while the first opposition is correct, the second has nothing to do with grammaticalization. Since the initial meaning is richer, more specific, it is also more palpable, more accessible to the imagination ("anschaulich") and, in this sense, more concrete; whereas the meanings of strongly grammaticalized signs, such as 'of', 'will' or 'and', do not yield mental images, cannot be illustrated and are, in this sense, more abstract. On the other hand, if "relational" is not just another word for "grammatical", but has its technical meaning of 'embodying a relation, i.e. having an open slot for an argument', then it seems clear that relationality is not affected by grammaticalization. More specifically, in the most straightforward cases relational lexemes yield relational grammatical formatives, and absolute lexemes yield absolute grammatical formatives. Cross-overs may occur, but are not part of the grammaticalization process (cf. 72). Typical examples include: Latin *de* > French *de*, both relational; Pre-Latin **ne-hilum* 'not a thread' > Latin *nihil* 'nothing', both absolute; Latin *ille* > French *le*, both relational, if determiners, both absolute (or only anaphorically relational), if pronouns; etc.

4 Parameters of grammaticalization

One point, however, may be conceded: The relationality (or absoluteness) of an item is part of its grammatical features. Grammaticalization rips off the lexical features until only the grammatical features are left.[5] Consequently, the relationality of an item is normally conserved while most of the original semantic features are lost in grammaticalization. Therefore, it is frequently the case that the end-product of the process signifies little more than a kind of grammatical relation. French *de* is again an example.

The second proposal which has some adherents today can be traced back to H. Frei (1929: 233):

> Examiné du point de vue le l'évolution, le langage présente un passage incessant du signe expressif au signe arbitraire. C'est ce qu'on pourrait appeler la loi de l'usure: plus le signe est employé fréquemment, plus les impressions qui se rattachent à sa forme et à sa signification s'émoussent. Du point de vue statique et fonctionnel, cette évolution est contre-balancée par un passage en sens inverse: plus le signe s'use, plus le besoin d'expressivité cherche à le renouveler, sémantiquement et formellement.

This passage has been quoted here in full because it contains a whole grammaticalization theory in a nutshell. We shall return to other aspects of it later on and concentrate here on the opposition 'expressive/arbitrary'. It implies the equivalence 'expressive = non-arbitrary = motivated'. This conception apparently relies on the fact that at the beginning of a grammaticalization scale we have periphrastic or even textually free constructions whose constructional meaning is motivated either by the syntax or even by functional sentence perspective. These are more expressive in the sense in which more transparent, more sumptuous constructions are more expressive than opaque or reduced ones. Compare, for example, the use of cleft-sentences with that of focus particles in focussation, the appositive juxtaposition of an anaphoric attribute to the use of a plain attribute in attribution, or the use of a relational noun and that of a simple adposition (e.g. *in back of* vs. *behind*) in adverbial relations. The same opposition is even valid for the single lexeme vs. grammatical formative. To signify DATIVE with the help of a coverb with the basic meaning 'give' is palpably more expressive than to use a mere *to* or even a case suffix for this purpose, because it makes the formation of a mental image for a grammatical concept possible; whereas Engl. *to* evokes no associations, might as well be called otherwise and is, in this sense, arbitrary. Indefinite pronouns and negations are further examples of categories which lose their initial emphasis in the course of grammaticalization.

---

[5] This is a major theme in Givón (1973).

4.2 Paradigmatic parameters

This concept of DEMOTIVATION (cf. the quotation from Hagège on p. 126 above) has been extended by recent writers, with farreaching consequences. Givón (1979c: 208–233) opposes, within the left half of a grammaticalization scale (Figure 2.1), the "pragmatic mode" to the "syntactic mode", characterizing the pragmatic mode as more transparent. Vincent (1980b: 170–172) equates 'weakly grammaticalized = pragmatically motivated = iconic' and 'strongly grammaticalized = unmotivated = arbitrary'. Finally, Plank (1979b: 622) opposes "functionally based coding" to "grammaticalized, functionally invariable language-particular coding", where the former observes only universal requirements of semantic distinctness, while the latter is largely arbitrary. Plank's equation 'pragmatically/functionally motivated = universal' and 'arbitrary = language-particular' can also be found in the two other sources quoted. I will defer a fuller discussion of the problems involved here until §§6.4 and 7.3.

We may anticipate that there is doubtless a grain of truth in these suggestions; but it is easy to overstate the case. There is an inveterate preconception in much of the linguistic literature which may be expressed by the equation 'grammaticalized = unmotivated = non-functional (or even dysfunctional)'. The reasoning behind this is, of course: if something is desemanticized, it ends up having no meaning; if it has no meaning, it contributes nothing to the message and is, therefore, functionless. Examples that have been raised repeatedly in the literature include the category of gender as it appears, e.g., in Latin or German, the English infinitive marker *to* and the *do* appearing in interrogative and negative sentences (cf. Sapir 1921: 97f , Lyons 1968: 421). We shall see in §4.2.3 that, quite on the contrary, the more grammaticalized an element gets, the more functional in its language system it becomes; and again, if something is not grammaticalized, it is not functional in its language system.

One particular type of demotivation deserves some attention here. As is commonly known, there is, within the formal process of REDUPLICATION, a gamut of completeness, leading from total reduplication, as in Indonesian *orang-orang* (man-man) 'men', via syllable reduplication, as in Hua *kire'-are'* (corn-RDP) 'lots of corn' (Haiman 1980: 222), to segment-reduplication, as in Latin *pe-pul-i* (RDP-drive.PF-1.SG) 'I drove'. Parallel to the decrease in substantive completeness, there is an increase in phonological regularity and thus formal grammaticalization. Again in parallel, we have a decrease in the iconicity of the meaning represented by the reduplication (cf. André 1978 and Heine & Reh 1984: 46–48). Full reduplication tends to signify intensification; for instance, with nouns, a multitude or collectivity, and with verbs, an intense or repeated action. More "domesticated" reduplication may signify grammatical meanings a bit more remote from the basis, such as plural or durativity. Arbitrary functions, such as the formation of

4 Parameters of grammaticalization

perfect stems in ancient Indo-European languages, are presumably only found in fully phonologized reduplication.

Thus, reduplication illustrates in a particularly clear fashion what is meant by demotivation in grammaticalization. The example might appear to be problematic, though, since it differs in a crucial respect from all the other instances of grammaticalization we have considered so far. Only here, a grammaticalization channel appears to be defined by a formal process, instead of by a function, or set of functions. On closer inspection, however, the exception proves to be a matter of perspective. We have taken the onomasiological perspective throughout, starting from functionally defined grammaticalization scales and occasionally narrowing down on a grammaticalization channel as a particular diachronic-structural instantiation of a scale. In a semasiological perspective, we could set up purely structural scales, based on means of expression such as prefixation, suffixation, reduplication etc. If we took such formal means as the point of departure and sought, in an inductive and semasiological procedure, the functions associated with them, this would lead to results of varying specificity. While all the functions fulfilled by prefixation might well turn out to have nothing in common, and similarly those fulfilled by suffixation and infixation – but this would have to be verified –, reduplication does appear to have a uniform functional basis, namely multiplication/intensification. This is doubtless a consequence of the fact that the formal process of reduplication is much more narrowly defined than the other ones, which correlates with the further fact that it is much less used in grammars than the other processes.

We should finally note that there is one aspect of the reduction of the paradigmatic weight of a sign in which the distinction between processes affecting the significans and processes affecting the significatum is not so easily made. This is the loss of the ability to inflect. This has been used as an independent criterion of grammaticalization in Givón (1975: 84); but it is an integral part of the reduction of the integrity of the sign. A clear example are coverbs; when these develop into adpositions or conjunctions, they cease to take affixes according to the verbal categories of the language. The history of the English modals is a related example.

Sometimes one inflectional subcategory becomes invariably associated with the grammaticalized lexical item and gets petrified on it (cf. p. 145 on fossilization). For example, relational nouns on their way towards adpositions first take only a limited number of case affixes, viz. only local ones. This is the situation in Quechua (see p. 86) and Hittite (p. 96–98). In a second step, the choice is reduced to one case affix, and this is then welded together with the noun to yield an adposition. This is the situation of the genuine postpositions of Turkish (see p. 85). German *würde* and *möchte* are auxiliaries of the subjunctive and desiderative, respectively. They only occur in finite forms of what is formally the past subjunctive and are no longer synchronically related to *werden* 'become' and *mögen* 'may, like'.

It would be wrong to explain the loss of the ability to inflect either by phonological attrition or by desemanticization alone. Both interact to constitute what might be called MORPHOLOGICAL DEGENERATION. What is lost is not some arbitrary phonological or semantic feature, but an inflectional category. The loss of all inflectional categories is the symptom of a change in status. A grammaticalized sign moves down the grammatical levels, from phrase via word form to morpheme. The last step, in particular, involves, in the first place, its transition from a major category to a minor one. We will have to take this point up in the next section.

4.2.2 Paradigmaticity

What is meant here by paradigmatic cohesion or paradigmaticity is the formal and semantic integration both of a paradigm as a whole and of a single subcategory into the paradigm of its generic category. This requires that the members of the paradigm be linked to each other by clear-cut paradigmatic relations, especially opposition and complementarity. The most superficial and evident aspect of paradigmaticity is the sheer SIZE OF THE PARADIGM. Consider the grammaticalization of local relational nouns to adpositions. In English, there is a fair number of such nouns as *front, back, top, bottom, interior* etc. which may be used to form periphrastic prepositions. These are opposed to a closed but still relatively large set of secondary local prepositions such as *beyond, before, within, amidst* etc. Finally, we have the small set of primary local prepositions including *in, on, at, from, to* and perhaps some others.

Similar numerical relationships may be found in the grammaticalization of – numeral or possessive – classifiers to noun classes and genders: the former may range in the dozens, whereas the latter are usually few, often only two. Again, consider personal pronouns (cf. §3.2.1.2). In Japanese, these are grammaticalized very little and agglomerate to a poorly integrated paradigm of at least twelve forms for the first and second persons (unmarked for number) which offer a choice among different social relationships (see Alpatov 1980 and Coulmas 1980). English, on the other hand, possesses fully grammaticalized personal pronouns forming a tightly knit paradigm of five distinct forms. Lastly, the grammaticalization of aspect to tense is always accompanied by a reduction in the size of

4 Parameters of grammaticalization

the paradigm. In the vast majority of languages, there are no more than three tenses, present, past and future, and often there are only two, either future and non-future (= REAL), e.g. in Dyirbal or in Turkish nominalized clauses, or past and non-past, e.g. in Walbiri. Aspect, on the other hand, can be differentiated in rich paradigms. Portuguese, for instance, has three tenses, with an analytic, slightly aspectual alternative for the synthetic future (*vou* + inf. $\simeq$ inf.-*ei*), but at least the aspectual forms shown in Table 4.2.

Table 4.2: TENSE/ASPECT periphrases in Portuguese

AUXILIARY		FULL VERB	MEANING
estou	*por*	+ inf.	inceptive
estou $\simeq$ *estou*	*a*	+ inf. + ger.	progressive
vou/ando		+ ger.	durative
venho $\simeq$ *venho*	*a*	+ inf. + ger.	resultative
acabo/venho	*de*	+ inf.	recent past
tenho		+ part.pass.	perfect

The distinction between open sets of lexical items and closed sets of grammatical(ized) items is related to that between MAJOR AND MINOR CATEGORIES or word classes (cf. Lyons 1968: 435f). A lexical item belongs, roughly, in one of the major classes of nouns, adjectives, numerals or verbs. The minor classes of grammatical items are, essentially, pronouns, auxiliaries (and the like), adpositions and conjunctions (particles and interjections remain unclassified). All the major classes have been shown to furnish items which enter into grammaticalization channels, and all the minor classes have been shown to be formed, or at least to receive members, through grammaticalization. For example, we have seen full verbs becoming auxiliaries, and nouns becoming numeral classifiers.

However, both the distinction between open and closed sets and the one between major and minor categories are gradual. Whether a word belongs already

4.2 Paradigmatic parameters

in the minor category of adpositions or yet in the major category of transitive verbs is a matter of degree of grammaticality. Sets are not either open or closed, but rather the fewer members they have the more closed they are. Furthermore, the distinction between major and minor categories reflects only certain segments at the beginning of a grammaticalization scale, since it presupposes words. The process, however, in which sets develop into paradigms and become ever smaller and more closed continues on the right half of a grammaticalization scale and concerns bound morphemes just as much as free morphemes.

The size of a paradigm is, to repeat it, a superficial and not always reliable aspect of paradigmaticity. Over and above its sheer size, the integration of the paradigm has more intrinsic and less easily quantifiable aspects. It also comprises the formal and functional HOMOGENEITY of the paradigm, i.e. a certain amount of similarity among its members and of regularity in their differences. For example, the Japanese case particles all have the canonical form (C)V, and the Turkish case suffixes have the form -(C)V(n). Latin personal endings on the present active verb are monophonematic in the singular and bi- or triphonematic in the plural, all but one allomorph ending in a consonant. All Latin negative indefinite pronouns begin with n. All English interrogative pronouns, with the partical exception of *how*, have an expression feature in common which has enabled the denomination of the class as "*wh-* pronouns". Bloomfield (1933: 256f) demonstrates how formally homogeneous the personal pronouns are in several unrelated languages.

On the semantic side, the members of a paradigm have a common semantic basis with varying differentiae specificae. This would be brought out by a componential analysis and is reflected in traditional terminology by the fact that there is a generic category name for the whole paradigm and oppositive names for the specific subcategories (e.g. local cases: locative, ablative, allative).

Such paradigmaticity is gradually reached in the process of grammaticalization. Categories grammaticalized very little do not constitute such tightly integrated paradigms. Consider, for example, the formal variation exhibited in the set of Portuguese aspects displayed above. Again, at the level of adpositions, many languages such as Mandarin have both pre- and postpositions, with rather heterogeneous functions (see Hagège 1975). At the level of case markers, most languages have only suffixes. Numeral classifiers often divide up into a number of heterogeneous subclasses with different distribution and formal properties; noun classes and genders are much more homogeneous.

The process of paradigmatic integration or PARADIGMATICIZATION leads to a levelling out of the differences with which the members were equipped originally.

Genetic differences among prepositions of different origins, which account for their different behavior as long as they are weakly grammaticalized, are adjusted when they develop into primary prepositions. This can be seen, e.g., in German *während* = Engl. *during*, which no longer behave as participles. In German, primary prepositions govern either the dative or the accusative, but not the genitive. Secondary prepositions of nominal origin do, of course, take the genitive; but the more grammaticalized they are, the more they prefer the dative. The fate of *wegen* 'because of' is widely known. Finally, the infinitives of ancient Greek derive from (locative) case forms (see Rix 1976: 196f, 237–239). In historical times, however, they are well integrated into the conjugation paradigm and participate in the verbal categories of tense, aspect and voice.

In many cases of paradigmaticization, grammaticalized elements join preexistent paradigms and assimilate to their other members. The ancient Romance synthetic future, which assimilates to the suffixal tense categories is a clear case in point. Such phenomena do not result exclusively from grammaticalization; analogical levelling plays a great role in them. This does not, however, mean that paradigmaticization can be reduced to the workings of analogy. The formation of new paradigms, as, e.g., the paradigm of the definite and indefinite articles, would be impossible if it were not part of the more comprehensive grammaticalization process.

In the writing of a grammar, there is the notorious problem of whether and to what extent PERIPHRASTIC CONSTRUCTIONS have to be admitted. Noone doubts that the synthetic verb forms and primary prepositions must be treated in a grammar; but disagreement arises when analytical verbs forms or compound prepositions are to be enumerated. The criterion that has commonly been employed by grammarians – though with different conclusions – is that of paradigmaticity. Thus *want* does not participate in analytic verb forms since *I want to write* is formed according to the same rules of syntax as *I intend to write* and similar constructions with an open set of governing verbs. But *will* does participate in analytic verb forms because there is a paradigm containing *I will write* and a few similar constructions.

The existence of a paradigm has even been made a presupposition of the correct application of the terms "analytic" or "periphrastic". Thus Matthews (1981: 55) defines: "When a form in a paradigm consists of two or more words it is PERIPHRASTIC." This implies that if there is no paradigm, there is no periphrastic word form, but merely a combination of words (cf. Žirmunskij 1966: 82–87). Whether or not there is a paradigm is, however, not always easy to decide or even in principle a matter of a yes-no decision. When the compound construc-

4.2 Paradigmatic parameters

tions are paralleled, in all relevant respects, by synthetic forms which belong to the same superparadigm, then the decision is facilitated. If such a parallelism does not obtain, as e.g. in the case of the Portuguese aspect formations, there can be only a more-or-less decision, and the question of whether such syntagms must be treated in the grammar becomes rather a question of the volume of the grammar.

At the right end of a grammaticalization scale, paradigms are not formed, but reduced. The most grammaticalized categories of a language system usually consist of a two-member paradigm, i.e. a binary opposition. Typical examples are number (singular/plural), gender (masculine/feminine), noun class (animate/inanimate, or human/non-human), tense (nonpast/past, or real/future), mood (indicative/subjunctive), etc. All of these can be privative oppositions; i.e. the opposition may consist only in the presence of a sign vs. its absence. This constitutes the highest degree of paradigmaticity. One more step of grammaticalization, and the paradigm ceases to exist. Its further fate may be called FOSSILIZATION (see Heine & Reh 1984: 35f). However, it is not meant that fossilization presupposes the reduction of the paradigm to a binary opposition. Anything that falls out of a paradigm in the process of its reduction may fossilize. Examples are the Germanic pronominal adverbs, e.g. Engl. *where, how, why* etc., which are fossilized remnants of cases that have fallen out of the pronominal paradigm, or the Germanic preterite-presents (see p. 29), which remind us that the synthetic perfect was once a member of the Indo-European tense paradigm. Such cases constitute the main argument for calling the last phase of grammaticalization "lexicalization" (as does Givón 1979c: 209). The fossilized forms can indeed no longer be obtained according to the rules of the grammar, but must be listed in the lexicon.

A further factor which accompanies paradigmaticization is increasing IRREGULARITY. At first, this seems to be in conflict with the general notion of grammaticalization as subjection to rules of grammar. However, this notion is not to be interpreted as increasing regularity. What it does mean has been explained on pp. 138–139: the rules governing the use of the grammaticalized item are less semantically motivated and increasingly arbitrary, purely formal. This includes the possibility of increasing irregularity as a consequence of the reduction of the paradigm and the desemanticization. The loss of semantic distinctions within a paradigm may mean that forms which had been opposed to each other become variants. Sometimes one variant does not consistently oust the other, but one of them becomes fixed on some lexemes and the other variant on other lexemes.

Some examples: The Latin perfect has a number of allomorphs, which are distributed according to conjugation class. Among them are the reduplication, as in *cu-curr-i* 'I ran', and an *-s*-suffix, as in *scrip-s-i* 'I wrote'. While the former continues a Proto-Indo-European perfect formative, the latter is a former aorist marker. The aorist itself was semantically fused with the perfect in Latin. The Latin future has basically two allomorphs, *-e-* and *-b*, which are again distributed according to conjugation class; e.g. *capi-e-t* 'he will seize', but *mone-b-it* 'he will admonish'. *-b-* comes from PIE **bhew-* 'become', while *-e-* is a former subjunctive sign. The inherited subjunctive itself was renovated by the inherited optative, which ceased to exist as such.

Apart from this morphological irregularity which is a direct consequence of paradigmaticization, there is also irregularity as a development of the ALLOMORPHY which arises mainly through morphological coalescence. For example, the accusative singular in Ancient Greek has a great many allomorphs which can hardly be covered by a synchronic rule; nevertheless, they have a common origin in the PIE suffix **-m*. The discussion of such phenomena belongs in the chapter on bondedness; but it is significant that distinct factors of grammaticalization bring about identical results.

Morphological irregularity may already affect the (grammaticalized) sign when it is yet a free morpheme; it is then called SUPPLETION. Examples: The English and German verb 'to be' is made up from three originally different verbs. *Is* = *ist* comes from PIE **Hes-* EXIST; *was* = *war* are remnants of Proto-Germanic **wes-* 'live'; and *been* or *bin* 'am' continue forms of PIE *bhew 'become'. Again, while Latin *ire* 'go' was almost exclusively a lexical verb with no suppletion, the same verb in French uses three stems, viz. *all-*, *va-* and *ir-*; and this has been grammaticalized to form an analytic future. While this is a frequent situation with grammatical words, it must be emphasized that suppletion is not restricted to these, but occurs also in lexemes, e.g. in *good – better*. The common denominator of all the suppletive paradigms is, however, the low semanticity of the stem. If the varying stems had a high semanticity, they would not be susceptible to integration into a paradigm.

4.2.3 Paradigmatic variability

Paradigmatic variability is the freedom with which the language user chooses a sign. The principal alternatives to choosing some sign are either choosing another member of the same paradigm or choosing no member of that paradigm, i.e. leaving the whole generic category unspecified. We will subdivide the discussion accordingly and deal first with intraparadigmatic, then with transparadigmatic variability. In both cases, the freedom of choice among various fillers of a given slot – including zero – is, of course, constrained by the context. This factor will be kept constant here as far as possible. We will ask whether, given a context, paradigmatic variation is at all allowed and how it is connected with the degree of grammaticality.

Starting now with INTRAPARADIGMATIC VARIABILITY, we must first specify that the kind of variation we are interested in is not free variation but the selection of alternatives which are in opposition. Free variation does not correlate with the degree of grammaticality and probably correlates with nothing, since it is in principle unsystematic. The selection of opposite members of the paradigm, however, is dictated by the grammar to the degree that the whole paradigm is grammaticalized. Therefore intraparadigmatic variability decreases with increasing grammaticalization.

One example of this has already been discussed (p. 64f), viz. that of numeral classifiers. Classifier systems of different languages vary somewhat along the parameter of intraparadigmatic variability, since in some of them a noun can be allocated relatively freely to a class not inherent in it, while in others there is little choice of the classifier, given a noun. Examples are the Burmese and the Mandarin systems, respectively. Noun classes and genders classify nouns, too; but here intraparadigmatic variability is on the whole reduced in comparison with numeral classifiers (see Serzisko 1981 and Lehmann 1982b: §6.3). The shift of the nominal class becomes increasingly a matter of lexical derivation which is possible only within well-defined limits. The gender in Indo-European languages, for example, is fixed for most nouns, except that motion is possible for some animate nouns such as Latin *lupus – lupa* 'wolf – she-wolf'.

Consider also free personal pronouns vs. personal agreement affixes. Given a transitive sentence in English or German, the choice of the object, including pronouns of varying person, number or gender, is, apart from selection restrictions, completely free. If the sentence is translated into a language with object agreement of the verb, such as Navaho, Ancash Quechua or Swahili, the choice of the pronominal element on the verb is no longer free, but determined by the nature of the nominal object.

As long as cases are weakly grammaticalized, they render the NP which they are attached to largely independent of the context and are rather freely substitutable.

E104   Hungarian
A gyerek játsz-ik az asztal-on.
DEF child cplay-3.GEN DEF table-SUPER
'The child is playing on the table.'

4 Parameters of grammaticalization

In E104, the case suffix on the noun may be substituted by several other local case suffixes such as -*nál* 'by', -*ban* 'in', and even non-local ones such as -*val* 'with'. When cases are more grammaticalized, they will require more specific contexts in order to signal different relations. They will, for instance, be combined with adpositions. We have seen on p. 98f how the choice of case is severely constrained if it combines with an adposition, to the point where the case is governed by the adposition and variability is reduced to zero. Similarly, the more grammaticalized cases are attracted into the valence of the verb, become governed by it and thus lose their intraparadigmatic variability.

This parameter is difficult to operationalize, firstly because substitutability itself is difficult to quantify, but more so because the dependency on the context varies enormously from one grammatical category to another. There are typical relational categories such as case, which are contextually bound to a large extent, and on the other hand such non-relational categories as nominal number or verbal tense, which can vary rather freely in any context, according to the meaning to be conveyed.

We now turn to what above has been called TRANSPARADIGMATIC VARIABILITY. By this we mean the freedom of the language user with regard to the paradigm as a whole. The paradigm represents a certain grammatical category, and its members, the subcategories (or values) of that category. There may then be a certain freedom in either specifying the category by using one of its subcategories, or leaving the whole category unspecified. To the extent that the latter option becomes constrained and finally impossible, the category becomes obligatory. We shall therefore use the term OBLIGATORINESS as a – more handy – converse equivalent of 'transparadigmatic variability'. Correspondingly, the reduction of transparadigmatic variability will occasionally be called by the neologism OBLIGATORIFICATION.

Obligatoriness of the category as a whole and restrictions on intraparadigmatic variability are sometimes difficult to keep apart, namely when the paradigm contains a formally unmarked member. For example, the use of the unmarked singular instead of the plural may either be an instance of intraparadigmatic variability or may indicate the optionality of the category of number. This shows that the parameters of intraparadigmatic variability and of obligatoriness (which I have kept distinct in earlier studies, e.g. Lehmann 1982b: 234ff) are so similar that they must be subsumed under one parameter of paradigmatic variability.

Examples of increasing obligatoriness are not difficult to come by. The category of number, which has just been mentioned, was already discussed from this viewpoint on p. 14. There we saw that the specification of nominal number in Turkish is obligatory only in specific contexts, whereas it must be specified for every noun in any context in Latin. The chapter on number (§3.3.1.1) provides a wealth of examples with varying degrees of obligatoriness. Recall also that numeral classifiers, whose high intraparadigmatic variability has been mentioned above, are generally optional in Persian.

Another typical example is the development of articles. A superficial examination of Latin texts shows that there is no syntactic rule which forces a determiner on a noun. More specifically, there is no tendency of definite nouns to be preceded by *ille* (D3) if there is no other demonstrative, and there is likewise no tendency of indefinite nouns to take *unus* 'one' in the absence of other indefinite determiners. Yet precisely these tendencies arise and take over to the point of obligatoriness in the development towards the modern Romance languages. In French, Italian, Spanish etc., it is in most contexts impossible to use a singular noun – and, with local variation, also a plural noun – without an article, that is, without specifying the category of definiteness. The same has, of course, happened in the Germanic languages. Details of this development in African languages are in Greenberg (1978: §3.3.–3.5).

The same increase in obligatoriness may be observed in the development of personal pronouns as discussed in §3.2.1.2. In Standard Italian the free personal pronouns are used in subject position for emphasis only; there is no tendency to insert them when the sentence otherwise has no subject. In Portuguese there is some sociolectal variation in this respect and precisely this tendency makes itself felt in the substandard sociolects. In French, finally, the subject position must not be left open but must be occupied by a personal pronoun if no NP is there. (Since these personal pronouns no longer carry any emphasis, the subsystem of emphatic pronouns has been renovated; see §7.2). A similar continuum can be observed in the modern Slavic languages.

It has been mentioned that paradigmatic variability depends on the CONTEXT. It is a principle of information theory that the conditioned probability of a sign usually differs from its absolute probability, and that these differences increase proportionally to an increase in the conditioning context. Limiting ourselves to the favorable contexts, we may say that the more we enlarge the context, the more a specific sign becomes obligatory. In Amharic, for instance, the verb has object agreement affixes only if the object is definite. Restricting the context of the agreement affixes to the verb, we would say that they are optional. Enlarging it to include the whole VP, we will say that they are obligatory in certain contexts and excluded in others. In languages such as Latin, the subjunctive is optional at the clause level. If one takes the introductory conjunction into account, many of them govern the subjunctive. Some conjunctions still admit either mood. However, once the context is enlarged to include the matrix verb, there is usually no longer a choice between indicative and subjunctive. An increase in the obligatoriness of a sign is therefore a decrease in the level of grammatical structure on which it is obligatory. This might be one possibility to operationalize the criterion of obligatoriness.

Another way of looking at the increase of obligatoriness is to view it as the dropping of restrictions posed on the nature of the context, that is, of SELECTION RESTRICTIONS (cf. Vincent 1980b: 56 and Serzisko 1981: 99f). The Amharic object suffix on the verb will gradually evolve into an unrestricted object agreement suffix to the extent that conditions on the nature of the object are loosened. The next step would be the appearance of the affix not only when the object is definite but also when it is human. This is essentially the situation in Swahili. The final extension, which includes agreement with indefinite non-human objects, is realized in Navaho. Restrictions on agreement may also be of a purely syntactic nature. Agreement at a relatively low level of grammaticalization is sometimes restricted to the constellation where the agreement triggerer precedes the agreeing term. With proceeding grammaticalization, agreement becomes obligatory independently of the position of the agreement triggerer. So here increasing obligatoriness may be seen as the dropping of a syntactic restriction. On the whole complex of agreement in connection with animacy and grammaticalization, see Comrie (1981a: 184f) and Lehmann (1982b: §6.2).

Another example was seen above on p. 72f. Infinite complements introduced by *for ... to* originated in sentences such as *I brought a book for him to read*, where the complement of *for*, the subsequent subordinate subject, is a beneficiary in the main clause and where the infinitive complement expresses an action which he is expected to be able to accomplish with the help of the benefaction. These conditions were then dropped, and consequently we use these structural means in sentences such as *For George to marry an unbaptized girl is highly unlikely*. Also in §3.3.2, we have seen how a verbum dicendi can be used to introduce indirect speech. When the restrictions on the nature of the embedded clause are eased, it may be grammaticalized to a conjunction introducing any kind of complement clause.

If a concept is highly grammaticalized, it becomes syntagmatically compatible with other concepts of the same semantic domain which are less grammaticalized and which would appear to contradict it (cf. Paul 1920: Ch. 15). For instance, sentence type is grammaticalized illocutionary force. An interrogative sentence may be used with the force of a request and then contain an adverb fitting that illocutionary force, e.g. *please*. Similarly, gender is so highly grammaticalized and, accordingly, carries so little information about sex that in gender languages, each gender is compatible with each sex. The same goes for the combination of tenses with temporal adverbs.

The dropping of restrictions on the use of a structural means implies that this becomes more ubiquitous, that its distribution is extended. For instance, definiteness markers start cooccurring first with other definite, then even with indefinite elements; cf. p. 41f. This EXPANSION has struck some authors as an essential characteristic of grammaticalization. Kuryłowicz (1965: 41) speaks of the "increase in the range" of a category, and likewise Lord (1976: 184–188) and Heine & Reh (1984: 39–41) have emphasized the role of expansion in grammaticalization. While there is no doubt that expansion occurs and is virtually indistinguishable from increasing obligatoriness, it does not seem advisable to isolate it as a criterion of grammaticalization, because expansion occurs also in analogical transfer. If a conjunction today introduces only indirect speech, but tomorrow also introduces clauses depending on verba sentiendi, this may be either a phenomenon of grammaticalization or one of analogical transfer. I will devote §5.4 to the distinction between these processes; but it may be anticipated here that it is far from clear, and therefore the expansion of distribution should be used with care as a criterion of grammaticalization.

Lack of paradigmatic variability thus accounts for the ubiquity of a feature in the texts of a language. Its textual frequency justifies the inference that it is important for the formation of grammatical structures in that language. The more grammaticalized a feature is, the higher is its SYSTEM RELEVANCE, at least up to a certain point. We are, for instance, justified in assuming that the article plays an important role in the systems of the Germanic, Romance and a lot of other languages precisely because of its pronounced obligatoriness; and the same goes for the noun classes in Bantu languages or the aspects of the Yucatec verb. We will pursue this point in §7.2. Suffice it here to say that the implications for system relevance have led some authors to regard obligatoriness as the essential feature of grammaticality (cf. also p. 14f). R. Jakobson (1959: 489) reports that F. Boas regarded "the obligatoriness of grammatical categories as the specific feature which distinguishes them from lexical meanings", and he characterizes grammar by the following task:

> "it determines those aspects of each experience that *must* be expressed."

And on p. 492:

> "Grammar, a *real ars obligatoria*, as the Schoolmen used to call it, imposes upon the speaker its yes-or-no decisions."

4 Parameters of grammaticalization

Because of its implications for system relevance, obligatoriness is doubtless an important factor in grammaticalization. Two considerations should, however, keep us from over-emphasizing its importance. First, if the obligatoriness of an element increases to the point that it becomes omnipresent, it becomes, at the same time, meaningless. Categories that are on the verge of this are the nominalizing -*s* of Plateau Penutian (see p. 41) and the suffix -*im* on all transitive verbs in Tok Pisin (see p. 45). But the processes which constitute grammaticalization go on, and so we get elements which are beyond the verge, that is, which no longer function in the grammar. These include the long vowel which terminates virtually all nouns in Hausa (see p. 60), the -*n*-infix inserted in the present stem of such Latin verbs as *tango* 'touch', and the reduplication of perfect verbs in Late Latin. These phenomena have ceased to play a role in the grammar. The point will be taken up in §5.3. Here it suffices to recall the considerations of p. 139 and to note that the functionality of an element in a language system does increase proportionately to its grammaticalization, but that there comes a point – which we have been regarding as the end of a grammaticalization scale – where the element loses, together with the last bit of semanticity, its grammatical function and is put on the shelf of linguistic history. This must be kept in mind if one wants to infer from obligatoriness to system relevance.

The second qualifying observation is simply that obligatoriness cannot be isolated from the other factors of grammaticality. While we might eventually consider this one parameter sufficient for the determination of the degree of grammaticality, it must not be overlooked that the others are necessary and therefore essential, too. Nothing can become obligatory in a grammar which is not also grammaticalized to a certain degree according to the other parameters. We shall return in §4.4.2 to the problem of the correlation among the parameters.

4.3 Syntagmatic parameters

4.3.1 Structural scope

The syntagmatic weight or structural scope of a grammatical means is the structural size of the construction which it helps to form. The structural size of a construction will be regarded, in the absence of more precise criteria, as being determined by its LEVEL OF GRAMMATICAL STRUCTURE (which, for many purposes, may be regarded as its constituent structure level). For example, the structural scope of a Turkish case suffix is the NP it follows, while the scope of a Latin case suffix is the noun (in the traditional sense). The structural scope of a sign decreases with increasing grammaticalization. Vincent (1980a: 56f) speaks of a "reduction or limitation in the subcategorization frame". The diagnostic lowering of the level of grammatical structure has been regarded by some as the essential feature of a process they called CONDENSATION (see p. 12) and which we will here subsume under grammaticalization (despite my qualms of p. 12f).

Let us illustrate the decrease in structural scope of a grammatical sign. The example of case markers just mentioned may be generalized (and idealized) as follows: A relational noun takes an NP with case as its complement; the same goes for an adposition. An agglutinative case affix attaches to a caseless NP, and a fusional case affix to a noun. Similarly, a demonstrative pronoun acts at the NP level, but the definite article is a noun affix in several languages. Recall also the observations on the intrusion of nominal categories into the NP by way of agreement (p. 62).

An auxiliary of the 'have' or 'be' type starts as a main verb which takes a nominalized VP as a complement; that is, it starts at the clause level. When it has become an auxiliary, it functions at the VP level. A relevant example is the formation of the Quechua habitual aspect described on pp. 33–34. The combination of a function verb with a full verb may first yield a serialized verb (something between VP and V), but ends up as an inflected verb. This may, in its turn, become an auxiliary, and so forth, so that we may even get all the way down to the stem level. A free personal pronoun in object position is an immediate constituent of a VP; but when it becomes an agreement affix, it merely helps to form a verb.

Examples are also available from levels above the clause level. Complex sentences formed by rules of topicalization and focussation may shrink to simple sentences as communicative sentence perspective becomes syntax (§3.4.2.3). We have also seen two clauses being integrated into one through grammaticalization of an anaphoric demonstrative to a copula (§3.1.2). A traditional hypothesis of long standing is the development of Indo-European hypotaxis out of parataxis, which implies the condensation of two sentences into one complex sentence. The genesis of the Indo-European correlative diptych mentioned on p. 123 is a case in point. Further grammaticalization in this channel involves nominalization: a subordinative conjunction such as English *that* forms a nominalized clause; but a nominalizing suffix such as *-ing* merely forms nominal VPs or verb forms (§3.1.6).

Some grammatical morphemes are birelational. Then we may consider their structural scope in both directions, as it were. The personal pronoun mentioned before is not only governed by the verb; it also contracts an anaphoric relation to an NP. As long as it is a free personal pronoun, the latter is a semantic relation at a level above the clause. Then the NP gradually intrudes into the clause, via

4 Parameters of grammaticalization

a left- or right-dislocation. Finally, when the personal pronoun has become an agreement affix, the referent NP may occupy the object position so that this relation has got down to the VP level and become a syntactic one. We may speculate that incorporation of the object further reduces this level.

It is now evident that we determine the grammatical level of the construction which a sign helps to form by the syntagmatic morphosyntactic relation(s) which it contracts. No use has been made here of semantic relations, of any notion of a sign "being valid for" or "concerning" a construction of a certain level. This must be stressed because fallacies of the following kind suggest themselves: Aspect may be grammaticalized to tense, and modality (as expressed, e.g. by modal verbs) may be grammaticalized to mood. Now aspect and modality are categories concerning the VP, while tense and mood are valid for the clause as a whole. (Let us grant this for the sake of argument and following Bazell 1949: 7.) Therefore in these cases grammaticalization is accompanied by an increase in the scope of a grammatical morpheme. Similar fallacies might be founded upon Traugott's (1980: 47) notion that

> grammatical markers shift over time from primarily referential meanings to less referential, more pragmatic, meanings

or, more detailed (1980: 47):

> Propositional meanings of grammatical markers may give rise to textual ones and textual meanings may give rise to interpersonal ones, but not vice versa.

To infer an increase in the structural level and thus in the scope of the grammatical marker would be fallacious, because these markers bear no grammatical relation to constituents at the higher levels mentioned; in particular, tense and mood bear no direct morphosyntactic relation to the clause as a whole. Their "being valid" for the clause is a matter of semantics.

In certain cases, there is an obvious divergence between structural and semantic scope of a grammatical operator. The meaning of the English modal verb *may* has developed from physical via deontic to epistemic possibility. This implies a widening of the semantic scope from the verbal action to the proposition. Similar developments are frequent in the case of tense, aspect and mood operators. This is a clear example that arbitrariness, absence of iconicity, accompanies increasing grammaticalization (cf. §4.2.1). Morphological structure is often not amenable to direct semantic interpretation. Possibly reduction of scope is the one factor which is most responsible for non-iconicity and arbitrariness in grammatical structure.

Also, the shrinking of structural scope in the course of grammaticalization ends at the stem level. The diverse structural scope of the affixes of one word does not reflect their grammaticality; i.e. it is not generally the case that inner affixes are more grammatical than outer affixes. Instead, inner affixes are generally derivational, while outer affixes are inflectional. Even among the inflectional affixes, no order according to grammaticality is observed. The reason lies in the mechanism of agglutination (see next section). If only morphemes (e.g. postpositions or person pronouns) agglutinated to hosts, then outer morphological layers would generally be more recent and therefore less grammatical, and shrinkage of scope would be regular. However, a whole inflected word form may agglutinate to a host, e.g. an auxiliary verb to a non-finite full verb. Then suddenly an inflectional affix may find itself wedged in between less grammatical morphemes. The result is some form of inner inflection, as in German compound adjectives like *hochwertig* (high:value:ADJVR) 'top-grade', comparative *höherwertig* (beside *hochwertiger*). The mechanism of agglutination of inflected forms also yields highly non-iconic sequential morphological structure. A notable example is the prefix sequence "subject agreement – tense/aspect – object agreement – verb stem" common in Bantu languages, which obviously results from the coalescence of a syntagm "inflected auxiliary – full verb". The possibility of coming up with a formal account of such structures and of the degree of systematicity of scope shrinking depends on a polycentric analysis of morphological structure which I will not try to vindicate here.

Condensation thus has to be taken with these provisos. The question nevertheless remains what the functional correlate of the phenomenon of structural scope is. P. Kiparsky (1968) has introduced the notion of PREDICATIVITY for the semantic aspect of structural scope. A sign is predicative if it can be used to predicate something on something else. Kiparsky's examples are temporal adverbs, which are predicative, and verbal tense morphemes, which are not; and his claim is that tense morphemes in the Indo-European languages have evolved from more predicative elements of Proto-Indo-European. We have seen in §3.1.6 that "temporal adverb > tense" is in fact a historically attested grammaticalization channel. The notion of predicativity has been taken up more recently by H. Seiler (1982) and been explicitly connected with that of semanticity. The idea is that the more semanticity an item displays, the more predicative force it has. Seiler's examples are techniques of nominal classification and individuation, such as numeral classification and noun class/gender, the former being more predicative than the lat-

4 Parameters of grammaticalization

ter. As we have seen in §3.2.1.3, the choice of the numeral classifier may indeed constitute a subordinate predication of itself, while noun class and gender are much less subject to discretionary choice and therefore contribute much more to assigning an item to a class than to predicating on it. Cf. also the observations in §4.2.3 on the syntagmatic compatibility of a gender with an apparently contradictory sex: it is always the sex that wins out.

In a related sense, the term RHEMATICITY has been used by K. Strunk (1980) for a property which items lose in the course of their grammaticalization. Discussing the grammaticalization of reflexivity in much the way I did in §3.2.1.3 above, Strunk finds that reflexive pronouns tend to be renovated or reinforced when they lose their rhematicity. If a reflexive pronoun is to emphasize the identity of the object with the subject, it must be able to carry the rheme of a sentence. If it is not rhematic in this sense, it will merely signify that the action abides in the sphere of the subject. For example, there comes a point in the development of Latin *se levare* where it can no longer be used to signify 'to lift oneself', but merely means 'to get up'. Then the reflexive will be reinforced, so that we get *sese levare* or Spanish *levarse a si mismo*. Rhematicity in this sense can obviously be regarded as a semantic or even communicative counterpart of the structural scope of an item: while a rhematic reflexive pronoun may form a VP with the governing verb, a non-rhematic reflexive helps to form an intransitive verb.

There are also possible connections between the parameter of structural scope and the EXPLICITNESS VS. ELLIPTICITY of a construction. These are discussed in Jakobson & Waugh (1979: 6f) as "two extreme aspects of linguistic operations", a view which the authors ascribe to Franciscus Sanctius Brocensis (16th cent). One may indeed consider that the periphrastic *habeo cantatum* 'I have sung' is more explicit than the synthetic *cantavi*. It seems, however, recommendable to restrict the terms 'explicit vs. elliptic' to a scale of proceeding syntagmatic abbreviation by omission of constituents in context; this appears also to be intended by Jakobson and Waugh. The reduction of structural scope is much more a condensation of a construction by a degradation to a lower level of constituent structure. The successive loss of specifications here is not a kind of contextual ellipticity, but a constitutional categorial restriction. Nevertheless, the difference is by no means clear-cut, and we will have to take up later the question of whether grammaticalization can be compensated for by explicitness.

At the end of this section, the question of the boundedness or open-endedness of grammaticalization scales poses itself with enhanced clarity. On the one hand, we have seen two clauses being condensed into one, and we are thus led to ask whether grammaticalization has any role to play above the sentence level. On the other hand, we have seen grammatical formatives being reduced to phonological alternations of morphemes (e.g. in apophony [ablaut]), and we are thus led to ask whether grammaticalization has any role to play below the morpheme level. These questions will be taken up in later chapters.

4.3.2 Bondedness

The syntagmatic cohesion or bondedness of a sign is the intimacy with which it is connected with another sign to which it bears a syntagmatic relation. The degree of bondedness of a sign varies from juxtaposition to merger, in proportion to its degree of grammaticality. The term "bondedness" appears to have first been used by W. Foley (1980) in order to describe the connection between head nouns and their adjuncts, his idea being, basically, that when an adjunct is reduced from a freely formed modifier to a mere grammatical determiner, its bondedness to the head noun increases. Foley posits a scale of bondedness and supports it empirically by the incidence of connecting particles in adnominal modification of Austronesian languages, which is greater in the more weakly bonded constructions. The German equivalent of "bondedness", viz. "Fügungsenge", had been used by H. Seiler (1975) to describe the degree of integration of a nominal term formed to name an object. Fügungsenge is loosest in descriptive terms, especially in transparent compounds, and most intimate in labelling terms, i.e. arbitrary monomorphemic nouns. We will return to this conception in our discussion of lexicalization (§5.2).

Any increase in bondedness will be called COALESCENCE. As this process can be observed fairly accurately at the level of phonology, a variety of terms have appeared in the literature to designate its phases. The first step away from juxtaposition is the subordination of the grammaticalized item under an adjacent accent, called cliticization. The next phase, in which it becomes an affix of another element, is agglutination; and the last phase, in which the grammaticalized item loses its morpheme identity, becoming an integral part of another morpheme, is fusion or merger. Some of these terms have also been used for the whole of the coalescence process. I will first treat coalescence as a process affecting the significans and later take up the question of its semantic counterpart.

Some examples of different degrees of bondedness or of coalescence may be reviewed before we go into greater theoretical detail. The Latin demonstrative *ille* is, as a determiner, juxtaposed to the nominal it determines. It yields the French definite article, which is proclitic, and the Romanian definite article, which is suffixal. As a pronoun, *ille* yields the oblique forms *le, la* etc. of several Romance languages, which are clitic to the verb and sometimes even treated as suffixes.

4 Parameters of grammaticalization

The German preposition *trotz* 'despite' is juxtaposed to the NP which it governs. More grammaticalized prepositions, e.g. *zu* 'to' and *an* 'at', tend to lose their accent and become proclitic. The result are characteristic fusional forms in combination with the definite article, as illustrated in E57 in §3.4.1.3. Case suffixes may be agglutinative, as they are in Turkish (e.g. *yıl-ın* 'year-GEN'), or fusional, as they are in Latin (e.g. *anni* 'year:GEN '). In the former case, the affix is separable from the stem, which can exist without the affix (e.g. *yıl* 'year'); in the latter case, stem and affix are inseparable, i.e. the stem necessarily appears in one of the forms defined by one of the affixes (e.g. *annus* 'year:NOM '). The greatest degree of fusion is reached in what has been traditionally called symbolism of the apophony (ablaut) and metaphony (umlaut) type, e.g. English *sing* vs. *sang* (PAST) or *foot* vs. *feet* (PL).

One might consider that the elementary necessary precondition for coalescence is that the grammaticalized item has some GRAMMATICAL RELATION to the element with which it is to coalesce. There is some truth in this. Collocations which come about only occasionally cannot coalesce; they are not amenable to grammaticalization at all. The Baltic languages, for instance, have a definiteness suffix on adjectives. The condition for the coalescence of a definiteness marker with an adjective is, evidently, that the expression of definiteness of an NP is bound to the presence of an adjective attribute, positioned immediately in front of the definiteness marker. In German and English, the collocation of the definite article with an adjective attribute is occasional, since it makes no difference for definite determination whether an adjective attribute is present or not. Here there is no basis for such a coalescence.

On the other hand, we know of cases of CLITICIZATION where there is no grammatical relation between the clitic element and its carrier. Cf. the Latin coordinator *-que*, which is appended to the first word of the second conjunct (as in *cum in ramo sedebat caseumque devorare in animo habebat* 'while it sat on a branch and had in mind to devour the cheese'). In Somali, subject personal pronouns are enclitic to the focus marker, even though both have nothing to do with each other (E100). In Coahuilteco (see Troike 1981), cross-referencing personal pronouns which function as subject agreement markers are attached to an oblique NP, mostly the object NP, which precedes the verb. In Yucatec Maya, subject pronouns precede the verb, and possessive pronouns precede the possessed noun; but both are enclitic to whatever happens to precede them. A multitude of such examples could be cited. We may learn from them that coalescence proceeds according to either of two potentially conflicting principles. One possibility is that the position of a grammaticalized item in a syntagm is defined by grammatical relations. Then it will be appended to such elements to which it bears a grammatical relation. Or its position in a syntagm is defined by sequential order relations, typically involving the number of constituents from a certain syntactic boundary on, and more typically the position after the first constituent of a clause. Then cliticization will not (necessarily) reflect grammatical relations. In the former case, coalescence will proceed along the trodden paths of grammaticalization, while in the latter case it will normally stop with cliticization. One might consider restricting the terms "clitic" and "cliticization" to the latter case, so that cliticization would not be an essential feature of grammaticalization. This would have an added advantage. If cliticization is the loss of accent and subordination under an adjacent one, and if all grammaticalization necessarily involved cliticization, it would be difficult to account for the existence of stressed inflectional affixes. Such affixes are rare, but do occur, especially in the archaic Indo-European languages. In Greek, for instance, the *-tó-* suffix forming a passive participle is stressed. (These cases must not, of course, be confused with those where an affix receives stress according to phonological rules of word accent.) It therefore appears advisable to regard cliticization as a typical, but not necessary ingredient of grammaticalization.

Before any phonological consequences of coalescence make themselves felt, there are syntactic symptoms to be observed. One of them is the inseparability of a grammatical formative under COORDINATION REDUCTION. That is, if the cohesion of the formative X with constituent A increases, "A-X and B-X" can no longer be reduced to "[A and B]-X", and similarly, "A-X and A-Y" can no longer be reduced to "A-[X and Y]" (cf. Mallinson & Blake 1981: 198–201). E105–E107 demonstrate impossibility of coordination reduction in the b-constructions and its possibility in their English a-counterparts.

E105   German

    a. *to describe and explain*

    b. *zu beschreiben und zu erklären*

E106   French

    a. *to the author or the editor*

    b. *à l'auteur ou au siège*

E107   Japanese (cf. Mallinson & Blake 1981: 201)

    a. *Sumie goes to and from Osaka.*

    b. *Sumie wa Oosaka ni to   Oosaka kara iku.*
       Sumie TOP Osaka DIR and Osaka ABL go

4 Parameters of grammaticalization

Examples E105 and E106 show that the bondedness of both German *zu* and French *à* is greater than that of English *to*, since they cannot be suppressed in coordination. E107 shows that the Japanese particles, often alleged to be postpositions, are, at any rate, more intimately bonded to their complements than are English prepositions, since they cannot be coordinated: **Oosaka ni to kara* is impossible. Incidentally, the two parts of the coordination criterion need not yield the same result. Thus, in Japanese it is perfectly possible to attach one case particle to two coordinated NPs, as in *Oosaka to Tookyoo ni* 'to Osaka and Tokyo', and the same is true of Turkish case suffixes.[6] One might speculate that the two halves of the coordination reduction criterion are related by an implication of the following kind: A-[X and Y] → [A and B]-X. That is, in coalescence, first the coordination of grammatical markers (belonging to the same paradigm) related to one constituent becomes impossible, then the combination of only one grammatical marker with a coordination of constituents becomes impossible. The latter is, of course, at the same time an instance of the reduction of the structural scope of a grammatical formative.

Another syntactic criterion to test the bondedness of a grammatical formative is the possibility of inserting material between it and the word it tends to attach to. Cf. Zwicky (1978) on decreasing insertability of material in lower level constituents. The test is generally effectuated by expanding the host constituent. Its application to English *to* + infinitive vs. German *zu* + infinitive is exemplified in E108.

E108 German

   a. *to fully describe*

   b. *vollständig zu beschreiben*

Here the expansion criterion converges with the coordination criterion in the result that bondedness in English *to* + infinitive is looser than in German *zu* + infinitive. Putting it more generally, the expansion test makes us see whether a grammatical formative is already so much grammaticalized as to be combinable only with a particular word form class, or whether it still attaches to a class of – potentially expanded – constituents.

UNIVERBATION is the traditional term for the welding of a syntagm into one word. Examples: German *keines Wegs* (lit. of no way) > *keineswegs* 'by no means', Proto-Greek *ἑοῖ αὐτῷ* (he:DAT.SG.M self:DAT.SG.M) > Attic *ἑαυτῷ* 'to himself' (cf.

---

[6] This is, in fact, one of the differences between agglutinative case suffixes and flexional ones of the ancient Indo-European type which first struck the eye of early typologists.

Wackernagel 1920/1924: II:82). The orthography is, of course, not always reliable. French *bon marché* 'cheap' behaves grammatically like one word, since it cannot be opposed to *mauvais marché* (but rather to *cher* 'expensive').[7]

If univerbation is to be considered within the scope of grammaticalization, the last example clearly shows that it does occur outside this domain, too. In fact, univerbation has traditionally been opposed to composition, this pair of terms being sometimes rendered in German by "Zusammenrückung vs. Zusammensetzung", respectively (cf. Žirmunskij 1966: 88). The difference between these two processes need not be clear-cut in every instance, but in principle it is this: Univerbation is restricted to the syntagmatic axis and may affect, in perhaps idiosyncratic ways, any two particular word forms which happen to be habitually used in collocation. Composition, as a schema of word-formation, presupposes a paradigm in analogy to which it proceeds and affects a class of stems according to a structural pattern. This characterization allows for the possibility that univerbation is an instance of coalescence as a constitutive process of grammaticalization, namely whenever at least one of the univerbated word forms is a grammatical formative, as in Greek ἑαυτῷ.

One might, in fact, ask whether there is any difference in principle between univerbation and AGGLUTINATION. The two are brought into close connection by F. de Saussure (1916: Part 3, Ch. VII, §§1f), who opposes agglutination to analogy as two driving forces of grammatical change, the former leading to univerbation, the latter to word formation (composition and derivation). We will return in §5.4 to the relation of grammaticalization to analogy and here remark only that univerbation should be kept distinct from agglutination for two reasons. The first lies in the potentially fortuitous, selective nature of univerbation. A univerbation such as *keineswegs* is possible everywhere and at any time, regardless of the existence or not of such models as *keinesfalls* 'in no case' or **jedenwegs*. Agglutination of a postposition as a case suffix to a noun, however, typically does not affect just one postposition, but a whole paradigm. Agglutination is not an occasional, but a systematic process.

The second reason for distinguishing agglutination and univerbation relates to a difference in scope: agglutination is not restricted to the word level, at least not in the same sense as univerbation. If a grammatical formative is univerbated with another word, it attaches to the latter as such and not as a representative of a possibly complex syntactic category. But precisely this typically happens in agglutination. The difference between an agglutinative and a fusional affix lies not only (as has sometimes been alleged, e.g. in Sapir 1921: Ch. V and Greenberg

---

[7] See Frei (1929: 109f), who calls the phenomenon "brachysemy".

4 Parameters of grammaticalization

1954) in the lesser degree of phonological adaptation exhibited or caused by the former. This is only the superficial consequence of the fact that the morphological bond between an agglutinative affix and its carrier is looser than that between a fusional affix and its carrier. Cf. the following examples from Altaic languages (Žirmunskij 1966: 71):

E109 Uzbek
ota, ona va dust-lar-dan salom
father mother and friend-PL-ABL greeting
'greetings from father(s), mother(s) and friends'

E110 Turkish
yarın gel-ir, al-ır-ım
tomorrow come-PRS take-PRS-1.GEN
'tomorrow I shall come and take'

E111 Turkish
ne y-iyor, ne iç-iyor, ne de söyl-üyor-du
neither eat-PROG nor drink-PROG nor also speak-PROG-PAST(3.GEN)
'he did not eat, nor drink, nor speak'

If we confined ourselves to comparing only Latin *amicis* '(from) the friends', *capiam* 'I will take' and *loquebatur* 'he spoke' with the relevant forms in the above examples, we might indeed be led to reducing the phenomenon to a phonological difference. What we have to compare, however, are the syntagms E109′–E111′.

E109′ Latin
a patre, matre et amicis salutationes

E110′ Latin
cras veniam atque capiam

E111′ Latin
non edebat, non bibebat, non loquebatur

The coordination test shows that the grammatical formatives ABL, 1.SG and PAST have to be repeated in Latin, because they are strictly bound to the word, whereas they may be combined with complex constituents in Uzbek und Turkish.

In a situation such as the latter one, it is, of course, essential to have independent criteria that one is, in fact, dealing with affixes. The criterion of structural scope, which one would be tempted to invoke here, has just been discarded, and we are left with morphological and phonological criteria. The morphological criterion concerns the fact that an affix – in contradistinction to a free morpheme – occupies a particular slot on a particular word class. This is the criterion of syntagmatic variability which we will turn to in the following section. The phonological criterion concerns the application of phonological rules to sequences which include the potential affix, such rules being otherwise known to apply to words. Turkish vowel harmony is an example; its application includes suffixes, but not postpositions. Accordingly we have *vapur ile* 'with a steamer', but *vapur-la* 'by steamer' (cf. p. 88). Furthermore, rules of sandhi and other assimilation rules operate in most languages to adapt an affix to a stem.

The more an affix is integrated into the word by such rules, the more agglutination gives way to FUSION. In classical morphological typology, a crucial feature distinguishing a language of the flexional ($\simeq$ fusional) type such as Sanskrit from a language of the agglutinative type such as Turkish was, in fact, the richness of sandhi rules to be found in the former; cf. Humboldt's (1836: 506–511) detailed discussion of Sanskrit sandhi. The common function of phonological rules setting in at the moment of agglutination and giving way to fusion might be designated, with Heine & Reh (1984: 17–20), by the term ADAPTATION.

Coalescence may be described as the weakening and final loss of boundaries. Hyman (1978: esp. §4) has set up a scale of boundaries rendered here in Figure 4.1.

$$\| \quad > \quad \#\# \quad > \quad \# \quad > \quad + \quad > \quad \emptyset$$

Figure 4.1: Scale of grammatical boundaries

This is to be read: clause boundary includes word boundary includes stem boundary includes morpheme boundary includes absence of boundary. The transitive inclusion relation from left to right means that if a phonological process applies across a given boundary, it also applies across the boundaries to its right; and when a boundary is weakened in coalescence, what is left is its neighbor on the right. Hyman argues that no phonological rule refers to the '+' boundary. Therefore loss of the '#' boundary would mean complete integration of a morpheme into a word. These ideas had been prepared by Kuryłowicz (1948: 211), who showed that the rules of syllabication, which in several languages such as German do not cross the word (or stem) boundary, nevertheless seize whatever comes to be agglutinated as an affix.

4 Parameters of grammaticalization

Fusion of grammatical formatives with stems leads to a variety of phenomena characteristic of the morphological structure of so-called flexional languages. One of them is the amalgamation or CUMULATION of several grammatical categories in one morpheme. In a Latin adjective form such as *bonō* (good:DAT.SG.M/N) it is not only difficult to localize a morpheme boundary, since the inflectional morpheme consists of a lengthening of the final vowel of the stem *bono-*; what is more, none of the three inflectional categories of case, number and gender has a separate morpheme, or morphological slot, for its expression; instead, they are cumulated in a case-number-gender morpheme. It is common for cumulation to affect affixal morphemes; but sometimes several grammatical categories may be agglomerated in a free morpheme. Cf. French *au* 'to the' < *à le*; more examples of portmanteau morphs in Jeffers & Zwicky (1980: §6).

Amalgamation naturally leads to lack of distinctness of inflectional morphemes. Polysemies or homonymies of endings are often only dispelled in agreement, as is familiar from Latin grammar. In German, this has been developed from a deficiency to a method, as has been shown by O. Werner (1979). Instead of expressing a bundle of inflectional categories on each of a set of agreeing constituents, we distribute its expression among these constituents, so that the exhaustive specification of these categories is afforded by none of the constituents in isolation, but only by the set taken together. A simple example is *kleiner Kinder* 'of small children'. *Kleiner* may be nom.sg.m. or gen.pl., whereas *Kinder* may be nom. or gen.pl. Taking both together, we get gen.pl., and the phrase can accordingly be used as a genitive complement, for instance to a verb such as *gedenken* 'commemorate'. At the same time we forfeit the possibility of representing such constituents by only one word as a carrier of the bundle of categories; *Kinder* alone, though potentially genitive plural, cannot constitute a genitive complement (it would have to be *der Kinder, einiger Kinder* or *von Kindern*). On the basis of such evidence, Werner is led to postulate a new morphological type, the "discontinuing type".

Another phenomenon of extreme fusion is what has traditionally been termed (by Humboldt and Sapir, among others) symbolism or SYMBOLIC EXPRESSION. This means that a grammatical category does not have a morpheme or segment reserved for its expression, but that it is embodied in the formal relation between two alternative forms of a stem. The examples of (qualitative) apophony (*sing* PRS vs. *sang* PAST) and metaphony (*tooth* SG vs. *teeth* PL) have already been mentioned. Other processes of symbolic expression include vowel lengthening (quantitative apophony), consonant mutation, accent shift and tone change. Vowel lengthening occurs in the Sanskrit guṇa and vṛddhi stem forms; consonant mutation in

4.3 Syntagmatic parameters

the grading of Finnish verb stems. For accent shift cf. Russian *ókna*, nom.pl. of 'window', with *okná*, gen.sg. Tone change occurs in Yucatec Maya deagentive verbs, e.g. *kach* 'break (tr.)' vs. *káach* 'break (intr.)'. These symbolic means may or may not be direct diachronic continuations of segmental formatives. Germanic umlaut is an indirect reflex, since it does not continue a former plural morpheme, but was triggered by one.

It is no great exaggeration if we say that the core of classical agglutination theory, with its stages of isolation, agglutination and fusion (=flexion), is embodied in the one grammaticalization parameter of bondedness or the corresponding process of coalescence. Relatively little thought has been devoted to the question of whether these rather easily discernible formal processes have anything corresponding to them on the semantic side.[8] Is there any such thing as semantic coalescence or "unification" (Žirmunskij 1966: §3); can we claim, as Bybee (1981: §3) does, that morphophonemic fusion diagrams semantic fusion?

This issue must be kept distinct from the unification of lexical meanings. Complex lexical meanings which have been formed by rules of word formation may subsequently be reduced to simple meanings, as when Pre-Latin *sim-plec-s* 'once folded' becomes French *simple*. Here fusion of the significans does reflect fusion of the significatum, but no grammaticalization is involved. This sort of process will be taken up in the chapter on lexicalization.

What we find in semantic bondedness is not so much the fusion of a grammatical with a lexical meaning; even in English *feet* the "plural" component is clearly distinct from the 'foot' component. Instead, we find an increase in the dependency of the grammatical meaning on the lexical meanings which it is attached to. The traditional notion of AUTOSEMANTIC VS. SYNSEMANTIC (or, alternatively, of (auto-)categorematic vs. syncategorematic) signs provides a suitable approach to this problem; cf. also Hjelmslev (1928: 230) on his notions of "semanteme" vs. "morpheme". Any full lexical noun can signify by itself a certain concept and can independently refer to a certain class of objects. But when it is grammaticalized to a noun of multitude to express collectivity, or to a numeral classifier to help individuate units in counting, it loses this ability and signifies a concept only in combination with another word. Similarly, any lexical verb can signify a certain kind of state, process or action or refer to individual instances of them. But when it is grammaticalized to a coverb or auxiliary, it forfeits this ability and needs another verb to help signify such things. This semantic dependency becomes even more pronounced with further grammaticalization. A number or gender marker

---

[8] One exception is von Humboldt (1836: 488–500), who has an intensive discussion of the essential differences between the three types.

4 Parameters of grammaticalization

does not signify a number or gender concept as such, but only insofar as these are features of other concepts. Similarly, a case or tense marker does not express an isolatable actant role or time concept, but only insofar as these are relations or categories of nominal or verbal concepts. This is, in fact, one of the semantic differences between the word *plurality* and the plural *-s*, or the word *past* and the suffix *-ed*.

The semantic dependency of synsemantic signs is particularly clear from the fact that they not only must be obligatorily combined with autosemantic signs, but they also can only be combined with specific classes of the latter. In English, grammatical plural is afforded a place in the classes of nouns and pronouns; it cannot be combined with adjectives, verbs (except *to be*) or any other lexical class.

When grammatical formatives become bound morphemes, they become morphologically dependent, subordinate to a lexeme. Some of them may have started by being syntactically subordinate to the word to which they are later affixed. A free personal pronoun occupying the object position of a transitive verb is governed by the latter. If it is grammaticalized to an agreement affix, its syntactic dependency is transformed into a morphological one; but the direction of dependency itself remains unchanged. This is not so in a major portion of the grammaticalization processes. Often the term which is subsequently grammaticalized starts as the head of the syntagm, either the governing or the modified term. Nouns of multitude in Bengali started as heads of possessive attributes, the latter becoming subsequently the lexical heads to which the former attached as plural suffixes (see Kölver 1982a: §2.1). The adverbial suffixes English *-ly*, Romance *-ment(e)* come from nouns to which the adjective was an attribute. Auxiliaries always start as syntactic main verbs, governing a lexical verb in a nominalized form. When they are attached to the latter as tense or aspect affixes, the lexical verb must have become the main verb (see p. 36f). The Japanese particle *no*, both in its attributive and in its nominalizing function, originally was the head of a possessive attribute. Dependent clauses derive diachronically from possessive attributes to their subordinating conjunctions also in other languages, such as Accadic.

One conclusion immediately suggested by this state of affairs is that morphological analysis can be made more precise. MORPHOLOGICAL RELATIONS could be seen as grammaticalizations of different syntactic relations. There would no longer be an unanalyzable relation between a stem of class x and an affix of slot y, but instead we might distinguish various relations of "morphological modification" and "morphological government" from x to y or vice versa. I suspect a promising line of research here, but will not pursue the matter further.

A second consequence that one must draw is that in the course of such grammaticalization processes, there must be a point of shift, of SYNTACTIC REANALYSIS. Consider the problem of case affixes. Firstly, there is no doubt that an adposition can govern a complement NP and that the complex phrase thus constituted is assigned a constituent category according to its head, i.e. it is an adpositional phrase. Secondly, there is no doubt that an NP may have an unmarked syntactic function, e.g. that of the direct object, that it may then have no case and thus simply be an NP. Thirdly, there is no doubt that an adposition may gradually evolve into a case affix and this may end up as zero, e.g. in the accusative. What constitutes a matter of doubt is the question of what the syntactic category of an NP with a case is. Should we locate it on this side of the turning point and say it is like an adpositional phrase; or should we locate it beyond the turning point, saying it is an NP? Or will we need a separate category for "cased" NPs? The latter solution appears particularly undesirable because then we could not forestall the danger of having to provide distinct syntactic categories for NPs with cases of different degrees of grammaticality, e.g. one "NP in a grammatical case" and another "NP in a concrete case", and so forth. Incidentally, I see here the crux of the whole enterprise of case grammar. In the field of constituent structure, we are particularly loath to accept gradual transitions. And yet, to all appearances, there is a gradual difference between an adpositional phrase and a noun phrase. Constituent structure, one of the last bastions of static structuralism, cannot be seen as formed by means of a series of binary decisions, but is the product of a set of operations which may inflate relations at some points and shrink them at other points. This is why we find different degrees of bondedness in grammatical structure.

4.3.3 Syntagmatic variability

The syntagmatic variability of a sign is the ease with which it can be shifted around in its context. In the case of a grammaticalized sign, this concerns mainly its positional mutability with respect to those constituents with which it enters into construction. Syntagmatic variability decreases with increasing grammaticalization.

The grammaticalization of adverbs to adpositions provides an example. An adverb which specifies an aspect of a local NP may often be juxtaposed to it on either side and sometimes even be separated from it (cf. p. 95). The more intimate its connection with the NP becomes, the more its position vis-à-vis the latter becomes fixed; it develops either into a preposition or into a postposition. At this point, it still enjoys a minimum of syntagmatic variability; it may, for instance, be coordinated with other adpositions. This last rest is lost when it becomes a case affix, which has to occupy a particular slot in a nominal affix series.

As authors have observed repeatedly (e.g. Matthews 1981: 256), the famous freedom of word order in Latin is subject to an exception: prepositions must normally precede their complements and got their name from this very fact. This exception turns out to be quite regular in the framework of grammaticalization theory, since prepositions are – along with conjunctions, for which similar restrictions obtain – the most strongly grammaticalized free morphemes of Latin. It is therefore to be expected that their syntagmatic variability is not much greater than that of bound morphemes.

Again, before a verb becomes an auxiliary, it may enjoy a certain positional freedom vis-à-vis the VP with which it combines. In Classical Latin, the parts of the construction *epistulam scriptam habeo* 'I have a letter written' could occur in any order. In Vulgar Latin, most of these options were doubtless lost, and we end up with Italian *ho scritto una lettera* 'I have written a letter', in which the sequence of auxiliary and full verb is invariable. The same can be observed when a personal pronoun develops into an agreement affix, or a demonstrative pronoun into a definite article. See Givón (1975: 84f) for loss of syntagmatic variability in serial verbs on their way to adpositions.

When a grammatical formative bears relations to two constituents, syntagmatic variability with respect to either of them may decrease at an uneven pace. Thus, when in a construction "verb – adverbial relator – NP", the bond between the adverbial relator and the NP is intensified, syntagmatic variability decreases here much more rapidly than in the relation between the verb and the adverbial NP. Only when the latter is grammaticalized to a governed NP, to a complement of the verb, its position vis-à-vis the verb tends to become fixed. Similarly, when a personal pronoun develops into an agreement affix, its syntagmatic variability decreases rapidly (cf. p. 43). At the same time, the NP to which it bears an anaphoric relation enters into a government relationship with the carrier of the agreement affix (most commonly the verb) and forfeits its own syntagmatic mobility, though much more slowly.

A phenomenon sometimes observed in grammaticalization is that the order in which the grammaticalized item is fixed in its construction differs from that order which was most natural when it was still a lexeme. This is, for instance, the situation in the development of the Romance auxiliary 'have' just mentioned. The unmarked sequence in Latin was either *epistulam scriptam habeo*, with the verb in final position, or *habeo epistulam scriptam*, with the verb in front of the object.

4.3 Syntagmatic parameters

Neither of these variations survived in Italian *ho scritto una lettera*. Similarly, Mallinson & Blake (1981: 423f) call attention to the fact that the formation of causative constructions with *fare* in Italian (and equally with *faire* in French) does not display that order which one would expect if general rules of syntax obtained. We find constructions such as those in E112 (cf. Comrie 1981a: 162).

E112 Italian

    a. *Faccio scrivere Maria la lettera.*

       'I have Mary write the letter.'

    b. *Gliela faccio scrivere.*

       'I have her write it.'

Since Mary and the letter are subject and object of the writing, respectively, one might expect *faccio Maria scrivere la lettera* and *faccio scrivergliela*; but instead, *faccio* and *scrivere* go together, the subject of the subordinate verb being demoted (cf. Comrie 1981a: §8.2). In German and similar languages, participles may grammaticalize to adpositions. While a participle, as a non-finite verb, governs its dependents to the left (e.g. *deinen Vorschlägen entsprechend* 'according to your suggestions'), the result of the grammaticalization is not a postpostion, but a preposition (*entsprechend deinen Vorschlägen*). Finally, Heine & Reh (1984: 132) show that while the unmarked position of time adverbs in Bari (Eastern Nilotic) is sentence-initial, that adverb which becomes a future marker shifts to a position between subject and verb, i.e. the position reserved for tense markers in Bari. Cf. also p. 39 above.

On the basis of such evidence, Heine & Reh suggest including "permutation" as one of the formal processes making up grammaticalization. It appears that one should rather conceive of such phenomena as POSITIONAL ADJUSTMENT than as permutation. Two principles seem to be involved here. First, while the syntagmatic variability of the grammaticalized item decreases, its bond with a particular class of words which it comes to modify grammatically becomes tighter. That is, whenever such positional adjustments occur, they will produce an order in which the grammaticalized item is adjacent to its lexical support. In this respect, positional adjustment is a consequence of coalescence. Second, as will be discussed in more detail below, the canalization of grammaticalization processes is due, to a great extent, to the existence of models which exert an analogical strain. The Bari example shows this very clearly. In the Italian causative construction, the governing grammatical verb is put in front of the governed full verb according to the model of the periphrastic verb forms. The latter in their turn, exemplified

4 Parameters of grammaticalization

by *ho scritto*, did not have a very strong model to follow. This may be inferred from the fact that besides *ho scritto*, we get *scriverò* < *scribere habeo*. The latter construction conforms rather to an older general syntactic pattern "governed – governing", which persisted most strongly in subordinate clauses, while the construction *ho scritto* conforms to a more recent pattern 'governing – governed'. Summarizing this consideration, we may say that there is no positional adjustment beyond the combined effects of coalescence and analogy.

In the beginning we appeared to dispose of a restricted concept of syntagmatic variability which concerned only the relation between a grammaticalized item and the constituent with which it forms a construction. But the complex constituent thus formed may contract a further grammatical relation to another constituent which may be mediated by the grammatical marker; recall the situation with case affixes and personal agreement affixes. The freedom of the order of such constituents is therefore also comprised under the concept of syntagmatic variability. Now consider that grammaticalization may reduce a grammatical marker to zero: we can still ask what happens to the syntagmatic variability of the constituents that had been related by this marker. In this way, the whole issue of word order and word order freedom emerges as one of the parameters of grammaticalization. The problem can obviously be tackled only in connection with the other grammaticalization parameters, and I will therefore return to it in the next chapter, which deals with their correlation.

4.4 Interaction of parameters

4.4.1 Quantifiability of the parameters

Before there can be a significant discussion of the correlation among the grammaticalization parameters, it is indispensable that they can assume measurable values independently of each other. Knowing in advance that we will not be able to stand up to the requirements of linguistic theory and method in this respect, we will at least make an effort at as much precision as possible. At least one condition for the quantifiability of the parameters is fulfilled: they are purely formal, i.e. they are indifferent as to the specific meanings or functions involved in the various grammaticalization channels.

The integrity of a sign is its meaning specificity and phonological size. I will assume these two aspects to correlate with each other; any lack of correspondence between them would not be a problem of grammaticalization theory. As was already said, the semantic specificity of a sign can be measured in terms of the number of propositions (as formal representations of semantic features) which are conjoined (rather than disjoined) in its semantic representation. A precise proposal has been made, and its applicability in principle has been demonstrated, in Lehmann (1978). To give a superficial idea of the magnitudes involved here, current semantic descriptions lead one to speculate that from five to twenty (rarely more) conjoined propositions are needed for the semantic representation of a lexical meaning, while the meaning (or function) of a grammatical formative may be specified with fewer, or by a disjunction of propositions. Concerning the size of the significans, we are on safer ground. Lexical items may be made up of an arbitrary length of segments; lexical morphemes may certainly contain more than three syllables (e.g. *inveterate*). In some languages such as Indonesian and Classical Arabic, there are comparatively few lexemes comprising less than two syllables; and in all languages the number of lexemes expressed only by one segment is very low, compared to the number of grammatical formatives so expressed (cf. Lehmann 1974: 115f). The latter very seldom comprise more than two syllables, very often no more than one or two segments, and occasionally even less than that, namely merely a feature on another morpheme. The latter case is impossible for the lexical morphemes of any language (cf. Moravcsik 1980). The mere counting of units could be refined if they were weighed differently according to their implicative potential; but such speculations are idle at the present low level of general sophistication. In any case, it is clear that this parameter may assume values from an arbitrary (but usually not too high) number down to zero.

Paradigmaticity has one aspect which is easily quantifiable, namely the sheer size of the paradigm in terms of number of members. The size of the Sanskrit case paradigm is eight, that of the English articles two. In general, paradigms may have from a dozen or (rarely) more members down to one member; lexical fields may, of course, have more. Unfortunately, this magnitude does not necessarily correlate with the cohesion of the paradigm as determined by its formal and functional homogeneity; a large paradigm may be homogeneous, and a small one may be heterogeneous. The homogeneity of a paradigm might be measured as the ratio of those features in which its members differ to those which they have in common. However, at present I have no idea whether in principle this would be feasible.

Paradigmatic variability is very difficult to quantify, since it must be made dependent on a number of contextual factors which differ from one paradigm to another. Abstracting away from such differences, paradigmatic variability boils down to the proportion of members of a paradigm which are mutually substitutable in a given context. Zero would have to be somehow included as a member

4 Parameters of grammaticalization

of any paradigm. The values then range from 100% if all members are possible in a given position, to 0% if only one member can occur in a given position and cannot even be omitted. Recall also that increasing obligatoriness means obligatoriness on decreasing levels of grammatical structure. Therefore the measure of structural scope, to be discussed now, may also be made use of in the quantification of obligatoriness.

Since the structural scope of a grammaticalized item is, roughly, the level of grammatical structure of that syntagm with which it contracts a grammatical relation, this parameter may be measured with respect to constituent structure configurations. As a first approximation, the structural scope of a sign might be defined as the maximal number of nodes dominated by that constituent with which it contracts a grammatical relation, recursion excluded. The value would range from about a dozen in the case of a clause to one in the case of a stem or word.

Bondedness is the most difficult parameter of all to quantify. I will not consider here the possibility of measuring the semantic dependence of a grammaticalized item and turn immediately to phonological cohesion. The problem of measuring it reminds one of Greenberg's (1954) agglutination index; but here we require a finer measure, because phonological bondedness is not to be determined for all the morphemes of a language but only for those belonging to a particular paradigm. A first attempt might consist in counting the phonological rules which operate across the boundary separating the grammatical formative from its co-constituent; but this could not account for those higher degrees of fusion where phonological adaptation is already morphologized. Another approach would be to determine the number of allomorphs per morpheme, because allomorphy usually increases with bondedness. But probably this is not completely reliable either, because there might be infixes with only one allomorph. For the time being, the best alternative would seem to consist in determining, with the help of grammatical tests such as those discussed in §4.3.2, the morphological status of a grammaticalized item as one of the following: (a) free, stressable morpheme, (b) clitic morpheme, (c) agglutinative affix, (d) fusional affix, (e) amalgamated in a flexional affix, (f) infix or symbolic alternation. These degrees of bondedness would be assigned integer values along an ordinal scale from six to one, so that the value decreases, with increasing bondedness, parallel to those of other parameters.

The syntagmatic variability of an item should be somehow determined by the number of positions that it may assume in a syntagm. This presupposes that we have an idea of which positions it might theoretically occupy. If we reduce the problem to binary constructions, made up of a grammatical formative and its coconstituent, we may say that there are, in principle, four positions for the former: either immediately before or after its coconstituent, or at some distance before or after it.[9] Then we might assign two points for each of the available positions and subtract one of them if the position is available only under certain restricted circumstances or if it is, on the contrary, obligatory under other circumstances. This yields a scale of values from seven to one along which syntagmatic variability decreases. The rough and tentative nature of this proposal is obvious. Methodological studies on the analysis of free vs. fixed word order are lacking in the literature; cf., at any rate, Steele (1978).

So much should suffice to show that all of the six criteria of grammaticalization are in principle operationalizable and yield parameters which are quantifiable independently of each other. Formulated in mathematical terms, grammaticalization is a vector whose variables are the six magnitudes which we have here been calling parameters. Any sign or paradigm of signs may be assigned a value along each of the parameters, and the six figures together can be taken to characterize its degree of grammaticality.

I have not yet succeeded in establishing a common formal basis for the quantification of the parameters; the six proposals for their quantification are still somewhat ad hoc and heterogeneous. However, their numerical behavior is roughly comparable: All of them have been designed to exhibit decreasing values with increasing grammaticalization. On the left they are open-ended. They assume manageable values at levels where interest in grammaticalization can reasonably set in and decrease steadily until they reach the opposite pole, which has the value "one" for all of them. If grammaticalization proceeds further, the parameter of integrity assumes the value "zero", whereas the others cease to be applicable (cf., however, §4.4.4). Thus the formal requirements for their comparison and for a test of their correlation are fulfilled in principle. In the following, I will refrain from actual quantification, partly because it is practically not yet possible, partly because what I want to show can be adequately shown at an informal level.

4.4.2 Correlation among the parameters

In the preceding sections, the six grammaticalization parameters were discussed, as far as possible, in mutual isolation. However, it was made clear from the start

---

[9] If the coconstituent of formative X is internally complex, consisting, say, of head A and modifier B, the sequence AXB is also possible. But it appears that this testifies more to the syntagmatic variability of B than to that of X.

4 Parameters of grammaticalization

that they are theoretically interconnected and must therefore be expected to correlate. Table 4.3 summarizes the behavior of the parameters and displays their correlation.

Table 4.3: Correlation of grammaticalization parameters

PARAMETER	WEAK GRAMMATICALIZATION	PROCESS →	STRONG GRAMMATICALIZATION
INTEGRITY	bundle of semantic features; possibly polysyllabic	attrition →	few semantic features; oligo- or monosegmental
PARADIGMATICITY	item participates loosely in semantic field	paradigmaticization →	small, tightly integrated paradigm
PARADIGMATIC VARIABILITY	free choice of items according to communicative intentions	obligatorification →	choice systematically constrained, use largely obligatory
STRUCTURAL SCOPE	item relates to constituent of arbitrary complexity	condensation →	item modifies word or stem
BONDEDNESS	item is independently juxtaposed	coalescence →	item is affix or even phonological feature of carrier
SYNTAGMATIC VARIABILITY	item can be shifted around freely	fixation →	item occupies fixed slot

Table 4.3 can be taken as the common denominator of all grammaticalization scales. It is our contention that a normal grammaticalization process obeys the following condition: an item which is grammaticalized in a construction will occupy a point on each of the six parameters in such a way that the six points are roughly on a vertical line. I will return in the next section to the question of what is meant by a normal grammaticalization process, and discuss here some theoretical considerations and empirical evidence which make such a correlation plausible.

Correlation of the paradigmatic parameters among each other is, to some extent, a logical necessity. "Meaning, or meaningfulness implies choice" (Lyons 1977: 33); and if more meaning is to be conveyed (semanticity), either the choice must be expanded (paradigmaticity), or it must be relieved from constraints (paradigmatic variability). Conversely, if an item is opposed only to a few similar ones or cannot but appear under certain circumstances, its semanticity will be correspondingly low. The well known correlation between desemanticization, dropping of selection restrictions and the rise of text frequency may be recalled here. Nevertheless, the dependence is not complete. Obviously a paradigm may

4.4 Interaction of parameters

contain members which are semantically not well distinct and thus have a relatively low semanticity; this occasionally occurs with noun classes and adpositions. Again, there are logical connections among some of the parameters of syntagmatic autonomy. The syntagmatic variability of an item can increase only if its structural scope likewise increases.

As for the relationship between the paradigmatic and syntagmatic parameters, it might be necessary to dispell a possible misunderstanding. It is sometimes said that in order to convey a meaning of a given specificity, the language user has a choice between paradigmatic and syntagmatic means. For example, if a German wants to specify a horse as black or white, he may either make up the expressions *schwarzes Pferd* and *weißes Pferd*, enlarging the message, or choose the words *Rappen* and *Schimmel*, drawing on a larger code, as it were. This is necessarily so, for reasons of information theory. However, two points must be observed here. First, there is no real alternative between paradigmatic and syntagmatic means. All the four expressions in question are items taken from a paradigm and are, at the same time, syntagms (embedded in larger syntagms). It is not possible to exclude the paradigmatic in favor of the syntagmatic, or vice versa. Second, the fundamental issue of grammaticalization is not how to convey a meaning of a given specificity, but rather how much freedom to invest in the construction of a linguistic sign, and, accordingly, with how much autonomy to invest the component signs. The autonomy which a sign enjoys in its paradigm is necessarily reflected by its autonomy in the syntagm; there is thus no complementarity, but parallelism.

Correlations among several of the parameters have long been observed (cf. also Heine & Reh 1984: 62–68). In a passage dealing with the freedom with which linguistic units are made up, R. Jakobson (1956) writes:

> Thus, in the combination of linguistic units there is an ascending scale of freedom. In the combination of distinctive features into phonemes, /243/ the freedom of the individual speaker is zero: the code has already established all the possibilities which may be utilized in the given language. Freedom to combine phonemes into words is circumscribed; it is limited to the marginal situation of word coinage. In forming sentences with words the speaker is less constrained. And finally, in the combination of sentences into utterances, the action of compulsory syntactic rules ceases, and the freedom of any individual speaker to create novel contexts increases substantially, although again the numerous stereotyped utterances are not to be overlooked.

4 Parameters of grammaticalization

Jakobson then goes on to establish combination (syntagmatic aspect) and selection (paradigmatic aspect) as the two fundamental modes of any language operation. His scale of freedom appears to involve two of our parameters in particular, the integrity and the syntagmatic variability of a sign. It is especially noteworthy that Jakobson prolongs the scale down to the phoneme and even the phonological feature. In §5.3 we will return to the problem of their integration into grammaticalization scales.

As an example of the correlation between integrity and syntagmatic variability, the German adpositions may be adduced. Some secondary adpositions, including *wegen* 'because of', *gemäß* 'in conformity with', *entsprechend* 'corresponding to', *zufolge* 'acccording to', *entlang* 'along', may be used either as prepositions or as postpositions. All the primary adpositions of the language are exclusively prepositions.

The negative correlation between semanticity and paradigmaticity has been confirmed by F. Serzisko in several writings on numeral classifiers (e.g. 1980: 23f). If there are comparatively few classifiers, they will have a comparatively unspecific meaning. If a language has a large paradigm of noun classes which have no semantic basis, this unstable situation tends to be settled by reducing the number of classes. Recall, furthermore, the discussion of adpositions (p. 101) and of cases (p. 119), which may be layered, within a language, in subparadigms of correlatively decreasing size and semanticity.

In discussing the same correlation, Langacker (1977: 112f) speaks of a "correlation between the gradients of semantic content and expressive salience". Langacker's notion of expressive salience comprises not only phonological integrity, but also major category status, with corresponding larger structural scope and lower bondedness. A further example of this relationship is the formation of possessive pronouns alongside personal pronouns. If the latter are weakly grammaticalized, it can happen that there are no special possessive pronouns; instead a regular genitive (or possessive construction) of the personal pronouns is formed. This is the case, e.g., in Japanese (high integrity, low paradigmaticity, low cohesion). If personal pronouns are highly grammaticalized, as, e.g. in English, there tends to be a subparadigm of possessive pronouns which cannot be derived from the personal ones by rules of grammar (values reverse).

Special attention has been devoted in the recent past to the correlation between structural scope and syntagmatic variability. It has been emphasized repeatedly (Givón 1979b: 205–209) that freedom of word order in a language is never greater at subconstituent level than at constituent level. A fine example is the NP containing a numeral and a numeral classifier (see Greenberg 1975: 29). The constituent structure is, irrespective of sequential order, as shown in Figure 4.2.

4.4 Interaction of parameters

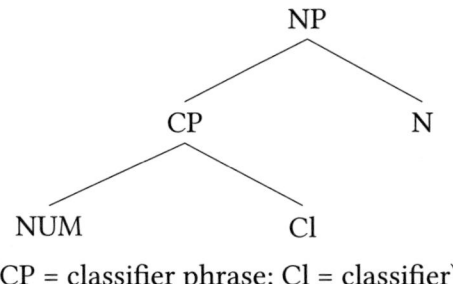

(CP = classifier phrase; Cl = classifier)

Figure 4.2: Structure of numeral classifier phrase

While the order of the numeral and the classifier within the CP is almost always fixed, the relative word order of the CP and the counted noun is variable in many languages, e.g. Malay. Ascending the levels of constituent structure, we usually find syntagmatic variability in the VP greater than in the NP (cf. Givón 1975: 92f), and in independent clauses greater than in subordinate ones. In Vedic, adverbs are normally constructed as preverbs in subordinate clauses, whereas they enjoy greater freedom in main clauses (correlation of structural scope, bondedness and syntagmatic variability, see p. 105f). With regard to main constituent order, mention may be made of the numerous languages such as German, Basque, Quechua and Turkish which have a rigid verb-final order in subordinate clauses, but varying degrees of freedom and deviation from verb-final order in main clauses (cf. Ross 1973). Such statements comprise, of course, the order among elements none of which need be grammaticalized or even equipped with a grammatical marker, and therefore provoke problems which we will deal with in §4.4.4.

So much should suffice to make a significant correlation among the six parameters plausible. Quantification along the lines sketched in §4.4.1 would certainly prove it. If linguistic theory were further developed, it would perhaps allow us to hierarchize the parameters, proving that some of them depend on the others and thus dispensing with them. It seems clear that such a relationship will not be shown within each of the pairs comprising a paradigmatic and a syntagmatic parameter. As has been argued convincingly by scholars such as de Saussure, Hjelmslev and Jakobson, the paradigmatic and the syntagmatic, or selection and combination, are two fundamental and mutually irreducible modes of any language operation. One might, however, consider that weight and variability are coordinate, while cohesion is subordinate to both of them. One might go further and postulate primacy for weight on account of the fact that the whole business of reinforcement appears to be essentially directed at restoring integrity. On the

4 Parameters of grammaticalization

other hand, it is good to remember that it is the parameter of syntagmatic cohesion that has seemed fundamental to the founders of agglutination theory, and that Jespersen proposed to call it coalescence theory. I therefore conclude that any attempt at hierarchizing the parameters would be premature.

Assuming now that the six parameters normally correlate and jointly constitute the grammaticalization of an item or a paradigm, we may compute its global degree of grammaticalization as a function of the six values. Items and paradigms may then be compared as to their grammaticality values. This may be done at a variety of levels. It has already been mentioned that a large paradigm can sometimes be split up into several subparadigms of different degrees of grammaticality; recall the example of the cases and the adpositions. Givón (1975: 86) shows how his criteria (which are included in mine) can be applied to the set of coverbs present in a language. As a result, the coverbs may be ordered on a scale between full verb and adposition. Differences among the items are gradual, and it may well be impossible to draw a line between coverb and adposition. The gradualness of the phenomena lies in the nature of grammaticalization itself. The fact that different degrees of grammaticality may be represented by the members of one synchronic paradigm is a consequence of the fact that grammaticalization need not seize all the relevant full verbs at once and transform them simultaneously, but acts upon verbs of a certain kind at any moment in language history that they become available; cf. p. 43 for personal pronouns.

At a somewhat higher level, we may compare grammatical paradigms within a language which are functionally similar. Obvious candidates are the various classes of more or less grammaticalized items which have filled the grammaticalization scales in Chapter 3. The paradigm of the cases will be compared with that of the adpositions, that of the auxiliaries with that of the synthetic aspects and this with the paradigm of tenses. The paradigm of the free personal pronouns, of the clitic personal pronouns and of the personal affixes (e.g. in the Romance languages) will be compared as to their degree of grammaticality. For one thing, this will confirm and make more precise the various grammaticalization scales that have been set up. Moreover, it will shed some light on the distance between functionally similar paradigms within a language. As we will see in §7.2, this differs from one language to another and contributes to its typological characterization.

Finally, functionally similar paradigms may be compared as to their degree of grammaticality at the cross-linguistic level. The Turkish case system can be compared to the Latin one, or the systems of auxiliary verbs of the Romance languages can be compared with each other. All such comparisons presuppose, of course, the functional similarity of the paradigms in question as a tertium comparationis (cf. pp. 132–134). If this is granted, the grammaticality values which may be assigned to the grammatical subsystems of a language may be taken to characterize the language. This point will also be taken up in §7.2.

4.4.3 Lack of correlation

In the same rather intuitive fashion in which we have found ourselves being able to assign degrees of grammaticality along each of the parameters and to judge on their correlation without having actually applied the measures, we can see that in some cases the parameters do not correlate. Grammaticalization according to one or the other of them may hasten ahead or lag behind. The following phenomena strike the eye as being unexpected within the general framework that has been developed.

Whenever an inflectional paradigm comprises more than a few subcategories, there is the prima facie suspicion that paradigmaticity is lower than other parameters of grammaticality. For example, Permyak has 17 (Comrie 1981b: 119) or even 21 (Austerlitz 1980: 238) cases, while the average number of cases in a language does not appear to be more than half a dozen. This example may perhaps be "explained away" by assuming several layers of cases, of differing degrees of grammaticality. The same explanation will not hold, however, for unusually extensive noun class sytems. Languages with two or three genders, such as the Indo-European ones, or around half a dozen classes (Pama-Nyungan, North-Caucasian, Swahili and other Bantu languages), appear to be the norm. However, the West-Atlantic language Ful is said (Heine, Schadeberg & Wolff 1981: 51) to possess "20 to 25 noun classes". Further inspection of this language would have to show, first of all, whether this figure has to be divided by two because noun class and number have been mixed up (as usual in African linguistics), and furthermore, whether Ful noun classes are, according to the other parameters, less grammaticalized than or as grammaticalized as the noun classes familiar from other Niger-Congo languages. It should be remembered that the sheer size of a paradigm is only one of the aspects of paradigmaticity, and that we perhaps tend to attribute too much weight to it due to the fact that it is the most directly quantifiable parameter of all.

Disproportions of quite a different kind may be observed when a sign is rather strongly grammaticalized according to all of the parameters except that it has a relatively large structural scope. The relative pronoun familiar from the more archaic Indo-European languages is an amalgamation of three grammatical concepts: a pronominal element which functions as the marker of a certain syntactic position in the relative clause; a conjunction which subordinates the relative

4 Parameters of grammaticalization

clause; and an attributor which links it with the head noun (details in Lehmann 1984: Ch. IV.4). It is common in languages for these three functions to be expressed separately; so there is certainly a basis for recognizing a high degree of bondedness in the Indo-European style relative pronoun. In fact, it is rather strongly grammaticalized according to all of the parameters, except that it serves to form finite subordinate clauses, thus operating at a high syntactic level.

Another disproportion between bondedness and the other parameters may be recognized in sentence sandhi phenomena. Phonological rules of assimilation and the like operate, in some languages such as Sanskrit and Ọwọn Afa Yoruba (Heine & Reh 1984: 26f), not only between the morphemes of a word, but also across word boundaries in a sentence. While the phenomenon in Yoruba might point to a specially tight relationship between verb and object, in Sanskrit it is completely general and does not have any obvious semantic counterpart. It is therefore not clear whether sentence sandhi should be viewed as a "hastening forward" of bondedness as against the other parameters.

In some languages to which discourse analysis has been applied, phenomena have emerged which might be characterized in terms of the parameter structural scope lagging behind the others. Wiesemann (1980) shows that in Kaingáng the sequencing of sentence adverbs and aspects in a chain of sentences obeys textual restrictions. We appear to be faced here with the grammaticalization, especially in terms of obligatorification, of structural phenomena which belong to a high level of grammatical structure.

Finally, the combination of *to* + infinitive in English is probably an example of bondedness lagging behind the other parameters. As we have seen (pp. 160–160f), *to* is relatively loosely bonded, whereas it must certainly be considered highly grammaticalized in terms of such parameters as semanticity and paradigmatic variability (obligatoriness).

The last example clearly shows how problematic such judgements are. In the passage referred to, we compared English *to* with German *zu* and found that the bondedness of German *zu* was higher. How can we justify saying that English *to* is relatively loosely bonded, rather than saying that bondedness of German *zu* has proceeded farther than the other grammaticalization parameters? Let us assume, for the moment, that such questions will receive an answer through the quantification of the parameters and pursue here the different question of how such disproportions among grammaticalization parameters, if they do exist, have to be incorporated into the theory.

Let me hasten to state that we have at present no explanation for a lack of correlation among the grammaticalization parameters. For one thing, we have no theoretical basis which would lead us to predict a 100% correlation, or a correlation of whatever percentage, for that matter. Insofar as no clear-cut theoretical principles are violated, there is no real exception that would require an explanation. But suppose we had a basis for saying that some of these disproportion phenomena are significant. We would then be able to distinguish between a normal grammaticalization process, in which all the parameters correlate to a high degree, and an exceptional one, in which some or all of the parameters assume values independently of each other. In order to explain the exceptional cases, we would have to look for two things: First, a principle which governs the structuring of language systems, which has rather the same structural scope as grammaticalization itself, but which may counteract it. Second, an analysis of how the two principles have interacted in the specific cases at hand, within each language system. The second task will not be approached in this book. The general principle which I will make responsible for lack of correlation in grammaticalization parameters is analogy. This will be treated in detail in §5.4. Here I will only call attention to the fact that such disproportions contribute to characterizing a language, to distinguishing it from other languages. If in the case system of a language all the grammaticalization parameter correlate neatly, this will be a language with a case system like dozens or hundreds of others. But if one or two parameters do not conform, paradigmaticity, e.g., being especially low, this makes the language unusual and contributes to its individuality. I will try to make this more precise in the chapter on typology.

4.4.4 Reduction to zero and fixation of word order

I have said that when integrity reaches the pole of maximal grammaticalization, namely when significans and significatum of a grammatical formative become zero, all the other grammaticalization parameters cease to be applicable. We may now modify this somewhat. First of all, one member of a paradigm may become zero, while the others subsist. The zero element may then remain a member of the paradigm, namely its unmarked member, and all the grammaticalization parameters continue to be applicable. Thus, in German nouns we reckon with four cases, including a nominative, although this is morphologically always zero. Moreover, even in situations where paradigms are not easy to establish, linguists have worked with zero formatives. This has been common in category conversion, for instance in the adjectivalization of nominals or the nominalization of clauses or verbals. This is often achieved without an overt "translative" functor, which may legitimately be hypostasized as a zero functor. In such a case, one of the grammaticalization parameters continues to be applicable, namely that of structural scope. Obviously, it is possible to determine the grammatical level of

4 Parameters of grammaticalization

a syntagm whose category is converted even if there is no translative functor. Now, the hypothesis of the correlation among grammaticalization parameters would appear to predict that zero translatives must have a minimal structural scope, i.e. occur only in the conversion of stems.

We return here to the problem raised in §3.3.2 in connection with the grammaticalization scale of nominalization. There we saw that nominalization of verbs by a zero affix is a common process, not only in English, but also in Mandarin. Here the structural scope of the nominalizer is indeed minimal. However, it is also possible, in English and Mandarin, to nominalize a whole finite clause (i.e. to embed it in an NP position) without an overt subordinator. Here the structural scope of the zero nominalizer is maximal. The reader is asked to verify the examples (e.g. E25 and E31 in §3.3.2) and note that they are strictly comparable. In both cases, the nominalizer, being semantically zero, achieves nothing by itself. The nominalizing force lies exclusively in the context. This is, in the case of a nominalized clause, the syntactic position of an NP, commonly the function of subject or direct object. In the case of a nominalized verb, it very often is the definite article, as in English, Arosi or Ancient Greek; in Bantu languages, the noun class prefixes fulfill the function of a nominalizing context. So do we have to recognize here another case of lacking correlation among grammaticalization parameters? Or is zero not necessarily the end of a grammaticalization process?

Zero grammatical formatives may indeed show up at various points on a grammaticalization scale, but with a different status. This becomes clear as soon as they are seen as members of paradigms. On the parameters of paradigmaticity and paradigmatic variability, the zero nominalizer in *I know she loves me* is quite different from that in *the love*. The zero complementizer participates in an open and heterogeneous paradigm of subordinating conjunctions (low paradigmaticity), many of which may be substituted for each other and by zero in many contexts (cf. *I know that/when/since/if she loves me* – high paradigmatic variability). The zero nominalizing affix, on the other hand, participates in no paradigm; instead it constitutes a paradigm in and of itself. In almost no context is there a choice of nominalizing a given verb either by zero or by some other affix. What we have, instead, is either of two things. We may have a set of nominalizing suffixes such as *-al* (*refusal*) or *-t* (*drift*); these are not interchangeable, but rather irregularly bound to specific subsets of verb stems: they are not grammaticalized, but lexicalized (see §5.2). Or we have the grammaticalized nominalizing suffix *–ing*. But this does not form a paradigm with zero, since it is less grammaticalized on all counts. For example, its structural scope is greater; cf. *her loving John*. The solution to our dilemma therefore lies in the remark made at the beginning

4.4 Interaction of parameters

of this section. If a whole paradigm of grammatical formatives becomes zero, this is indeed the end of grammaticalization. But quite apart from this, one member of a paradigm may be zero, or a sign may be simply optional. The zero appearing here is not an index of high grammaticalization, but, on the contrary, of low paradigmaticity and absence of obligatoriness, thus of low grammaticalization. In fact, such zeros will typically occur at the beginning of a grammaticalization scale, since optionality decreases further to the end.

An analog to this situation in nominalization may be found in adverbial or case relations. In §3.4.1.4 we saw that adverbs juxtaposed to an NP may be at the origin of adpositions and later case affixes. Such constructions have a very low degree of grammaticality; and the adverb may be substituted by a host of others, or it may be simply lacking, for instance in a sentence such as E65. At the opposite pole of the scale, we have zero case endings, as in English or the Romance languages. They form a closed paradigm, namely that of the cases dependent on verbal government, and they are not optional (substitutable by overt affixes); they are completely grammaticalized. This shows that it is essential to distinguish between the reduction of a grammatical paradigm to zero and such a "zero formative" which is merely an optional (weakly grammaticalized) formative.

One instance of a grammaticalization parameter which may still be measured even if a paradigm is reduced to zero has just been shown to be its structural scope. Another one is syntagmatic variability, when this is suitably extended to grammatical relations not necessarily contracted by the grammatical formative itself. I have occasionally referred to a distinction between UNIRELATIONAL AND BIRELATIONAL GRAMMATICAL FORMATIVES. Unirelational formatives, such as gender and number markers on nouns, or tense markers on verbs, contract only one grammatical relation, namely the one which in the course of grammaticalization becomes the morphological relation to their carrier. Birelational formatives contract, in addition to this primary relation, a secondary, less intimate one to another constituent. The most important birelational formatives are pronominal elements marking cross-reference and adverbial/adpositional elements marking case relations. Both of these mainly express a relation between a verb and an NP, the difference being that the pronominal elements attach to the verb and refer to the NP, while case markers attach to the NP and refer to the verb. Their ultimate function, namely to signal which NP is related to the verb in which way, is similar, but they achieve it in quite different ways. In particular, the locus of personal agreement affixes is the pure syntactic relations, because these tend to inhere in the carrier of such affixes, while the locus of case affixes is the more concrete relations, because these do not inhere in relational terms, but instead

4 Parameters of grammaticalization

are freely assumed by more independent, marginal actants (cf. the discussion in §3.4.2.1 and Lehmann 1983: §4). Nevertheless, both agreement affixes and cases may be grammaticalized to zero, with the consequence that – renovations apart – the syntactic relation has no overt expression. It is commonly assumed that in such cases the relation is expressed by the sequential ordering of the relata. My purpose here is to show how this structural means, which is fundamentally different in nature from segmental means, can come to substitute the latter. It will become clear that there is no simple alternative – either segmental means or sequential ordering –, but that the two are always and regularly connected with each other through grammaticalization.

In §3.2.1.2 we saw that the agglutination of a personal pronoun to its governing term as an agreement affix (primary relation) is accompanied by a tightening of the anaphoric (secondary) relation between it and the NP it refers to. This NP is gradually attracted into the sphere of the carrier of the agreement affix, called the relational term. The relation between the pronominal element and the NP gradually turns into a relation between the relational term and the NP, mediated by the agreement marker; and in the end, when the agreement marker becomes zero, it is a direct syntactic relation of government between the relational term and the NP. This is a grammaticalization process, as we have seen in §3.4.2. Therefore, the syntagmatic variability of the NP vis-à-vis its relational partner – first the pronoun, then the relational term – decreases gradually. From maximal variability at the pre-agreement stage, it reduces to the availability of a few positions within the clause; and finally, when the NP is subject to government without a grammatical marker and grammaticalization is highest, the syntagmatic variability score may even be reduced to one. The result is the fixed position of the unmarked subject, direct object and possessive attribute vis-à-vis their governors in some languages such as Chinese, English or Bambara.

A similar course is taken by an NP which starts by bearing a marked adverbial relation to the verb. To the degree that this is grammaticalized, not only does the adverbial relator become attached to the NP as a case marker (primary relation); but also the NP changes from an adjunct in a marginal position (secondary relation) to a complement in a more central position. When it is attracted into the government of the verb, the case tends to become zero. A natural part of this grammaticalization process is again the decrease in the syntagmatic variability of the NP vis-à-vis its governor.

The point of this discussion is that we do not get a simple dichotomy of fixed vs. free word order, nor one of segmental vs. positional means. Instead, fixed word order is to be seen as low syntagmatic variability, within the whole framework of grammaticalization. In §3.4.2.3 we saw that there is a gradience of grammaticalization from functional sentence perspective to syntax. In the same sense, Meillet (1912: 147f) had already noted that word order in Latin was free and signalled "expressive nuances", while in French it was fixed and signalled syntactic relations; and this change, said Meillet, was a grammaticalization process. Consider, as an example not yet repeated, attribution. On p. 76, we saw that agreement markers on attributes result from the grammaticalization of personal pronouns serving as the anaphoric heads of the attributes (primary relation). At this stage, syntagmatic variability of the attribute vis-à-vis the referent of the pronoun – the subsequent head of attribution – (secondary relation) is maximal. As the pronoun becomes an agreement affix, the attribute comes nearer to its head. This is the situation in Latin, where syntagmatic variability of adjective attributes would have a value – according to the numerical scale of §4.4.1 – of somewhere between three and seven, depending on style. As agreement is reduced, syntagmatic variability decreases; in French, the value would be two, because both the positions immediately before and after the head are available, but only under certain constraints. In English, where there is no agreement of adjective attributes, their order with respect to the head is fixed, i.e. their syntagmatic variability score is one.

We are now prepared to take up a problem which we had raised and left open on p. 6. There we noted a contradiction between the otherwise parallel scales of grammatical concepts set up by W. v. Humboldt and E. Sapir. Expression of grammatical concepts, or rather relations, by position is arranged near the beginning of the scale (at stage II) by Humboldt, but near its end by Sapir. At first blush, it might appear that Humboldt was wrong and Sapir was right, since fixed word order has just been analyzed as low syntagmatic variability, and syntagmatic variability reaches its low point at the end, not at the beginning, of a grammaticalization scale. Closer inspection of the problem, however, reveals that Humboldt and Sapir meant different things and are both right.

Suppose there is a birelational grammatical formative Z which attaches to constituent X and relates it to Y. Then syntagmatic variability may be observed both within the primary relation Z-X and within the secondary relation Z-Y, and it will be greater in the latter than in the former. Now if Z is reduced to zero, we get a direct relation Y-X, and syntagmatic variability in this relation will be lower than if X and Y were related by segmental means. Given that Z is birelational, the output of the grammaticalization scale in which it is reduced to zero is not the bare X, but X in the non-segmentally expressed relation Z to Y, with a certain, relatively low degree of syntagmatic variability between X and Y. Suppose now

4 Parameters of grammaticalization

that Y is, in its turn, grammaticalized. This means that the construction X-Y, with the very same syntagmatic variability as before, is the input to a grammaticalization scale. In its course, Y will attach to X, and syntagmatic variability between them will again be annulled.

Possible examples of this development are serial verb constructions. In one variant, Y is a coverb, X its nominal complement and Z the case marker of X. Here the first grammaticalization scale leads from whatever its initial element is to an affixal case marker (Z affixed to X), and the second one leads from a serial verb (coverb) to a case marker (Y affixed to X). In another variant, Y is a serial verb assuming an aspectual function, X is the full verb and Z a complementizer or nominalizer subordinating the full verb. In this variant, the first grammaticalization scale leads from whatever its initial element is to a nominalizing affix (Z affixed to X), and the second one leads from a serial verb to an aspect marker (Y affixed to X). In both variants, as long as Z ist still present, Y is not yet a serial verb; but it may be one as soon as Z is zero.

Having now established that one and the same construction, with a given degree of syntagmatic variability, may both be the output of one grammaticalization scale and the input to another one (or even to the same one), we can see that both Humboldt and Sapir had the construction X-Y in mind. But Sapir was looking at it as the output of the first grammaticalization channel, where the relation expressed by Z is increasingly expressed by the fixed order of X and Y; while Humboldt was looking at it as the input to the second grammaticalization channel, where Y is still independent, but has fixed word order in relation to X.

This problem could not have arisen if syntagmatic variability between X and Y were greatest at the moment where Y enters a grammaticalization scale and lowest at the moment where it is about to disappear. (Then both Humboldt and Sapir would be wrong, because the notion of word order would be inapplicable to the construction X-Z, and word order would be completely free in the construction X-Y.) In reality, however, the phase of the parameter of syntagmatic variability is somewhat displaced as against the others, since it normally reaches its lowest point already at the stage where Z is agglutinated to X and then cannot decrease further while Z is gradually reduced to zero. On the other hand, at the beginning of a grammaticalization scale, the order between X and Y is not maximally free; it decreases long before Y shows the first symptoms of grammaticalization. In the case of a birelational Z, it is therefore not only theoretically sound to include its secondary relation into the account, but it is methodologically profitable, since once Z is agglutinated to X, no further decrease in its syntagmatic variability can be observed, whereas it becomes increasingly interesting to observe syntagmatic variability in the secondary relation to Y.

4.4 Interaction of parameters

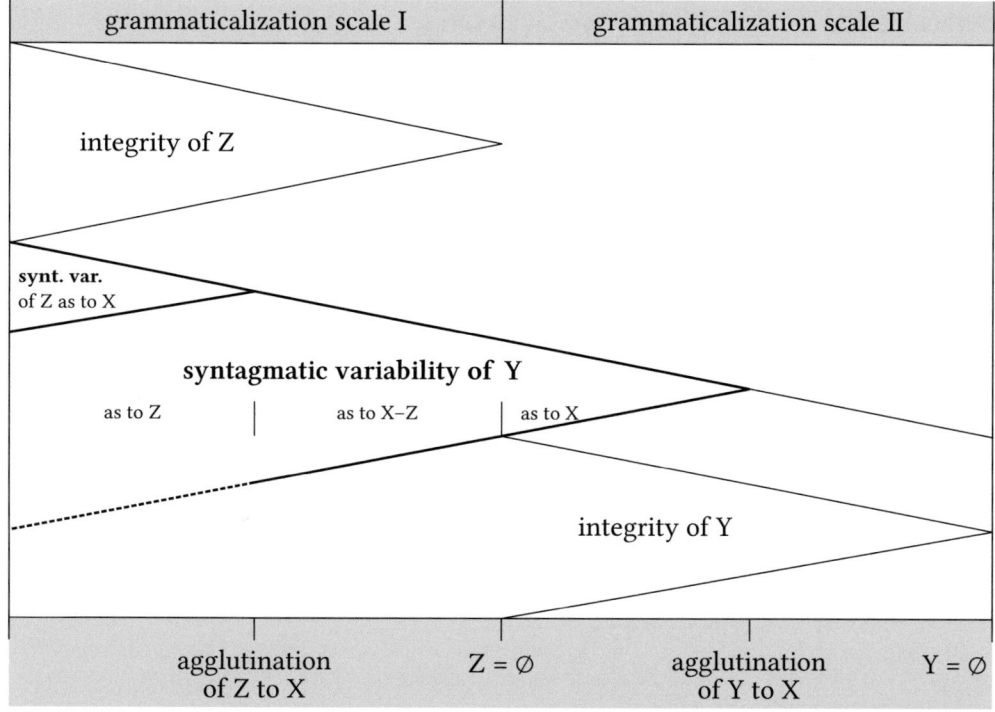

Figure 4.3: Reduction to zero and fixation of word order

Figure 4.3 sums up this discussion by displaying two things at once: first, the behavior of syntagmatic variability in both the primary and the secondary grammatical relations of Z while this is reduced to zero; and second, the phase-displacement of syntagmatic variability as against the other grammaticalization parameters, here represented by integrity.

The picture is to be read as follows: One side of each of the two wedges symbolizing decrease in syntagmatic variability has been prolonged to the right, both to suggest that the notion continues to be applicable even after the agglutination stage, but that no further decrease occurs, and to illustrate how the carrier of the affix becomes the reference point for the secondary grammatical relation and exhibits syntagmatic variability with respect to a third term. We also see that at the point where Z becomes zero, word order between X and Y is already fairly fixed.

We may anticipate that the subsumption of word order in the framework of grammaticalization will lead to a new appraisal of the attempts to typologize languages according to their word-order patterns. This will be done in §7.2.

The last lesson that this discussion teaches concerns the level at which gram-

4 Parameters of grammaticalization

maticalization works. A view that concentrates on the historical fate of single words and morphemes is too atomistic. Grammaticalization reduces not only the integrity, but also the scope of a sign. This means that it shifts signs down the hierarchy of grammatical levels, and it does this simultaneously to a given sign and to the sign of which the former is a proper grammatical part. One cannot but agree with Givón's (1979: 94) proposal "to treat syntacticization and the rise of grammatical morphology as two mutually dependent parts of the same process."

Epilogue to the third edition

More than thirty years after the original non-publication of *Thoughts on grammaticalization*, a revised edition might seem overdue. Such a revision would, however, require adequate consideration of all the work published in the field during this period, which in turn would imply rewriting the entire text. (Some parts of it may deserve it that somebody take on this task.) Neither would it be easy to prolong the account of the research history offered in Chapter 1 by these past decades, which have seen several times the amount of research on grammaticalization published in the preceding centuries. Instead of all this, I will confine myself to some topics treated in the present book. Some of these remarks are apologetic in nature, for which I ask the reader's indulgence.

Research in grammaticalization over these decades has brought forward a large set of empirical insights into both the synchronic functioning and the diachronic dynamism of essential parts of the grammar of numerous languages over the world. Our understanding of the origins and workings of such fields of grammar as tense, aspect and mood, case relators, personal pronouns and indices, and of grammatical operations such as determination, auxiliation and negation continues to profit from the perspective afforded by grammaticalization theory. And sure enough, it is now permitted to speak of a theory of this strand of research, since the fundamentals of grammaticalization have become sufficiently clear over the years. The following points may deserve some attention:

A scientific definition of a concept mediates between theory and method. In order to assign the concept its place in a theory, the definition must presuppose a set of more elementary concepts and be compatible with another set of concepts akin to it. The concept of grammaticalization receives its place in the framework of a theory of language as a human activity bound up with the history and culture of a social community. The main theoretical problem to be faced here is the dichotomy between a static and a dynamic view of language. Apart from certain restrictions which I will return to, grammaticalization is, in a dynamic view of language, what grammar is in a static view. A definition of grammaticalization whose definiens includes the concept of grammar bases a dynamic concept on the static view and is bound to fail to the extent that grammaticalization is precisely the kind of process which traverses the boundary between grammar and such aspects of the use of linguistic signs as remain outside grammar, like discourse and the lexicon. It therefore seems more profitable to base this definition on more general and possibly dynamic concepts of linguistic activity. It is for this reason that grammaticalization of a linguistic sign has been conceived as reduction of the speaker's freedom in using it, which implies its increasing subjection to constraints specific of the particular language.

The methodological role of a definition is fulfilled by its operationalization. Since grammaticalization is a gradual process, operationalization of this concept does not answer the question whether something is or is not grammaticalized, but to what degree it is grammaticalized. Methods must be deduced from the theory, and §4.1 goes to some lengths to provide such a foundation. The freedom of the speaker is converted into the autonomy of the sign, and this is measured by a set of parameters. These must be as formal as possible, not only in the interest of methodological reliability and validity, but also in the sense of pertaining to linguistic structure rather than substance. This, again, follows from the nature of the concept: the increasing subjection of the grammaticalized unit to rules of the particular language implies its increasing contribution to linguistic structure rather than to the sense of the message. Attempts to capture grammaticalization by semantic criteria have therefore failed. Instead, the six parameters spelling out the autonomy of the linguistic sign have proved their applicability in a large number of empirical cases.

Grammaticalization starts from different sources, runs through different phases and takes different forms constrained by the type of language in which it occurs. It has been clear from the beginning that the six parameters do not always run in parallel; nor do they need to do so, for the reasons just mentioned. The concept must therefore be a prototypical one (cf. Wiemer 2014). Examples of the prototype are provided by the 'going-to' future in English and other languages or by the development of a dative construction out of a benefactive construction, e.g. in current Portuguese. The transition of a derivational morpheme to an inflectional one, for instance, is more peripheral, since syntagmatic cohesion does not grow.

In order to model the prototypicality of the concept, one might consider as prototypical cases of grammaticalization such cases in which all six parameters correlate and accept as marginal such cases in which at least half of them correlate. This, however, seems a bit mechanistic. One may reach greater validity here by realizing that the three janus-headed principal parameters relate to the idea of the structural autonomy of the linguistic sign to different degrees. The parameter most directly reflecting the speaker's freedom in using a sign is its variability. Enhanced cohesion may be considered as a symptom of reduced variability. At any rate, these two parameters are purely structural ones. The parameter of weight is more problematic.[10] On the one hand, it is internally not quite consistent, as integrity is not exactly the paradigmatic counterpart of structural scope. On the other, integrity is not a purely structural parameter, since it tries to capture the substance of the sign in formal terms. Consequently, until the integrity parameter is repaired, the three principal parameters may be ranked as follows:

1. Variability

2. Cohesion

3. Weight

The operationalization of a prototypical concept of grammaticalization may then be based on this ranking of the criteria.

The most encompassing concept which one might term "grammaticalization" is probably the process by which anything becomes part of grammar. This, however, is not a unitary process, since there are many different ways in which this may happen. Such a wide concept would include, among many other things, the morphologization of a phonological contrast. There are quite a number of processes of grammatical change which bear paradigmatic and syntagmatic relations to grammaticalization and which have to be excluded from the latter concept simply because there are empirical cases in which any one of these processes occurs in isolation. Worth of particular mention here are analogical change and reanalysis. These are important in grammatical variation. However, they differ from grammaticalization in that they do not (necessarily) reduce the autonomy of the sign. And they may or may not cooccur, in a given historical case, with each other or with grammaticalization. Consequently, grammaticalization cannot be reduced to any other process of grammatical variation.

The two main aspects of a complete process of grammaticalization are the recruitment of new material for grammatical function and the subjection of this material to rules of grammar leading to its final reduction to zero. For convenience, these may be described as two subsequent phases in a diachronic perspective. As a matter of fact, however, even the first deployment of a lexical formative or a free construction to fulfill a grammatical function already involves an incipient subjection to rules of grammar. Anyway, the two aspects reflect the two

---

[10] This subdivision of the three principal parameters is first suggested in Lehmann (1995).

Epilogue to the third edition

main forces driving grammaticalization: Extravagance (Haspelmath 1999 after Lehmann 1985a) is responsible for the incessant re-entry into the spiral; automatization (Lehmann 2004 after Givón 1989) is responsible for its incessant passage down to the pole of pure structural function. Both of these forces are directed, which means that grammaticalization takes similar forms in different languages and different areas of grammar. Each of them has a logical opposite, viz. understatement (or parsimony) and reflection; but these are far from being antagonists on a par with the former two.

The question of the unidirectionality of grammaticalization has caused much stronger a stir in the linguistic community than any other aspect of this phenomenon. One of the most hotly debated issues in the theory of grammaticalization concerns the existence or otherwise of degrammaticalization, i.e. the inverse process to grammaticalization. While most specialists agree that most of the evidence for degrammaticalization adduced so far is defective in one or another way and that very few if any examples of degrammaticalization stand up to closer scrutiny, let alone emerge as prototypical instances of this concept, this state of affairs seems theoretically interesting only if it can be turned into a theorem. The theorem says: Grammaticalization is a unidirectional process; a process running in the inverse direction of grammaticalization, thus, does not exist.

This thesis should be understood as an empirical claim (cf. Lehmann 2004: §4.2). As such, it may be true or false. The idea that it may be true is apparently so provocative that it has triggered a wealth of literature aimed to falsify it. By common standards of scientific dispute, the falsification of a thesis is all the more impressive if it has been seriously upheld in the specialized literature (preferably, by somebody else). Thus, a *locus classicus* for the thesis is sought. This has been detected, more than once, in *Thoughts on grammaticalization*. Here are four representative references to previous editions:

> a search for counterevidence [to unidirectionality], a task that Lehmann regards as largely futile given that grammaticalization is "an irreversible process" (1995:16).

(Howe 2010: 569)

> the term [degrammaticalization] was introduced by Lehmann for a phenomenon which he believed to be non-existent:
>
> "Various authors (Givón 1975:96, Langacker 1977:103f, Vincent 1980[I]:56–60) have claimed that grammaticalization is unidirectional; that is, an irreversible process [...] there is no *degrammaticalization*." (Lehmann 1995 [1982]:16, emphasis original)

(Norde 2010: 123)

> However, unidirectionality has also been defined as a constraint on grammatical change in general (Heine, Claudi, and Hünnemeyer 1991; Heine 1994 and 1997; Lehmann 1995 [1982]; ...)
> (Norde 2009: 50)

> Lehmann (1995a[1982]: 16) takes change of this type to be unidirectional and is thus led to claim that degrammaticalization does not exist.
> (Börjars & Nigel 2011: 163)

And here is the actual wording of the paragraph in question:

> Various authors (Givón 1975:96, Langacker 1977:103f, Vincent 1980[I]:56–60) have claimed that grammaticalization is unidirectional; that is, it is an irreversible process, the scale in F1 cannot be run through from right to left, there is no *degrammaticalization*. Others have adduced examples in favor of degrammaticalization. The few that have come to my knowledge will be briefly discussed.
> (Lehmann 2002b: 14; unchanged from the earlier editions)

The passage, thus, does not propose the thesis in question and instead ascribes it to other researchers. The quotations adduced before are, therefore, perfect examples of inadmissible quotations taken out of context and of misrepresentation of published views, respectively.

What the text, admittedly, does say towards the end of the discussion introduced by the previous quotation, is the following:

> We may therefore conclude this discussion with the observation that no cogent examples of degrammaticalization have been found.
> (Lehmann 2002b: 17)

This, again, may or may not be a misrepresentation of the research situation obtaining in 2002; but it is obviously not a theoretical claim on the non-existence of degrammaticalization.

Just to forestall any misunderstandings: The current state of research is essentially the same. I.e., the thesis of the non-existence of degrammaticalization is an empirical hypothesis which has not yet been thoroughly falsified. Some examples have been adduced in the literature (in particular, in Norde 2009) that come rather close to being empirical evidence of degrammaticalization. Should a completely convincing case be found – something that no current theory is in

Epilogue to the third edition

a position to exclude –, then it would merit considerable interest. The theory of grammaticalization, however, would be only marginally affected. Empirical linguistic theorems are generally subject to a couple of exceptions – language is an activity of human beings, who (fortunately) sometimes oppose the general trend.

At the time of this writing, the most recent tendency in the field is to marry grammaticalization with construction grammar. Here again, some authors have misrepresented the approach taken in this book. It has been characterized as focused on the isolated morpheme or word and been opposed to "constructionalization", assumed to be taking the appropriate broader perspective. These critics apparently have failed to map the traditional structuralist concept of the set of syntagmatic relations of a linguistic unit relied on in Chapter 4 onto the contemporary notion of the construction. Neither have they, apparently, appreciated §4.4, which proposes a passage in step of the grammaticalization of a linguistic sign and of the construction containing it. Construction grammar is a conception of grammar which pays equal attention to the structure and meaning of complex linguistic signs and consequently does recommend itself as a model for the description of the steps involved in grammaticalization in a language.

On the other hand, all the cases of grammaticalization discussed in this book have it in common that they do contain some item which becomes a (more) grammatical formative by grammaticalization. In later publications (Lehmann 2002b: §2.3), I have entertained the possibility of the grammaticalization of a construction irrespectively of the presence of a particular item which may be said to be grammaticalized. This may or may not be a fruitful extension of the concept. However, two things should be noted: First, it is not clear how the parameters of grammaticalization would apply to such cases. The parameters themselves would have to be suitably extended or be replaced by better ones. Second, every extension of the concept of grammaticalization runs the risk of depriving it of its force to identify a genuine phenomenon in linguistic life which cannot be reduced to anything else.

Some construction grammarians have offered a new edition of the behavior pattern known from the model ousted by construction grammar, viz. generative grammar: previous approaches are either misguided or superfluous. Thus, we don't need grammaticalization, since all it can tell us is taken care of by our constructionalization. This replicates the earlier generativist rhetorical figure: Grammaticalization is not needed, since our device of reanalysis is more than sufficient to account for the phenomena in question. These critics have failed to understand the nature of a monotonous directed variation. Consider the following numerical sequence: 0 1 3 6 10. Mathematician A has mastered elementary arithmetic. He will say: You have to analyze this as a set of pairs x and y. The relationship between the members of the first pair is: $x + 1 = y$. The relationship in the second pair is: $x + 2 = y$. In the third pair, it is $x + 3 = y$. And in the final pair, the relationship is $x + 4 = y$. Mathematician B has mastered analysis. He accepts such a binary subdivision as a first step in understanding the principle of the numerical sequence, but then goes on: This is a strictly monotonically increasing sequence, generated by the function $x_i + i = y$. Faced with a phenomenon like the evolution of the English immediate future out of a motion-cum-purpose construction, the grammarian – no matter whether the generative or the construction grammarian – acts like mathematician A, applying their analytic devices of reanalysis or constructionalization to every single step in the diachronic sequence. The grammaticalizationist acts like mathematician B, applying the concept of grammaticalization to the entire sequence and thus capturing its principle. Grammaticalization theory will only be truly supplanted by a theory embodying this kind of higher-level principle.

References

Alpatov, V.M. 1980. Sistema ličnych mestoimenij 1-go i 2-go lica v sovremennom japonskom jazyke. In Igor F. Vardul' (ed.), 3–26. Moskva: Nauka.
Anderson, Stephen R. 1977. On mechanisms by which languages become ergative. In Charles N. Li (ed.), 317–363. Austin & London: University of Texas Press.
André, Jacques. 1978. *Les mots a redoublement en latin.* Paris: Klincksieck.
Arens, Hans. 1969. *Sprachwissenschaft: Der Gang ihrer Entwicklung von der Antike bis zur Gegenwart.* 2nd edn. Freiburg & München: Karl Alber.
Ashby, William J. 1981. The loss of the negative particle *ne* in French: a syntactic change in progress. *Language* 57. 674–687.
Austerlitz, Robert. 1980. Typology and universals on a Eurasian east-west continuum. In Gunter Brettschneider & Christian Lehmann (eds.), *Wege zur Universalienforschung. Sprachwissenschaftliche Beiträge zum 60. Geburtstag von Hansjakob Seiler*, 235–244. Tübingen: G. Narr.
Bazell, Charles E. 1949. Syntactic relations and linguistic typology. *Cahiers Ferdinand de Saussure* 8. 5–20.
Benveniste, Emile. 1968. Mutations of linguistic categories. In W.P. Lehmann & Y. Malkiel (eds.), *Directions for historical linguistics. A symposium*, 83–94. Austin & London: University of Texas Press.
Bloch, Jules. 1954. The grammatical structure of Dravidian languages. Deccan College Hand-Book Series (3).
Bloomfield, Leonard. 1933. *Language.* New York etc: Holt, Rinehart & Winston.
Bolinger, Dwight L. 1978. Intonation across languages. In Joseph H. Greenberg (ed.), vol. 1, 471–524. 4 vols. Stanford: Stanford University Press.
Bopp, Franz. 1816. *Über das Conjugationssystem der Sanskritsprache in Vergleichung mit jenem der griechischen, lateinischen, persischen und germanischen Sprache* (Documenta semiotica - Serie 1). Reprint 1975. Frankfurt am Main: Andreäsche Buchhandlung.
Bopp, Franz. 1833-52. *Vergleichende Grammatik des Sanskrit, Zend, Griechischen, Lateinischen, Litauischen, Altslawischen, Gothischen und Deutschen.* Berlin.
Bossong, Georg. 1979. Typologie der Hypotaxe. *Folia Linguistica* 13. 33–54.
Brettschneider, Gunter. 1978. Baskisch. *Studium Linguistik* 5. 67–75.

References

Brettschneider, Gunter. 1980. Zur Typologie komplexer Sätze. In Gunter Brettschneider & Christian Lehmann (eds.), *Wege zur Universalienforschung. Sprachwissenschaftliche Beiträge zum 60. Geburtstag von Hansjakob Seiler*, 192–198. Tübingen: G. Narr.

Brettschneider, Gunter & Christian Lehmann (eds.). 1980. *Wege zur Universalienforschung. Sprachwissenschaftliche Beiträge zum 60. Geburtstag von Hansjakob Seiler*. Tübingen: G. Narr.

Bybee, Joan L. 1981. What's a possible inflectional category. SUNY at Buffalo.

Börjars, Kersti & Vincent Nigel. 2011. Grammaticalization and directionality. In Heiko Narrog & Bernd Heine (eds.), *The Oxford handbook of grammaticalization* (Oxford Handbooks in Linguistics), 163–176. Oxford, etc.: Oxford University Press.

Capell, Arthur. 1971. *Arosi grammar*. Canberra: Australian National University.

Clark, Marybeth. 1979. Coverbs: evidence for the derivation of prepositions from verbs — new evidence from Hmong. *Working Papers in Linguistic* 11(2). 1–12.

Cole, Desmond T. 1955. *An introduction to Tswana grammar*. London etc: Longmans, Green & Co.

Cole, Peter. 1982. *Imbabura Quechua* (LDS 5). Amsterdam: North-Holland.

Comrie, Bernard. 1981a. *Language universals and linguistic typology: Syntax and morphology*. Oxford: B. Blackwell.

Comrie, Bernard. 1981b. *The languages of the Soviet Union* (Cambridge Language Surveys). Cambridge: Cambridge University Press.

Coseriu, Eugenio. 1974. *Synchronie, Diachronie und Geschichte. Das Problem des Sprachwandels*. Übersetzt von Helga Sohre. München: W. Fink.

Coseriu, Eugenio. 1979. Verbinhalt, Aktanten, Diathese. Zur japanischen Ukemi-Bildung. In K.H. Ezawa K. & Rensch (ed.), *Sprache und Sprachen. Festschrift für Eberhard Zwirner zum 80. Geburtstag*, 35–55. Tübingen: M. Niemeyer.

Coulmas, Florian. 1980. Zur Personaldeixis im Japanischen. *Papiere zur Linguistik* 23(2). 3–19.

Davies, John. 1981. *Kobon* (LDS 3). Amsterdam: North-Holland.

de Condillac, Étienne Bonnot. 1746. *Essai sur l'origine des connaissances humaines*. Paris.

de Saussure, Ferdinand. 1916. *Cours de linguistique générale*. Charles Bally (ed.). Paris: Payot.

Delbrück, Berthold. 1888. *Altindische Syntax* (Syntaktische Forschungen 5). Reprint: Tübingen: M. Niemeyer, 1976; Darmstadt: Wissenschaftliche Buchgesellschaft. Halle: M. Niemeyer.

References

Dillon, George L. 1977. *Introduction to contemporary linguistic semantics* (Foundations of Modern Linguistics). Englewood Cliffs, NJ: Prentice-Hall.

Dixon, Robert M.W. 1972. *The Dyirbal language of North Queensland* (Cambridge Studies in Linguistics 9). Cambridge & London: Cambridge University Press.

Dixon, Robert M.W. 1979. Ergativity. *Language* 55. 59–138.

Edmondson, Jerrold A. 1978. Ergative languages, accessibility hierarchies governing reflexives and questions of formal analysis. In W. Abraham (ed.), *Valence, semantic case, and grammatical relations*, 633–660. Amsterdam: J. Benjamins.

Falkenstein, A. 1959. *Das Sumerische* (Handbuch der Orientalistik, 1. Abteilung, 2. Band, 1. Abschnitt, Lfg. 1). Leiden: Brill.

Faltz, Leonard M. 1977. *Reflexivization. A study in universal syntax.* University Microfilms 77-31, 345. University of California, Berkeley PhD thesis.

Foley, William A. 1980. Toward a universal typology of the noun phrase. *Studies in Language* 4. 171–199.

Frei, Henri. 1929. *La grammaire des fautes. Introduction à la linguistique fonctionnelle.* Paris: Geuthner, Genève: Kundig, Leipzig: O. Harrassowitz. Reprint: Genève: Slatkine Reprints, 1971.

Gary, Judith Olmstedt & Saad Gamal-Eldin. 1982. *Cairene Egyptian colloquial Arabic.* Amsterdam: North-Holland.

Givón, Talmy. 1971. Historical syntax and synchronic morphology: An archaeologist's field trip. *Chicago Linguistic Society* 7. 394–415.

Givón, Talmy. 1973. The time-axis phenomenon. *Language* 49. 890–925.

Givón, Talmy. 1975. Serial verbs and syntactic change: Niger-Congo. In Charles N. Li (ed.), 47–112. Austin & London: University of Texas Press.

Givón, Talmy. 1978. Definiteness and referentiality. In Joseph H. Greenberg (ed.), vol. 4, 291–330. 4 vols. Stanford: Stanford University Press.

Givón, Talmy. 1979a. From discourse to syntax: grammar as a processing strategy. In T. Givón (ed.), *Discourse and syntax* (Syntax and semantics 12), 81–112. New York etc: Academic Press.

Givón, Talmy. 1979b. Language typology in Africa: a critical review. *Journal of African Languages and Linguistics* 1. 199–224.

Givón, Talmy. 1979c. *On understanding grammar* (Perspectives in Neurolinguistics and Psycholinguistics). New York etc: Academic Press.

Givón, Talmy. 1980. The drift away from ergativity: Diachronic potentials in Sherpa. *Folia Linguistica Historica* 1. 41–60.

Givón, Talmy. 1981. On the development of the numeral 'one' as an indefinite marker. *Folia Linguistica Historica* 2. 35–54.

Givón, Talmy. 1989. Mind, code and context. Essays in pragmatics. Ch. 7.

Greenberg, Joseph H. 1954. A quantitative approach to the morphological typology of language. In R.F. Spencer (ed.), *Method and perspective in anthropology. Papers in honour of Wilson D. Wallis*, 192–220. Minneapolis: University of Minnesota Press.

Greenberg, Joseph H. 1975. Dynamic aspects of word order in the numeral classifier. In Charles N. Li (ed.), 27–45. Austin & London: University of Texas Press.

Greenberg, Joseph H. (ed.). 1978. *Universals of human language*. 4 vols. Stanford: Stanford University Press.

Greenberg, Joseph H. 1980. Circumfixes and typological change. In Elizabeth C. Traugott et al. (eds.) (Current Issues in Linguistic Theory 14), 233–241. Amsterdam: J. Benjamins.

Haas, Mary R. 1941. *Tunica*. New York: J. J. Augustin (Extract from *Handbook of American Indian Languages*, IV).

Haas, Mary R. 1977. From auxiliary verb phrase to inflectional suffix. In Charles N. Li (ed.), 525–537. Austin & London: University of Texas Press.

Hagège, Claude. 1975. Le problème linguistique des prépositions et la solution chinoise. Collection Linguistique (71).

Hagège, Claude. 1978. Du thème au thème en passant par le sujet. Pour une théorie cyclique. *La linguistique* 14(2). 3–38.

Haiman, John. 1980. *Hua. A Papuan language of Eastern Highlands of New Guinea* (Studies in Language Companion Series 5). Amsterdam: J. Benjamins.

Hale, Kenneth L. 1976. The adjoined relative clause in Australia. In R.M.W. Dixon (ed.), *Grammatical categories in Australian languages*, 78–105. Canberra: Australian Institute of Aboriginal Studies.

Haspelmath, Martin. 1999. Why is grammaticalization irreversible? *Linguistics* 37(6). 1043–1068.

Haudry, Jean. 1980. La 'syntaxe des désinences' en indo-européen. *Bulletin de la Société de Linguistique de Paris* 75. 131–166.

Heine, Bernd. 1980. Language typology and linguistic reconstruction: The Niger-Congo case. *Journal of African Languages and Linguistics* 2. 95–112.

Heine, Bernd & Mechthild Reh. 1984. *Grammaticalization and reanalysis in African languages*. Hamburg: H. Buske.

Heine, Bernd, Thilo C. Schadeberg & Ekkehard Wolff (eds.). 1981. *Die Sprachen Afrikas*. Hamburg: H. Buske.

Hewitt, B. George. 1979. *Abkhaz* (LDS 2). Amsterdam: North-Holland.

Hjelmslev, Louis. 1928. Principes de grammaire générale. Det Kongelige Danske Videnskabernes Selskab, Historisk-filosofiske Meddelelser 16 (1).

Hodge, Carleton T. 1970. The linguistic cycle. *Language Sciences* 13. 1–7.

Howe, Chad. 2010. Review of Muriel Norde. 2009. Degrammaticalization. Oxford: Oxford University Press. *Folia Linguistica* 44(2). 569–577.

Huang, Shuan-fan. 1978. Historical change of prepositions and emergence of SOV order. *Canadian Journal of Chinese Linguistics* 6. 212–242.

Hyman, Larry M. 1975. On the change from SOV to SVO: evidence from Niger-Congo. In Charles N. Li (ed.), 113–147. Austin & London: University of Texas Press.

Hyman, Larry M. 1978. Word demarcation. In Joseph H. Greenberg (ed.), 1:443–470. 4 vols. Stanford: Stanford University Press.

Ineichen, Gustav. 1980. Zur Beurteilung der lateinischen *habeo*-Periphrasen. In Gunter Brettschneider & Christian Lehmann (eds.), *Wege zur Universalienforschung. Sprachwissenschaftliche Beiträge zum 60. Geburtstag von Hansjakob Seiler*, 218–221. Tübingen: G. Narr.

Jakobson, Roman. 1936. Beitrag zur allgemeinen Kasuslehre. Gesamtbedeutungen der russischen Kasus. In Eric P. Hamp, Fred W. Householder & Robert Austerlitz (eds.), *Readings in linguistics*, vol. 2, 51–89. different year: 1966. Chicago & London: University of Chicago Press.

Jakobson, Roman. 1956. Two aspects of language and two types of aphasic disturbances. In Roman Jakobson & Morris Halle (eds.), *Fundamentals of language*, 53–87. 's-Gravenhage: Mouton & Co.

Jakobson, Roman. 1959. Boas' view of grammatical meaning. In Roman Jakobson (ed.), *Word and language* (Selected writings 2), 489–496. alternating year= 1971. The Hague & Paris: Mouton.

Jakobson, Roman & Linda R. Waugh. 1979. *The sound shape of language*. Brighton: Harvester Press.

Janda, Richard D. 1980. On the decline of declensional systems: the overall loss of OE nominal case inflections and the ME reanalysis of *-es* as *his*. In Elizabeth C. Traugott et al. (eds.) (Current Issues in Linguistic Theory 14), 243–252. Amsterdam: J. Benjamins.

Jeffers, Robert J. & Arnold M. Zwicky. 1980. The evolution of clitics. In Elizabeth C. Traugott et al. (eds.) (Current Issues in Linguistic Theory 14), 221–231. Amsterdam: J. Benjamins.

Jespersen, Otto. 1922. *Language. Its nature, development and origin*. London: G. Allen & Unwin.

Jespersen, Otto. 1940. *A Modern English grammar on historical principles. Part V: Syntax*. 7 vols. Copenhagen & London: E. Munksgaard & G. Allen & Unwin.

Jorden, Eleanor Harz. 1962. *Beginning Japanese*. New Haven & London: Yale University Press.

References

Kachru, Yamuna. 1980. Towards a typology of compound verbs in South Asian languages. *Studies in the Linguistic Sciences* 10(1). 113–124.

Kahr, Joan Casper. 1975. Adpositions and locationals: typology and diachronic development. *Working Papers on Language Universals* 19. 21–54.

Kahr, Joan Casper. 1976. The renewal of case morphology: sources and constraints. *Working Papers on Language Universals* 20. 107–151.

Kiparsky, Paul. 1968. Tense and mood in Indo-European syntax. *Foundations of Language* 4. 30–57.

Krahe, Hans. 1967. Formenlehre. *Germanische Sprachwissenschaft* 2(780). Sammlung Gröschen.

Kuno, Susumu. 1973. The structure of the Japanese language. *Current Studies in Linguistics Series* (3).

Kuryłowicz, Jerzy. 1948. Contributions à la théorie de la syllabe. *Bulletin de la Société Polonaise de Linguistique* 8. 80–114.

Kuryłowicz, Jerzy. 1965. The evolution of grammatical categories. *Diogenes* 51. 55–71.

Kölver, Ulrike. 1982a. Interaktion von nominalen Kategorien am Beispiel der Entwicklung des modernen Bengali. In Hansjakob Seiler & Christian Lehmann (eds.) (LUS 1, I), 244–251. Tübingen: G. Narr.

Kölver, Ulrike. 1982b. Klassifikatorkonstruktionen in Thai, Vietnamesisch und Chinesisch. Ein Beitrag zur Dimension der Apprehension. In Hansjakob Seiler & Christian Lehmann (eds.) (LUS 1, I), 180–185. Tübingen: G. Narr.

Kölver, Ulrike. 1985. Kasusrelationen im Birmanischen. In F. Plank (ed.), *Relational typology* (Trends in Linguistics 28), 195–212. Berlin & New York: Mouton.

Labov, William. 1971. On the adequacy of natural languages: I. The development of tense. First draft, Febr. 20, 1971. Univ. of Pennsylvania: Trier: LAUT, B23, 1977.

Langacker, Ronald W. 1977. Syntactic reanalysis. In Charles N. Li (ed.), 57–139. Austin & London: University of Texas Press.

Lehmann, Christian. 1974. Isomorphismus im sprachlichen Zeichen. In H. Seiler (ed.), vol. 2: Arbeiten des Kölner Universalienprojekts 1973/74 (Linguistic Workshop), 98–123. München: W. Fink.

Lehmann, Christian. 1978. On measuring semantic complexity. A contribution to a rapprochement of semantics and statistical linguistics. *Georgetown University Papers on Languages and Linguistics* 14. 83–120.

Lehmann, Christian. 1982a. Nominalisierung – Typisierung von Propositionen. In Hansjakob Seiler & Christian Lehmann (eds.) (LUS 1, I), 64–82. Tübingen: G. Narr.

Lehmann, Christian. 1982b. Universal and typological aspects of agreement. In H. Seiler & F.J. Stachowiak (eds.), *Apprehension*, vol. 2, 201–267. Tübingen: G. Narr.

Lehmann, Christian. 1983. Rektion und syntaktische Relationen. *Folia Linguistica* 17. 339–378.

Lehmann, Christian. 1984. *Der Relativsatz. Typologie seiner Strukturen — Theorie seiner Funktionen — Kompendium seiner Grammatik* (LUS 3). Tübingen: G. Narr.

Lehmann, Christian. 1985a. Grammaticalization: Synchronic variation and diachronic change. *Lingua e Stile* 20. 303–318.

Lehmann, Christian. 1985b. The role of grammaticalization in linguistic typology. In Hansjakob Seiler & Gunter Brettschneider (eds.), *Language invariants and mental operations. International interdisciplinary conference held at Gummersbach/Cologne, Germany, Sept. 18–23, 1983*, vol. 5 (LUS), 41–52. Tübungen: G. Narr.

Lehmann, Christian. 1986. Grammaticalization and linguistic typology. *General Linguistics* 26. 3–23.

Lehmann, Christian. 1987. Sprachwandel und Typologie. In Norbert Boretzky et al. (eds.), *Beiträge zum 3. Essener Kolloquium über Sprachwandel und seine bestimmenden Faktoren, vom 30.9. – 2.10.1987 [sic; i.e. 1986] an der Universität Essen*, vol. 4 (Bochum-Essener Beiträge zur Sprachwandelforschung), 201–225. Bochum: N. Brockmeyer.

Lehmann, Christian. 1989a. Grammatikalisierung und Lexikalisierung. *Zeitschrift für Phonetik, Sprachwissenschaft und Kommunikationsforschung* 42. 11–19.

Lehmann, Christian. 1989b. Markedness and grammaticalization. In Olga M. Tomić (ed.), *Markedness in synchrony and diachrony* (Trends in Linguistics, Studies and Monographs 39), 175–190. Berlin & New York: Mouton de Gruyter.

Lehmann, Christian. 1992. Word order change by grammaticalization. In Marinel Gerritsen & Dieter Stein (eds.), *Internal and external factors in syntactic change* (Trends in Linguistics 61), 395–416. Berlin & New York: Mouton de Gruyter.

Lehmann, Christian. 1993. Theoretical implications of processes of grammaticalization. In William A. Foley (ed.), *The role of theory in language description* (Trends in Linguistics 69), 315–340. Berlin & New York: Mouton de Gruyter.

Lehmann, Christian. 1995. Synsemantika. In Joachim Jacobs et al. (eds.), *Syntax. Ein internationales Handbuch zeitgenössischer Forschung*, vol. 2 (Handbücher der Sprach- und Kommunikationswissenschaft 9), 1251–1266. Berlin: W. de Gruyter.

References

Lehmann, Christian. 2002a. New reflections on grammaticalization and lexicalization. In Ilse Wischer & Gabriele Diewald (eds.), *New reflections on grammaticalization* (TSL 49), 1–18. Amsterdam & Philadelphia: J. Benjamins.

Lehmann, Christian. 2002b. *Thoughts on grammaticalization.* Second, revised edition (ASSidUE 9). Erfurt: Seminar für Sprachwissenschaft der Universität.

Lehmann, Christian. 2004. Theory and method in grammaticalization. *Zeitschrift für Germanistische Linguistik* 32(2): *Themenschwerpunkt: Grammatikalisierung.* [publ. 2005], 152–187.

Li, Charles N. & Sandra A. Thompson. 1974. Historical change of word-order: A case study in Chinese and its implications. In John M. Anderson & Charles Jones (eds.), *Historical linguistics: Proceedings of the first International Conference on Historical Linguistics, Edinburgh 2nd-7th Sept. 1973*, vol. 1, 199–217. Amsterdam & Oxford: North-Holland, New York: American Elsevier.

Li, Charles N. & Sandra A. Thompson. 1976. Subject and topic: A new typology of languages. In Charles N. Li & Sandra A. Thompson (eds.), *Subject and topic*, 457–489. New York etc: Academic Press.

Li, Charles N. & Sandra A. Thompson. 1977. A mechanism for the development of copula morphemes. In Charles N. Li (ed.), 419–444. Austin & London: University of Texas Press.

Lightfoot, David W. 1979. *Principles of diachronic syntax* (Cambridge Studies in Linguistics 23). Cambridge: University Press.

Lord, Carol. 1976. Evidence for syntactic reanalysis: from verb to complementizer in Kwa. In Sanford B. Steever, Carol A. Walker & Salikoko S. Mufwene (eds.), *Papers from the parasession on diachronic syntax. April 22, 1976*, 179–191. Chicago: CLS.

Lyons, John. 1968. *Introduction to theoretical linguistics.* Cambridge: University Press.

Lyons, John. 1977. *Semantics.* 2 Vols. Cambridge etc: Cambridge University Press.

Malkiel, Yakov. 1957. Diachronic hypercharacterization in Romance. *Archivum Linguisticum* 9 and 10. 79–113 and 1–36.

Mallinson, Graham & Barry J. Blake. 1981. *Language typology. Cross-linguistic studies in syntax* (North-Holland Linguistic Series 46). Amsterdam etc: North-Holland.

Martinet, André (ed.). 1968. *Le langage* (Encyclopédie de la Pléiade 25). Paris: Gallimard.

Matthews, Peter H. 1981. *Syntax* (Cambridge Textbooks in Linguistics). Cambridge: Cambridge University Press.

Meillet, Antoine. 1912. L'évolution des formes grammaticales. *Scientia (Rivista di Scienza)* 12(26). Reprint: Meillet 1921:130-148, 6.

Meillet, Antoine. 1915. Le renouvellement des conjonctions. *Annuaire de l'École Pratique des Hautes Études, section historique et philologique.* Reprint: Meillet 1921:159-174.

Meillet, Antoine. 1934. *Introduction à l'étude des langues indo-européennes.* 7th edn. 1st:1903; 8th unchanged edition: 1937. Paris: Hachette.

Meinhof, Carl. 1936. *Die Entstehung flektierender Sprachen.* Berlin: D. Reimer.

Mel'čuk, Igor A. 1976. On suppletion. *Linguistics* 170. 45–90.

Merlan, Francesca. 1982. *Mangarayi* (LDS 4). Amsterdam: North Holland.

Misteli, Franz. 1893. *Charakeristik der hauptsächlichsten Typen des Sprachbaues: Neubearbeitung des Werkes von Prof. H. Steinthal (1861).* Berlin: F. Dümmler.

Moinfar, Moh. Djafar. 1980. Les classificateurs en persan. In Gunter Brettschneider & Christian Lehmann (eds.), *Wege zur Universalienforschung. Sprachwissenschaftliche Beiträge zum 60. Geburtstag von Hansjakob Seiler,* 317–320. Tübingen: G. Narr.

Moravcsik, Edith A. 1980. Some crosslinguistic generalizations about motivated symbolism. In Gunter Brettschneider & Christian Lehmann (eds.), *Wege zur Universalienforschung. Sprachwissenschaftliche Beiträge zum 60. Geburtstag von Hansjakob Seiler,* 23–28. Tübingen: G. Narr.

Mosel, Ulrike. 1980. *Tolai and Tok Pisin. the influence of the substratum on the development of New Guinea Pidgin* (Pacific Linguistics, Series B 73). Canberra: Australian National University.

Norde, Muriel. 2009. *Degrammaticalization.* Oxford & New York: Oxford University Press.

Norde, Muriel. 2010. Degrammaticalization. three common controversies. In Katerina Stathi, Elke Gehweiler & Ekkehard König (eds.), *Grammaticalization. Current views and issues* (Studies in Language Companion Series 119), 123–150. Amsterdam & Philadelphia.

Paul, Hermann. 1920. *Prinzipien der Sprachgeschichte.* 5th edn. Tübingen: M. Niemeyer.

Plank, Frans. 1979a. Exklusivierung, Reflexivierung, Identifizierung, relationale Auszeichnung. Variationen zu einem semantisch-pragmatischen Thema. In I. Rosengren (ed.), *Sprache und Pragmatik. Lunder Symposium 1978,* 330–354. Lund: CWK Gleerup.

Plank, Frans. 1979b. The functional basis of case systems and declension classes: from Latin to Old French. *Linguistics* 17. 611–640.

References

Polomé, Edgar C. 1967. *Swahili language handbook* (Language Handbook Series). Washington: Center for Applied linguistics.

Pulgram, Ernst. 1978. *Italic, Latin, Italian. 600 B.C. to A.D. 1260. texts and commentaries* (Indogermanische Bibliothek, 1. Reihe). C. Winter.

Qvonje, Jørn Ivar. 1979. Die Grammatikalisierung der Präposition *na* im Bulgarischen. *Folia Linguistica Historica* 1. 317–351.

Ramat, Paolo. 1980. *Introduzione alla linguistica germanica* (Linguistica Generale e Storica 16). Bologna: Pàtron.

Ramat, Paolo. 1983. Ein Beispiel von 'Reanalysis', typologisch betrachtet. *Folia Linguistica* 16. 365–383.

Reid, Aileen A. et al. 1968. *Totonac: From clause to discourse.* Norman: SIL of the University of Oklahoma.

Rix, Helmut. 1976. *Historische Grammatik des Griechischen. Laut- und Formenlehre.* Darmstadt: Wissenschaftliche Buchgesellschaft.

Ronneberger-Sibold, Elke. 1980. *Sprachverwendung – Sprachsystem. Ökonomie und Wandel* (Linguistische Arbeiten 87). Tübingen: M. Niemeyer.

Ross, John R. 1973. The penthouse principle and the order of constituents. In Corum et al. (eds.), *You take the high node and I'll take the low node. Papers from the Comparative Syntax Festival*, 397–422. Chicago: CLS.

Rosén, Haiim B. 1980. Weiteres über die Entstehung der periphrastischen "Perfekt"-formen im Lateinischen: Zum Begriff "Zustand des Akt(resultats)besitzes". In Gunter Brettschneider & Christian Lehmann (eds.), *Wege zur Universalienforschung. Sprachwissenschaftliche Beiträge zum 60. Geburtstag von Hansjakob Seiler*, 311–316. Tübingen: G. Narr.

Sankoff, Gillian. 1977. Variability and explanation in language and culture: cliticization in New Guinea Tok Pisin. In Muriel Saville-Troike (ed.), *Linguistics and anthropology*, 59–73. Washington: Georgetown University Press (GURTLL 1977).

Sankoff, Gillian & Suzanne Laberge. 1974. On the acquisition of native speakers by a language. In David DeCamp & Ian F. Hancock (eds.), *Pidgins and creoles. Current trends and prospects*, 73–84. Washington: Georgetown University Press.

Sapir, Edward. 1921. *Language. An introduction to the study of speech.* New York: Harcourt, Brace & World.

Sasse, Hans-Jürgen. 1977a. A note on WH-movement. *Lingua* 41. 343–354.

Sasse, Hans-Jürgen. 1977b. Gedanken über Wortstellungsveränderung. *Papiere zur Linguistik* 13f. 82–142.

Seebold, Elmar. 1971. Versuch über die Herkunft der indogermanischen Personalendungssysteme. *Zeitschrift für vergleichende Sprachforschung* 85. 185–210.

Seiler, Hansjakob. 1973. On the semantosyntactic configuration 'possessor of an act'. In Braj B. Kachru et al. (eds.), *Issues in linguistics: Papers in honor of Henry and Renée Kahane*, 836–853. Urbana etc: University of Illinois Press.

Seiler, Hansjakob. 1975. Die Prinzipien der deskriptiven und der etikettierenden Benennung. In H. Seiler (ed.), *Linguistic workshop III. Arbeiten des Kölner Universalienprojekts 1974*, 2–57. München: W. Fink.

Seiler, Hansjakob. 1978. The Cologne project on language universals: Questions, objectives, and prospects. In (TBL 111), 11–25. Tübingen: G. Narr.

Seiler, Hansjakob. 1982. Das sprachliche Erfassen von Gegenständen (Apprehension). In Hansjakob Seiler & Christian Lehmann (eds.) (LUS 1, I), 3–11. Tübingen: G. Narr.

Seiler, Hansjakob. 1983. *Possession as an operational dimension of language* (LUS 2). Tübingen: G. Narr.

Serzisko, Fritz. 1980. Sprachen mit Zahlklassifikatoren: Analyse und Vergleich. In *Arbeiten des Kölner Universalienprojektes*, vol. 37. Köln: Institut für Sprachwissenschaft der Universität.

Serzisko, Fritz. 1981. Gender, noun class and numeral classification: a scale of classificatory techniques. In *Arbeiten des Kölner Universalienprojektes*, vol. 40, 93–126. Köln: Institut für Sprachwissenschaft der Universität.

Serzisko, Fritz. 1982. Temporäre Klassifikation: Ihre Variationsbreite in Sprachen mit Zahlklassifikatoren. In Hansjakob Seiler & Christian Lehmann (eds.) (LUS 1, I), 147–159. Tübingen: G. Narr.

Stammerjohann, Harro (ed.). 1975. *Handbuch der Linguistik: Allgemeine und angewandte Sprachwissenschaft*. Darmstadt & München: Wissenschaftliche Buchgesellschaft & Nymphenburg.

Starke, Frank. 1977. Die Funktionen der dimensionalen Kasus und Adverbien im Althethitischen. StBoT (23).

Steele, Susan. 1978. Word order variation: a typological study. In Joseph H. Greenberg (ed.), vol. 4, 585–624. 4 vols. Stanford: Stanford University Press.

Strunk, Klaus. 1980. Zum indogermanischen Medium und konkurrierenden Kategorien. In Gunter Brettschneider & Christian Lehmann (eds.), *Wege zur Universalienforschung. Sprachwissenschaftliche Beiträge zum 60. Geburtstag von Hansjakob Seiler*, 321–337. Tübingen: G. Narr.

Syromjatnikov, N.A. 1980. Zakonomernosti razvitija ličnych mestoimenij v novojaponskom jazyke. In Igor F. Vardul' (ed.), 104–126. Moskva: Nauka.

References

Szemerényi, Oswald J.L. 1970. *Einführung in die vergleichende Sprachwissenschaft*. Darmstadt: Wissenschaftliche Buchgesellschaft (Die Altertumswissenschaft).

Tauli, Valter. 1966. Structural tendencies in Uralic languages. Indiana University Publications, Uralic and Altaic Series (17).

Traugott, Elizabeth C. 1980. Meaning-change in the development of grammatical markers. *Language Sciences* 2. 44–61.

Troike, Rudolph C. 1981. Subject-object concord in Coahuilteco. *Language* 57. 658–673.

Ultan, Russell. 1978. The nature of future tenses. In Joseph H. Greenberg (ed.), vol. 3, 83–123. 4 vols. Stanford: Stanford University Press.

van Roey, Jacques. 1974. *A contrastive description of English and Dutch noun phrases*. Bruxelles: AIMAV; Paris: Didier.

Vater, Heinz. 1979. Determinantien. Teil I: Abgrenzung, Syntax. KLAGE (6).

Vincent, Nigel. 1980a. Iconic and symbolic aspects of syntax: Prospects for reconstruction. In P. Ramat et al. (eds.), *Linguistic reconstruction and Indo-European syntax. Proceedings of the colloquium of the 'Indogermanische Gesellschaft', University of Pavia, 6–7 September 1979*, 47–68. Amsterdam: J. Benjamins.

Vincent, Nigel. 1980b. Some issues in the theory of word order. *York Papers in Linguistics* 8. 167–179.

von der Gabelentz, Georg. 1891. *Die Sprachwissenschaft. Ihre Aufgaben, Methoden und bisherigen Ergebnisse*. Leipzig: Weigel Nachf. 2. überarbeitete Aufl.: Leipzig: Tauchnitz, 1901.

von Humboldt, Wilhelm. 1822. Über das Entstehen der grammatischen Formen und ihren Einfluß auf die Ideenentwicklung. *Abhandlungen der Akademie der Wissenschaften zu Berlin*. Reprint: Humboldt 1972:31-63.

von Humboldt, Wilhelm. 1836. *Über die Verschiedenheit des menschlichen Sprachbaues und ihren Einfluß auf die geistige Entwicklung des Menschengeschlechtes*. Reprint: Humboldt 1972:368-756.

von Schlegel, August Wilhelm. 1818. *Observations sur la langue et la littérature provençales*. Paris: Librairie grecque-latine-allemande.

Wackernagel, Jakob. 1920/1924. *Vorlesungen über Syntax, mit besonderer Berücksichtigung von Griechisch, Lateinisch und Deutsch*. 2 vols. Basel: Birkhäuser & Co.

Weinreich, Uriel. 1963. On the semantic structure of language. In J.H. Greenberg (ed.), *Universals of language. Report of a conference held at Dobbs Ferry, New York, April 13-15, 1961*, 114–171. Cambridge, Mass: MIT Press. 2. ed. 1966.

Welmers, William E. 1973. *African language structures*. Berkeley etc: University of California Press.

Wendt, Heinz F. 1972. *Langenscheidts praktisches Lehrbuch Türkisch*. Berlin etc: Langenscheidt.

Werner, Otmar. 1979. Kongruenz wird zu Diskontinuität im Deutschen. In B. Brogyanyi (ed.), *Festschrift for Oswald Szemerényi on the occasion of his 65th birthday*, 959–988. Amsterdam: J. Benjamins.

Wiemer, Björn. 2014. Quo vadis grammaticalization theory? Why complex language change is like words. *Folia Linguistica* 48. 425–467.

Wiesemann, Ursula. 1980. Events and non-events in Kaingáng discourse. In Gunter Brettschneider & Christian Lehmann (eds.), *Wege zur Universalienforschung. Sprachwissenschaftliche Beiträge zum 60. Geburtstag von Hansjakob Seiler*, 419–433. Tübingen: G. Narr.

Woodbury, Anthony C. 1977. Greenlandic Eskimo, ergativity, and relational grammar. In Peter Cole & Jerrold M. Sadock (eds.), *Grammatical relations*, vol. 8 (Syntax and semantics), 307–336. New York etc: Academic Press.

Zwicky, Arnold M. 1978. Arguing for constituency. *Papers from the Regional Meeting of the Chicago Linguistic Society* 14. 503–512.

Žirmunskij, V. M. 1966. The word and its boundaries. *Linguistics* 27. 65–91.

Name index

Alpatov, V.M., 141
Anderson, Stephen R., 118
André, Jacques, 139
Arens, Hans, 1, 3
Ashby, William J., 120
Austerlitz, Robert, 81, 179

Bazell, Charles E., 131, 154
Benveniste, Emile, 23, 30, 31
Blake, Barry J., 30, 44, 74, 81, 83, 95, 117, 121, 122, 159, 169
Bloch, Jules, 114
Bloomfield, Leonard, 143
Bolinger, Dwight L., 11, 127
Bopp, Franz, 3
Bossong, Georg, 65, 67–69
Brettschneider, Gunter, 88, 100
Bybee, Joan L., 165
Börjars, Kersti, 193

Capell, Arthur, 104
Clark, Marybeth, 111, 112
Cole, Desmond T., 76
Cole, Peter, 33, 48, 54, 78, 86, 87, 117, 124, 127
Comrie, Bernard, 15, 100, 121, 150, 169, 179
Coseriu, Eugenio, x, 31, 88
Coulmas, Florian, 141

Davies, John, 56, 95
de Condillac, Étienne Bonnot, 1

de Saussure, Ferdinand, 161
Delbrück, Berthold, 46, 105
Dillon, George L., 119
Dixon, Robert M.W., 91, 117

Edmondson, Jerrold A., 45, 51

Falkenstein, A., 110
Faltz, Leonard M., 45, 49, 50, 52
Foley, William A., 157
Frei, Henri, 29, 51, 71, 103, 138, 161

Gamal-Eldin, Saad, 49, 55
Gary, Judith Olmstedt, 49, 55
Givón, Talmy, 6, 11, 15, 18, 21, 27, 31–34, 36, 38, 41, 56, 58, 111, 112, 117, 118, 120, 121, 126, 138–140, 145, 168, 176–178, 192
Greenberg, Joseph H., 41, 60, 100, 149, 161, 176

Haas, Mary R., 28, 31, 32
Hagège, Claude, 111, 115, 120, 126, 143
Haiman, John, 61, 139
Hale, Kenneth L., 91
Haspelmath, Martin, 192
Haudry, Jean, 92
Heine, Bernd, 22, 27, 31–33, 38, 39, 56, 60, 61, 134, 135, 139, 145, 151, 163, 169, 175, 179, 180
Hewitt, B. George, 33, 44, 48, 55, 61, 62, 70, 109
Hjelmslev, Louis, 165

Name index

Hodge, Carleton T., 6
Howe, Chad, 192
Huang, Shuan-fan, 111
Hyman, Larry M., 111, 122, 163

Ineichen, Gustav, 31

Jakobson, Roman, 26, 136, 151, 156, 175
Janda, Richard D., 21
Jeffers, Robert J., 20, 164
Jespersen, Otto, 49, 71
Jorden, Eleanor Harz, 73, 82, 83, 121, 125, 126

Kachru, Yamuna, 114
Kahr, Joan Casper, 19, 26, 81, 87, 89–92, 96, 100, 102, 103, 110, 111
Kiparsky, Paul, 155
Krahe, Hans, 57
Kuno, Susumu, 66
Kuryłowicz, Jerzy, 18, 60, 151, 163
Kölver, Ulrike, 60, 62, 63, 117, 125, 166

Laberge, Suzanne, 39
Labov, William, 39
Langacker, Ronald W., 13, 18, 52, 176
Lehmann, Christian, xi, xii, 19, 20, 42, 43, 57, 62, 63, 65, 74, 76, 88, 93, 120, 123, 124, 127, 130, 134, 136, 147, 148, 150, 171, 180, 184, 191–194
Li, Charles N., 12, 29, 111, 120, 121
Lightfoot, David W., 22, 30, 111
Lord, Carol, 65, 66, 70, 151
Lyons, John, 139, 142, 174

Malkiel, Yakov, 25
Mallinson, Graham, 30, 44, 74, 81, 83, 95, 117, 121, 122, 159, 169

Martinet, André, 13
Matthews, Peter H., 36, 94, 116, 144, 168
Meillet, Antoine, 8, 23, 27, 31, 35, 58, 69, 88, 127, 130, 131, 134, 185
Meinhof, Carl, 70
Mel'čuk, Igor A., 14
Merlan, Francesca, 43, 47, 57, 61, 78, 92, 95, 100, 101
Misteli, Franz, 55, 68
Moinfar, Moh. Djafar, 63
Moravcsik, Edith A., 171
Mosel, Ulrike, 37, 38, 61

Nigel, Vincent, 193
Norde, Muriel, 192, 193

Paul, Hermann, 150
Plank, Frans, 45, 139
Polomé, Edgar C., 110
Pulgram, Ernst, 17

Qvonje, Jørn Ivar, 87

Ramat, Paolo, 31, 76, 94
Reh, Mechthild, 22, 27, 31–33, 38, 39, 56, 60, 61, 134, 135, 139, 145, 151, 163, 169, 175, 180
Reid, Aileen A., 108, 109
Rix, Helmut, 32, 144
Ronneberger-Sibold, Elke, 15, 30, 123, 131
Ross, John R., 177
Rosén, Haiim B., 31

Sankoff, Gillian, 39, 45, 120, 126
Sapir, Edward, 5, 15, 92, 137, 139, 161
Sasse, Hans-Jürgen, 37, 53, 111, 124
Schadeberg, Thilo C., 179
Seebold, Elmar, 17

Name index

Seiler, Hansjakob, x, 28, 31, 81, 118, 155, 157
Serzisko, Fritz, 63, 64, 147, 150
Stammerjohann, Harro, 1
Starke, Frank, 97, 98, 105
Steele, Susan, 173
Strunk, Klaus, 45, 52, 156
Syromjatnikov, N.A., 42
Szemerényi, Oswald J.L., 17, 50, 70

Tauli, Valter, 23, 25, 90
Thompson, Sandra A., 12, 29, 111, 120, 121
Traugott, Elizabeth C., 23, 35, 137, 154
Troike, Rudolph C., 158

Ultan, Russell, 31

van Roey, Jacques, 132
Vater, Heinz, 89
Vincent, Nigel, 18, 120, 122, 139, 150, 153
von der Gabelentz, Georg, 43
von Humboldt, Wilhelm, x, 44, 136, 165
von Schlegel, August Wilhelm, 22

Wackernagel, Jakob, 161
Waugh, Linda R., 156
Weinreich, Uriel, 132, 136
Welmers, William E., 37, 76, 112, 113
Wendt, Heinz F., 47, 67, 82, 88
Werner, Otmar, 164
Wiemer, Björn, 190
Wiesemann, Ursula, 180
Wolff, Ekkehard, 179
Woodbury, Anthony C., 89

Zwicky, Arnold M., 20, 160, 164

Žirmunskij, V. M., 28, 32, 33, 137, 144, 161, 162, 165

Name index